L AND SINGULAR to whom these Presents shall come

d Marshall John Fisher Swan Knight Commander of the Royal Victorian Order Garter Principal King of Arms
ng! Whereas The Very Reverend   Priest in the Roman Catholic Church and of the
            in London Provost of the said Oratory Bachelor of Divinity of the University of London and Master
niversity of Cambridge hath represented unto The Most Noble Miles Francis Stapleton Duke of Norfolk Knight
er of the Garter Knight Grand Cross of the Royal Victorian Order Companion of the Most Honourable Order
Order of the British Empire upon whom has been conferred the Decoration of the Military Cross Earl Marshal
                                was founded by the Fathers of the Congregation of the London Oratory
orm-entry Grammar School in 1963 and in 1970 expanded and became a six-form-entry voluntary-aided
rls into the sixth-form: That on the Twentieth day of April 1989 the Secretary of State for Education and
rred upon him by the Education Reform Act 1988 Section 62 (ii) approved proposals for the said London Ora-
hool on the First day of September 1989 conducted by a Governing Body the building and grounds of the said
f the London Oratory Charity as administered under a scheme made by the Charity Commission on the
y a Trust Deed dated the Thirteenth day of December 1973 and as further amended by the London Oratory
th day of September 1992: That the Governing Body of The London Oratory School being desirous of having
e as Chairman of the London Oratory Charity Trustees and Chairman of the Governors of The London Ora-
Crest as are deemed suitable to be borne and used by The London Oratory School on Seals or otherwise
l bearing date the Seventh day of March 1995 authorize and direct Me to grant and assign such Arms and
of the Letters Patent of My Office granted by The Queen's Most Excellent Majesty do by these Presents
- Gules a Bar wavy Argent between three Mullets of eight points Or And for the Crest upon a Helm with a
therefrom to the sinister a Pennant Argent charged with six Gouttes in fess Gules Mantled Bleu
tory School aforesaid on Seals or otherwise in accordance with the Laws of Arms In witness whereof

THE LONDON ORATORY SCHOOL
A Celebration of 150 Years

THE LONDON ORATORY SCHOOL
A Celebration of 150 Years

Pauline Devereux

John Dennis Patrick Hogan (left) and friend c. 1930.

The London Oratory School: A Celebration of 150 Years

2013 © The London Oratory School and Third Millennium Publishing Limited

First published in 2013 by Third Millennium Publishing Limited, a subsidiary of Third Millennium Information Limited.

2–5 Benjamin Street
London
United Kingdom
EC1M 5QL
www.tmiltd.com

ISBN: 978 1 906507 87 9

All rights reserved. No part of this publication may be reproduced or transmitted in any form or by any means, electronic or mechanical, including photocopying, recording, or any storage or retrieval system, without permission in writing from the copyright owner concerned.

British Library Cataloguing in Publication Data
A CIP catalogue record for this book is available from the British Library.

Project Manager	Susan Millership
Design	Susan Pugsley and Matt Wilson
Production	Bonnie Murray
Reprographics	Studio Fasoli, Verona, Italy
Printing	Gorenjski Tisk, Slovenia

Photo Acknowledgements

Many of the photographs in the book are from the school's collection or from the library of the Oratory Church. The school and TMI Publishers would also like to thank Julian Andrews, Paul Flanagan, Maciek Krula, André Camara and Jackie McRoberts for their images as well as the following individuals and organisations: pp 4, 26 (left), 27, 29 (top), 30 (top), 31 (top), 32, 107 courtesy of Pat Frith; p12 (left) Helen Thompson; p22 (right) ©John Frost Newspapers/Mary Evans Picture Library; p23 Christophe du Parc; p34 Alamy; p37 (left) courtesy of Wandsworth Heritage Service, (right)©Lincolnshire Echo; p38 ©Helen McRoberts; p40 (left) Richard O'Sullivan (right) Topham/Picturepoint; p45 © Duffy Archive; pp46, 47, 82 and 83 (left) Bernard Liengme; pp46/47 (top) Kevin Lynch; p56 The Press Association; p94 (right) Cunard Press Office; p119 (left) Lafayette photography, Cambridge; pp119 (top)and 129 (top) © Mike Moran; p126 ©Planet News/Science & Society Picture Library; p128 Brian Cheesman; p134 (left) Jon Combe; p136 (top) Ian Davidson; p137 (top) Alan Meakin; p149 Richard Bond. Rower on back cover © Bill Scott.

Every effort has been made to trace copyright holders and to obtain their permission for the use of copyright material. TMI Publisher apologises for any errors or omissions in the above list and would be grateful if notified of any corrections that should be incorporated in future editions of this book.

Contents

Foreword 7
Author's Note 9

PART I Foundation to Seagrave Road, 1863–1969
1 Foundation and Early Years, 1863–1914 11
      The Oratorians in England 16
2 The First World War 21
3 The Inter-War Years 25
4 The Second World War 35
5 The Post-War Years, 1945–69 43

PART II Seagrave Road, from 1970 onwards
6 1970 to the Present Day 51

PART III An Oratory Education
7 Religious Life 67
      School Chaplains 78
8 Academic Life 81
9 The Creative Arts 89
      The John McIntosh Arts Centre 89
      Art 91
      Music 96
      Drama 106
10 Sport 115
11 School Journeys 133
12 Clubs and Societies 143
13 The Cadet Force 149
14 *Respice Finem*: Look to the End 157

Appendices
Heads of School since moving from Stewart's Grove to Seagrave Road 161
List of Subscribers 162
Governors, Staff And Pupils 166
Index 173

Foreword

Much has changed since the Fathers of the Oratory opened a school in Bury Street, Chelsea back in 1863. The first headmaster presided over a small number of boys providing a Catholic education for a modest fee. Today I have the privilege of leading a state school of almost 1,400 pupils located in Fulham: a Catholic school serving the capital, with a national reputation for excellence.

Yet despite the many and obvious changes that have occurred during the past 150 years, many of the values and traditions have remained at the heart of the school to create an enduring school spirit. But how to capture that spirit and create a worthy memorial for its 150th anniversary? We are indeed fortunate that our author, Pauline Devereux, Deputy Headmaster and a long-serving history teacher at the school, has met that challenge and delivered a portrait of the school formed from a rigorous and critical study. The result, here for us all to prize, is impressive.

This portrait is neither a narrative nor a catalogue of accomplishments, although it contains great stories and achievements. It is a synthesis of many intangibles that make up what Oratorians above all know to be the 'spirit of the school'. In that spirit are to be found the beliefs, the dedication, the work, the privations and the successes and failures of all who have passed through the doors of the school.

In the quest to create this history, many strands have been drawn together. The themed approach casts light on the life of the school and complements the earlier sections that reflect upon the school's development in a historical and social context, capturing its individuality. Within these broad themes there are some wonderful vignettes, flavoured by candid observations and anecdotes from Old Oratorians. It is a rich and diverse story, supplemented with photographs and illustrations from our own archives, interspersed with more recent acquisitions.

In these pages an old boy will hear many familiar echoes of school life, and others will gain a better understanding of the school's inner workings. For current staff, parents and pupils, the book shows how the school was formed and marked its stamp over all who passed within its sphere. For everyone else it demonstrates the achievement of a great religious order and how Saint Philip's precept of obedience, humility and humour can be utilised towards a profound and enduring influence for good.

I would like to offer my sincere thanks to Pauline Devereux for writing this history. This is an unfinished story which, it is hoped, marks a beginning. Its ultimate value lies in providing the impetus for others to supplement the history, and ensuring that considerations on the future of The London Oratory School will always account for the strands of the past that underpin our enduring values.

This book is for all who have ever been associated with the school in any capacity: pupil, staff, parent, governor or friend. It tells our story; I hope you enjoy it as much as I did.

David McFadden
Headmaster, 2013

Author's Note

Credit for the idea of writing this book to coincide with the school's 150 years goes to Headmaster David McFadden. His faith in the project, and in the author, helped to turn the idea into reality.

Father Rupert McHardy and Father George Bowen of The London Oratory have assisted in providing material from the Library of the London Oratory. I am grateful to the many current and former Oratorians, and friends and associates of the school who have assisted in this work in a variety of ways. Although not always identified, it is hoped they will find evidence of the value of their contributions in the pages ahead.

Pauline Devereux
2013

A note on sources

Throughout the text sources are acknowledged only where a direct quote is made. School log books are referred to as log followed by date of the relevant entry. References to The Oratory Parish Magazine, with relevant volume and page number are noted as PM, vol., p. The month is also cited if page numbers repeat in a volume. The Oratorian, school newsletter, is cited as Orat. followed by volume and issue number. The Oratorian, school magazine, is shown as Orat. followed by the year of issue. Other sources are referred to in the text. Specific contributions from pupils, staff and associates of the school, past and present, are acknowledged by name and, where appropriate, followed by their years at the school.

PART I
Foundation and Early Years, 1863–1914

Generations of pupils of The London Oratory School have started their school years by learning about the life and work of St Philip Neri, who lived in the 16th century, and thereby have established themselves in a history that spans almost 500 years. It was St Philip who founded the Congregation of the Oratory in Rome in 1575, and many years later, in 1847, it was John Henry Newman who established the first Oratory in England, in Birmingham. Two years later Father Faber came to open an Oratory in London.

On arriving in London Father Faber established the community at King William Street (now William IV Street), just off the Strand. This part of London was a mix of wealth and poverty. Here were the elegant squares and refined houses of the well-to-do and just a short walk away were the narrow alleys and squalid hovels of the poor. Having established their House in this area the Fathers debated how best to fulfil their mission. In the example and spirit of St Philip, Oratorians practise a wider social role beyond their priestly duties; that mission has often been amongst the sick and outcast of society. The Fathers in London moved in a new direction and decided to found a school for poor children. It was estimated that about 30,000 children were living in poverty in London in the mid 19th century. Many of these children dressed in rags, hence the name of the movement which advocated the education of such children. Ragged Schools were established most often by Evangelical or Nonconformist religious groups, who ran simple one-room establishments to give children the basics of an education. After the Irish Potato Famine brought huge numbers of Catholic Irish immigrants to England, the need for Roman Catholic schools for the poor was recognised, and it was against this background that the Fathers of the Oratory decided to base their mission in London. There was a need to educate Catholic children; Father Hutchison of the Oratory in London wrote to Newman in Birmingham to explain that 'there are in London hardly less than 18,000 Catholic children, almost

Opposite: St Philip Neri from a painting in the Chiesa Nuova, Rome, a copy of which hangs in the school Chapel.

Right: Father Hutchison of the Oratory recognised the urgent need for Catholic schools for the children of the poor in London.

The London Oratory School – *Part I: Foundation to Seagrave Road, 1863–1969*

Above: The school in Bury Street, founded in 1863.

Above left: The Ragged School Museum in London's East End tells the story of the Ragged School Movement. The first school founded by the Oratory Fathers in London was a ragged school in Covent Garden.

all Irish, who are not attending any Catholic school, and who are, therefore, either running wild in the streets … or being tempted to renounce their religion by the rewards held out to their parents and themselves if they attend the Protestant Ragged School'.

In October 1851 the Oratory Fathers opened the Ragged School at 6 Rose Street, Covent Garden. It was soon inundated with hundreds of children, and the school moved to larger premises in Dunne's Passage, off Oxford Street, one year later. Then in 1854 the running of the school passed into the charge first of the Brothers of Christian Instruction and then to the Xaverian Brothers. The school moved in 1858 to a new building in Charles Street, Drury Lane (later Macklin Street), built to accommodate the expanding numbers. The format moved away from the ragged school model to that of an Industrial School where, alongside the rudiments of an education, children were prepared for a trade. In 1860 the Oratorians resumed charge of the school, but three years later they withdrew and handed charge to the Archdiocese. The school still functions as a primary school in the Archdiocese today, St Joseph's Macklin Street.

The reasons for withdrawing from the school had been many. These included changes in the laws relating to different types of schools and financial and economic considerations. The illness and subsequent deaths in 1863 of two of the key figures in establishing the Oratory in London, Father Faber and Father Hutchinson, also had an impact. The fact that since 1854, at the request of the Archdiocese of Westminster, the Oratory Fathers had moved their London home to a vacant parish in Brompton was, however, to be the most significant factor in terms of the history of The London Oratory School.

The Fathers of the Oratory had not abandoned their role in education and had opened a small school for boys in 1856 in Marlborough Square after the move to Brompton. In 1863, at the request of Cardinal Wiseman, they opened a school for boys in Bury Street, and in the same year they announced the intention of establishing a Middle School. This was the beginning of The London Oratory School of today. The thread is not a single one; there were, as we have seen, a number of different schools under the auspices of the Oratory, and it would be some years yet before the Boys Central School, of which today's school is the direct descendant, would emerge. The year 1863, however, has to be the starting point for tracing the story of the school, as with the establishment of their school in 1863 the Fathers of the London Oratory began an association: a commitment and a tradition of providing for the Catholic education of London boys which remains at the heart of the school.

The early school in Bury Street provided a Catholic education for a modest fee. When in 1880 the Elementary Education Act ensured that children attended school up to the age of 12 (and in a further Act in 1891 this education

12

Right: Headmaster Mr Duffy with boys, c.1900.

Below: Oratory schoolchildren, 1907.

was to be free) the Oratory Middle School (officially the Brompton and Chelsea Catholic Middle School) was founded in premises on Sydney Street. It later moved on to the Bury Street site with the Boys' School. Records for this period are scant, but it seems probable that the two schools functioned alongside each other. The Headmaster of the Middle School was originally Mr Westerman (who held the post without pay) and later Mr Robertson. Within a year of opening, the Middle School had enrolled 60 pupils drawn from six different boroughs, and this number grew steadily until it settled at around 100 pupils for a number of years. The annual fee for the school was £4.

In 1888 Mr J M Duffy succeeded Mr Robertson in the Middle School, while Mr Robert Thomas was Headmaster of the Oratory Boys' School. *The Clapham Observer* of 1909 records the death of Mr Thomas, who had been 'Headmaster of the Brompton Oratory Boys' School' for 40 years. When he died in 1909, just a short while after his retirement, the boys of the Oratory School mourned the loss of 'a man of singular piety and refinement, and a teacher of outstanding ability'. The newspaper account of Mr Thomas's funeral relates how the Oratory boys sang 'Cardinal Newman's 'Hymn for the Holy Souls' and 'Jesus, the Very Thought of Thee' as they stood around the grave, their faces bearing witness of their grief'. The flag of St George was flown at half mast on the school building to mark the respect in which this former Headmaster was held, and Mr Duffy attended the funeral with the Oratory boys.

Early records of the Middle School tell of the regular visits of the Fathers, often to test the boys on their studies. The Reverend Father Sebastian Bowden, The Reverend

Father Charles Bowden, The Reverend Father Jarrett and The Reverend Father McCall paid many visits in the early years, taking a very close interest in the school and the progress of the pupils. Father Sebastian Bowden was the original force behind the foundation of the Middle School and was the first to hold the position of School Manager. He died in 1920, and was the last of the Fathers to have been personally acquainted with Father Faber, who had first established the community in London.

Although the school was flourishing and getting good reports from Inspectors, a constant issue in these early years was the matter of attendance. The number on the Middle School roll seems to have been around 110 boys at this time. The Headmaster was required to keep a note in the school log book of the pattern of attendance and often noted that attendance was low. Even in the late 19th century Headmasters were vexed by the problem of pupils returning late from holidays, with a number of Oratory pupils spending time 'away in the country' and failing to report in on the first day of the new term. At this time, however, illness is more often the cause of absence, with regular reference to sickness causing a drop in attendance. Boys were more exposed to the elements than today as they travelled to and from school, and break times were

The door of the Oratory Primary School in Cale Street today. The Oratory Middle School for boys moved into these premises in 1901.

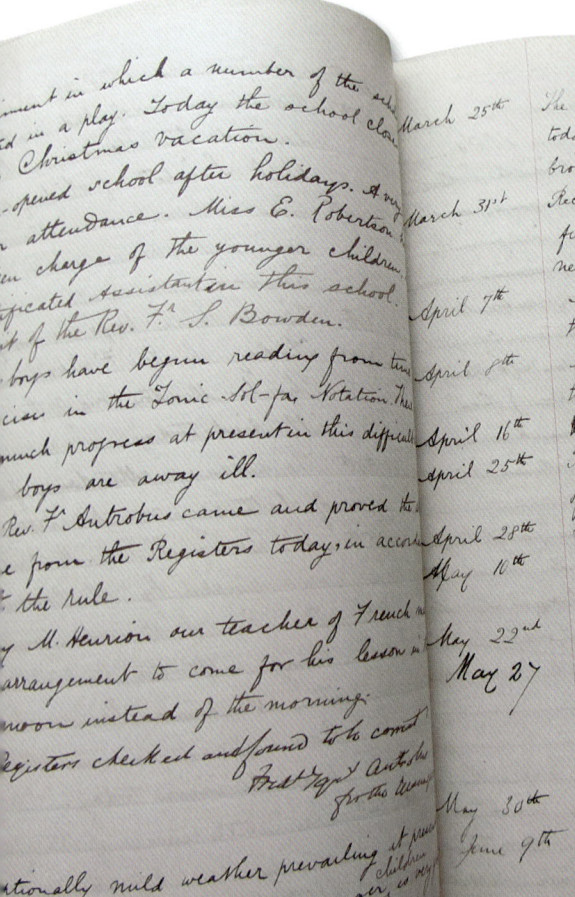

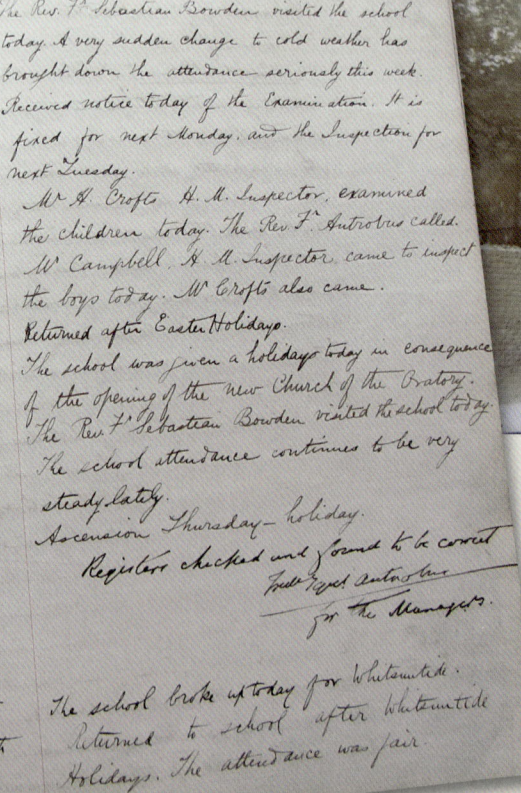

Left: Pages from the school log book of 1882. Visits from the Fathers and a holiday to mark the opening of the 'new Oratory Church' on 25 April are among the events noted here.

Above: The school building on Cale Street in the early 20th century.

1 / *Foundation and Early Years, 1863–1914*

Above: A classroom in the school, *c.*1900.

Right: John Menzies Duffy, Headmaster 1888–1930.

In 1904 all the denominational schools in London came to be placed under the control of the London County Council, with the council paying the day-to-day costs of the school and school managers being responsible for the buildings. The benefits of an Oratory education were widely appreciated and as numbers grew pressure was put on London County Council to make a clearer distinction between the different status and mission of the schools under the auspices of the Oratory, and so in 1905 they were designated as four institutions: Oratory Boys Free School, Oratory Boys Middle School, Oratory Girls and Infants, and Oratory Girls and Infants Middle School. (The 1905 designation did not use apostrophes in the names of the schools and this form is followed in the text.)

Throughout this period of change John Menzies Duffy, who had become Headmaster at the Oratory Middle School in 1888, remained in his position. If he thought the school was now in a settled period he was far from the truth. As war approached in 1914 boys who had once attended the school would be heeding the call to fight for king and country. When the war was over a new phase of Oratory education would soon emerge and Mr Duffy would be seeing the school through some interesting times.

observed outside whatever the weather. On 3 May 1882 'the wet weather of the last day or two' is cited as the reason for low attendance. Just one week later 'a covered walkway has been constructed in the playground for the convenience of the children during wet weather'. This was not sufficient to keep ailments at bay, however, with about 'half the children absent through sickness together with wet weather' in October that same year. The fluctuating attendance remained an issue and in an attempt to address the matter in 1892, 'The Reverend Father Antrobus [began] giving tickets … to all boys who have not missed a single attendance during the past month'. The importance of regular attendance and success at school was understood from the earliest days. In all the extant records of the school regular checks on attendance feature prominently.

Alongside these developments in educating boys the Oratory had also overseen the establishment of a school for girls. When St Wilfrid's Convent in Cale Street (formerly Bond Street) was bought by the Daughters of the Cross in 1870 they took over the education of the girls, and in 1901 the Middle School boys were established in a new home in the Cale Street premises, where they enjoyed the comfort of surroundings more conducive to healthy study, where 'the light is excellent' (log 9.09.1901).

The London Oratory School – Part I: Foundation to Seagrave Road, 1863–1969

THE ORATORIANS IN ENGLAND

Above: The Fathers of The London Oratory, 1877.

Top right: Cardinal Newman.

Far right: The temporary Church and the Oratory House in 1854.

John Henry Newman, 1801-90

John Henry Newman was born in London on 21 February 1801. His early religious formation owed much to his French mother, who was of Huguenot descent, and he grew up in a Calvinist tradition. In 1817 he went up to Trinity College, Oxford, and after completing his degree in 1822, was elected a fellow of Oriel College. By this time he was developing those High Church ideals that would in due course lead him to Roman Catholicism. In 1824 Newman was ordained as an Anglican priest and in 1828 he was appointed Vicar of the church of St Mary the Virgin in Oxford. Here he earned a reputation for the quality of his sermons, and he began to publish writings which show the increasing sympathy he was developing for Catholicism. He had been profoundly influenced by the sermon given in 1833 by John Keble which heralded the start of the Oxford movement within the Anglican Church. In the *Tracts for the Times* Newman expressed his thoughts on spiritual and theological matters; the most significant of these was Tract 90, in which he argued that the Thirty-Nine Articles of the Church of England were essentially Catholic in doctrine. This was controversial and split the Oxford movement. Establishment figures were much displeased, while others took this as enough to convince them to convert to Catholicism. Newman himself wrestled with his own position and in 1843 withdrew from the city to the parish of Littlemore on the outskirts of Oxford. Two years later he was received into the Catholic Church by the Passionist priest Blessed Dominic Barberi. Along with Newman a number of his Oxford friends, including Ambrose St John, had been received into the Church. Nicholas Wiseman, later first Archbishop of Westminster, whom Newman had met on a visit to Italy in 1832, offered the old Oscott Seminary buildings near Birmingham for their use. Later Newman renamed the building Maryvale, and it remains a centre for Catholic study to this day.

Newman travelled to Rome in 1846 where he spent a year and a half in study and preparation for the priesthood, and he was ordained in 1847. While in Rome Newman had been attracted to the Congregation of the Oratory and in 1848 he returned to England with permission from the Pope to

1 / *Foundation and Early Years, 1863–1914*

exposition of his religious opinions and their origins. In 1865 he wrote the beautiful poem 'The Dream of Gerontius', and in 1870 his *Essay in aid of a Grammar of Assent* was published. In this work he explained his assertion that Catholic belief is reasonable and can be sustained by rational argument.

In 1878 Pope Leo XIII hoped to make Newman a cardinal. At first Newman was reluctant but he eventually accepted, having been assured it would not entail him leaving his Oratory in Birmingham. Newman lived for 11 more years, and at his death the streets of Birmingham were lined with mourners.

For the pupils of The London Oratory School, Newman is a patron and spirtual guide. It is, however, to another Oratorian, Father Faber, that we must look to trace the events that led to the establishment of the Oratory in London and of The London Oratory School.

establish an Oratory in Birmingham. The Oratorian way of life had particular appeal for Newman; as a community of priests living in an independent congregation it would be possible for him and his close followers to remain together in their work. The Oratory House which was established in Birmingham was the first of the three Oratorian communities in England. A short time later he oversaw the building of a new house in Hagley Road, Birmingham, which was to remain his home until his death.

Newman was invited in 1854 to take the position of Rector at the Catholic University which was being planned for Dublin. This led Newman to write *The Idea of a University* and began an interest in education which influenced the foundation of a school in Birmingham, and from there the Oratory School, Reading.

For over 40 years Newman ministered to his parish, especially to the poor and afflicted. He wrote extensively and his works show his sharpness of mind, powers of rhetoric and literary style. In 1864, in response to the accusation by Charles Kingsley, Anglican clergyman, Professor of Modern History and author, that Catholic clergy had never regarded truth as a virtue, Newman wrote the *Apologia pro Vita Sua*, a remarkable

17

The London Oratory School – Part I: Foundation to Seagrave Road, 1863–1969

Father Frederick William Faber, 1814–63

Frederick William Faber was received into the Catholic Church in 1845. After education at Shrewsbury and Harrow he went on to study at Balliol and University College, Oxford, becoming a Fellow of the latter in 1837. He was ordained in the Anglican Church in 1839. He was possessed of a powerful mind and a colourful personality and was by now part of Newman's circle. His own writings began to show an inclination towards Roman Catholicism, especially evident in his *Life of St Wilfrid*, published in 1844. On 17 November 1845 he was received into the Catholic Church, two years later he was ordained and in 1848 he joined the newly established Congregation of the Oratory in Birmingham. Newman felt they were not meant to work together and decided to split the community into two, sending Father Faber to establish a community in London, which opened in 1849, in King William Street, near the Strand, and was later to move to Brompton. It is Father Faber, therefore, who, in bringing the Oratory to London, began the tradition that gave the school its foundation.

Father Sebastian Bowden, 1836–1920

'Always a priest, but he was a soldier priest, a scholar and a high spirited English gentleman' (The Times, Sept. 1920).

Father Sebastian Bowden was directly responsible for the establishment of the Boys Middle School. Born in 1836 he was the son of Henry Bowden, whose brother John was a great friend of John Henry Newman. John Bowden had converted to Catholicism and the rest of his family followed his example. His two sons, Sebastian's cousins, both became members of the Congregation of the Oratory.

Sebastian was educated at Eton until forced to leave aged 16, when his own father converted to Catholicism. Sebastian himself converted a short time later. After a brief spell as an undergraduate at Newman's university in Dublin he joined the Army and was an officer in the Scots Guards for 12 years.

He joined the London Oratory in 1868 – his two cousins Father John and Father Charles Bowden were already members of the Congregation – and he was ordained a priest in 1870. He was influential in some of the building and decorative work of this time, most notably St Wilfrid's and St Joseph's Halls. It was when he was appointed Parish Priest in 1880 that he established the Oratory Middle School.

Father S Bowden was a suitable patron for the boys of the Oratory Middle School. As a boy he had played football and cricket for Eton and had a lifelong interest in sport. Even when well advanced in age he liked to 'spend an afternoon at Lord's or the Chelsea Football Ground' and from the beginning he encouraged sporting activity for the boys in the school. He was a keen swimmer and while still at school had been awarded a medal of the Royal Humane Society for 'jumping into the river

Above: Cartoon of Father Faber and novices, 1848.

Left: Father Faber as a young man.

1 / *Foundation and Early Years, 1863–1914*

Above: Father Sebastian Bowden.

Right: Father Edward Crewse.

and saving a man's life'. His own academic credentials were well established and his military background not only added a certain heroic quality for the schoolboys but underpinned Father Bowden's approach to the running of the school and his emphasis on character building. He valued military precision and drilling, stressing the importance of qualities such as punctuality, telling the novices in his charge that 'punctuality is an excellent form of self discipline, and its absence betrays an undisciplined mind. Punctuality is said to be the politeness of princes, but it is also that of an Oratorian.' He was also an excellent preacher and no doubt could enthral the young pupils of the school. While he could be direct in his opinions, he was not averse to using sarcastic humour, and he possessed an infectious enthusiasm which must have encouraged the boys in their endeavours.

When Father Bowden died in 1920 aged 84 he was mourned by many: fellow clergy, parishioners, family and friends – amongst them staff and pupils who recognised his significant influence in advancing and defining 'an Oratory education' for Catholic boys in London.

Father Ralph Kerr, 1874–1932

As Chairman of Managers Father Kerr was closely involved with the development and progress of the Oratory Boys Central School. 'Our interest and troubles were his' commented the Headmaster when paying tribute after the untimely death of Father Kerr in October 1932. Father Kerr had a genuine interest in educational matters and had played an important role not only in advancing and safeguarding Catholic education in London but also by his interest in government policy on a wider scale.

Boys and girls from the Central School sang a Requiem Mass in the Oratory Church on 25 October for the repose of the soul of Father Kerr. Father Kerr's brother Captain Philip Kerr arranged for every boy in the school to receive a photograph and prayer card in his memory.

Father Edward Crewse, 1865–1935

In announcing the death of Father Crewse in 1935 the Headmaster noted the gratitude owed to him, as he was the Superior of The London Oratory when the Central School was formed in 1921, and he always took a great interest in the school's affairs. He attended all school functions and was particularly keen on sport: 'he was never a spectator at games; he joined in the games with the boys, football, cricket, swimming, boxing, athletics, he entered into them all.' He was a driving force behind the view that the school buildings and facilities should be of the highest standard and was prepared to commit to the financial burden of the building projects at the school and to insist on fine materials and good equipment at every level.

2

THE FIRST WORLD WAR

Opposite: Pupils on the annual Battlefields Tour visit the Thiepval Memorial to the Missing on the Somme.

Below: The school War Memorial.

Visitors to The London Oratory School today will see the War Memorial in the Choir Transept of the Chapel with the exhortation to 'PRAY FOR THE SOULS OF THE PAST SCHOLARS OF THIS SCHOOL WHO DIED FOR THEIR COUNTRY'. On this bronze tablet there are 21 names recorded under the First World War. The Memorial was made after the Second World War, when it was decided to record the casualties of both wars.

The names for 1914–18 include R Fenessy, P Hanvey, H Murray, W O'Malley – most likely all of Irish extraction, bearing witness to the Irish Catholic backgrounds of the families from which the school still drew many of its pupils at this time. In drawing up the list of the First World War, names were no doubt recalled by those who had known these 'boys' before they went to war, and some details were communicated by word of mouth. This might explain why the spelling of some of the more unusual names were not quite accurate. Harry Pragnell and Stanley Veacock, for example, appear on the memorial as 'Pragnall' and 'Veocock', while 'R Fenessy' is missing one letter from his true name, Fennessy, and 'F Balkins' has acquired an extra letter (his name was actually Balkin). Research has established their correct identities and enables us to learn about the contributions made by each to the war. Given the enormous number of lives lost in the First World War and the paucity of school records from this era we cannot necessarily recount in detail the war experiences of all old boys, but as current and former pupils who have studied the First World War in their history lessons will know, the conflict which was to be 'the war to end all wars' exposed men to the most horrendous field of battle and made extraordinary demands on them, physically and mentally. Those members of the school who died in the First World War are remembered to this day. Each year the history department takes a group of pupils to visit the sites of the War in Belgium and France, during which it has become established practice to include a visit to an individual grave or memorial associated with a former pupil and there to remember all those members of the school who died in the war. What surprises many pupils today is the fact that so many of those who were killed in the war were there because they volunteered to go, choosing to enlist before conscription was introduced.

The outbreak of war in 1914 had prompted a call for volunteers, and men from all over the country and all walks of life felt the call of duty. The old boys of the Oratory were no exception. Many of those from the school who paid the ultimate sacrifice were volunteers – some had been members of the Oratory Cadet Corps, some served with the London Territorial Divisions. Old Oratorians are represented across the different services. It is no surprise that most of the 21 on the memorial served in the Army, but at least one, Alfred Rorke, joined the Royal Navy Volunteer

The London Oratory School – Part I: Foundation to Seagrave Road, 1863–1969

Force, while Richard Fennessy served with the Royal Marine Light Infantry, Stanley Veacock was in the Royal Flying Corps and Francis Toms volunteered with the Royal Naval Air Service.

Richard Fennessy of the Royal Marine Light Infantry was one of the first to fall in the Great War, killed in action when his vessel, HMS *Aboukir*, was torpedoed in the North Sea in September 1914. In October 1916 Alfred Rorke joined the Royal Naval Volunteer Reserve, from where some of the naval ratings were drawn to join the British Expeditionary Forces in France. Sub-Lieutenant Rorke had been enlisted into Hawke Battalion and was soon on duty in the trenches. He was wounded in the neck and chest in action on 4 February 1917 and was brought to a casualty clearing station where he died eight days later. He is buried in Varennes Military Cemetery.

A grave in the Churchyard of St Thomas of Canterbury in Fulham, the parish in which the school is now situated, marks the last resting place of Francis Hamilton Toms, Flight Sub-Lieutenant in the Royal Naval Air Service. The inscription tells us that 'he voluntarily returned from Brazil, and gave his life in the service of his country.' We do not know what work Francis Toms was doing in Brazil, but on hearing the call for volunteers he came back to London and joined up with the Royal Naval Air Service. The main training ground for pilots was Chingford Aerodrome and it was here Sub-Lieutenant Toms was sent (and where he may have encountered Ivor Novello, who was also based at the aerodrome, although Mr Novello was never to qualify as a pilot). It was at Chingford in February 1916 that Francis Hamilton Toms was killed while on active service. There were many accidents at this airfield, which was described as 'a strip of fogbound and soggy meadowland' (*Loughton & District Historical Society newsletter* 189). The King George Reservoir and nearby Epping Forest proved hazardous to pilots and tragically some, including Francis Toms, were to die in accidents at the base.

Another flyer, Stanley Veacock, is buried in Hazebrouck Military Cemetery in Northern France. A Lieutenant in the Royal Flying Corps, Stanley Veacock had been a member of 20 Squadron. The Squadron was highly decorated for service during the war and boasted 40 flying aces, one of whom, Thomas Mottershead, was awarded a posthumous VC. Four Distinguished Conduct Medals and over 60 Military Crosses and Military Medals were awarded to men of the Squadron. Although never decorated we can believe that Lieutenant Veacock was one of those airmen flying over Northern France attacking the German planes flown by men such as Baron Von Richtofen (the Red Baron). Stanley Veacock was fatally wounded in action on 17 October 1917 and is buried in France.

France is the resting place of other Old Oratorians of the First World War. Robert Farr was killed on 1 July 1916, the first day of the Somme, on which there were 60,000 casualties, with 20,000 deaths. He was just 19 years old. His grave lies in Ancre British Military Cemetery at Beaumont Hamel. For the past 30 years Oratory boys have visited Beaumont Hamel and have walked across the ground of the battle where Robert Farr fought and fell, retracing the movement of the men in the first stages of the Battle of the Somme. The Somme Campaign continued until November 1916. Frank Balkin, serving with the King's Royal Rifle Corps, died on Friday 15 September 1916 in the Battle of Flers-Courcelette, which began on this date, and was the first battle at which tanks were used by the British Army. 'Imagine Hampstead Heath made of cocoa powder, and the natural surface folds further complicated by countless shell-holes, each deep enough to hold a man, and everywhere meandering crevices where men live below the surface of the ground and you will get some idea of the terrain of the attack' (*The 47th London Division Report*, 15 Sept. 1916). It

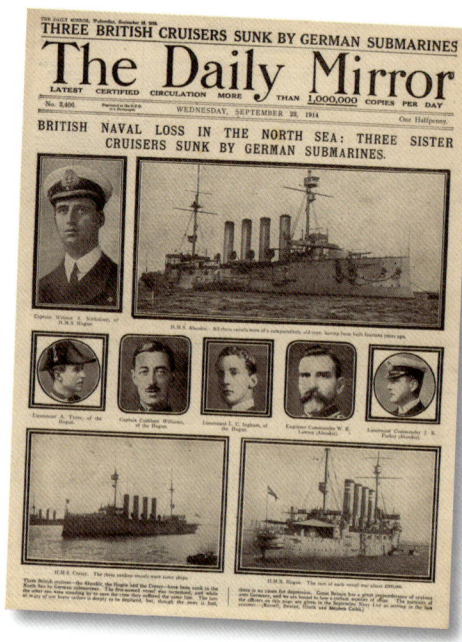

Above: The *Daily Mirror* report of the sinking of three British cruisers by German U boats, including HMS *Aboukir*, the vessel on which Richard Fennessy, Old Oratorian, was serving when he was killed.

Left: The grave of Old Oratorian Francis Hamilton Toms in the churchyard of St Thomas's Church, Fulham.

Right: Gatien du Parc was sent to the school after his family left Belgium at the start of the war. He joined the Belgian Army in 1917.

Below: A plaque on the door of the old school in Cale Street commemorates the hospitality shown to the Belgian evacuees.

is perhaps not surprising that the tanks made little headway and became stuck. The attack turned into a desperate battle with heavy casualties; Frank Balkin was one of the many.

On the very same day that Frank Balkin died another Old Oratorian fell in battle. This was Sergeant Harry Pragnell who, serving with the Royal Engineers, would have played an important role in the preparation for the battle in the days leading up to 15 September. What poignant evidence of the impact of the war on a generation: two Old Oratorians, dying on the same day within a short distance of each other. They were only two of the thousands of men to die in the Battle of the Somme, but two whose names on our school memorial remind us of the horror and price paid by a generation. Sergeant Pragnell was awarded the Military Medal for his action on the day before the battle and is now buried in Fricourt Military Cemetery. Pupils who visit his grave on Battlefields Tours today survey the beautiful, quiet surroundings and consider the sacrifice made over this land nearly 100 years ago. Many of those who fell in the War have no known grave and Michael Duffy, son of the Headmaster John Menzies Duffy, is one. He had been with the London Regiment and was then sent with the Royal Irish Rifles to France, where he was killed in action at the Battle of Cambrai in November 1917. Oratory boys over the years have searched for and found his name on the Thiepval Memorial to the Missing on the Somme.

As well as the aforementioned Military Medal won by Sergeant H Pragnell, three other Oratory scholars were decorated for service in the War. A holiday was granted on 28 January 1918 'on account of the distinctions gained' by the four. Like Sergeant Pragnell, Sergeant H Wilson was awarded the Military Medal. One Old Oratorian, Ernest Allen, won both the Military Medal and the Croix de Guerre. He was to go on to a successful career as an actor and is better known by his stage name, Alan Mowbray. Other recipients of medals were Lieutenant B Hegarty, who won the Distinguished Conduct Medal, and Captain H Kemp of the Royal Flying Corps, who was awarded the Military Cross.

While these former pupils were serving king and country abroad the pupils of the time were still at school in London, where their numbers had been boosted by the arrival of a group of 40 Belgian children, sent there as evacuees after Belgium was occupied by the Germans in 1914. The class had arrived in September 1915 accompanied by their teacher Mr Leslaeghe and later by Mademoiselle Lombaertes. A note in the school log shows that she and her charges were all recorded as absent from school on 15 November 1917, to mark the King's Feast, a national holiday in Belgium. The overseas visitors took over the school hall as a classroom, necessitating the relocation of 'Drill' for the rest of the school. Some of the Belgian pupils left the school as soon as they were of age to serve in the Belgian Army. Gatien du Parc Locmaria, who fought on the Belgian Front from 1917, had been a pupil at the school. He was gassed and wounded but survived the war and went on to a long and fruitful life. Gatien's son Yves has written an account of his father's life in which he shares recollections of the time he spent at the Oratory. Gatien and his brother Alain had not come to London with the Belgian evacuees. Their mother was English and they left Belgium just before the war began and came to the family estate in Ashford. There they offered hospitality to many Belgians, including soldiers on leave from the trenches.

Another pupil at the school during the First World War was T W Hendrick, who in 1981, at the age of 75, shared his recollections of his wartime schooldays. 'We frequently saw a weeping mother arrive at the school to tell a boy that his father or elder brother had been killed in action.'

The boys of the Oratory seem to have continued their studies through the war years, although they would be missing some of their teachers who had joined up. Mr J B Young was probably the first to do so; he enlisted on 31 August 1914. Mr Hayes went in February 1916 and Mr Brown a few months later. Mr Young and Mr Brown are mentioned in later school records, indicating they survived the war, but it seems Mr Hayes may not have survived. On 11 November 1918 the school was granted a half-day holiday to mark the Armistice.

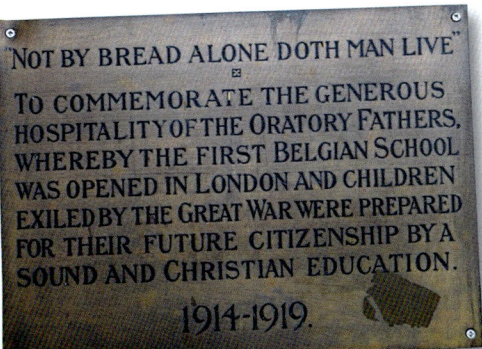

THE INTER-WAR YEARS

The Education Act of 1918 raised the school leaving age to 14, and the London County Council sought to cater for the older ages by opening more Central Schools. Central Schools were free schools for children aged 11 to 15 which provided a good general education with a practical slant, aimed at preparing young people for trade or commerce. They had been part of the London system since 1911, when with about half of London's young people staying in education beyond the then compulsory age of 12 it was recognised that the authorities needed to consider ways to meet the demand for greater provision, while endeavouring to ensure young people were being prepared to take their place in a world recovering from the economic and social impact of the First World War.

The Oratory Parish Magazine of January 1921 notes that 'December 1920 is likely to be an important date in the history of the Oratory Schools'. The reason for this is that the proposal for the Oratory Middle School for boys and the one for girls to convert to Central Schools was accepted by the London County Council. 'They will be the first Catholic Central Schools in London', boasted the parish; in fact they were to be the first in England. This would not be the only time in the history of The London Oratory School when a bold initiative was taken in what was firmly believed to be the best interests of the pupils it served. In establishing the Oratory Central Schools the following stipulations were applied:

(i) Pupils were drawn from all the Catholic schools 'within a reasonable distance'

(ii) Pupils must be 11 years old and will be selected by examination
(iii) Children will remain at the school until they are 16 years old
(iv) The school will have a commercial bias.

Opposite: The Vestibule, Stewart's Grove, with the statue of St Philip which is now in the school Chapel.

Right: The Oratory began to publish a monthly magazine in 1921 containing spiritual and historical writings as well as recording events in the life of the parish and the schools.

The London Oratory School – *Part I: Foundation to Seagrave Road, 1863–1969*

Left: The boys and girls of the Oratory Central Schools in 1933.

Below: The school newsletter and the parish magazine both issued regular appeals for contributions to the building fund.

It was to take nearly 18 months for the necessary arrangements to be completed. The school log entry for 4 September 1922 records 'the official title of the school as ordered by the Board of Education is Chelsea, Oratory Boys Central School, no 7384' (as this first record does not use an apostrophe in the title this is the form followed in the text). In establishing the Central Schools the Fathers had been driven by the recognition that in a time of considerable change and expansion in education 'the same facilities of education should be given to those who regard definite religious teaching as an essential part of education, as those who attach no such importance to teaching of that character', and that consequently there was a need to provide 'a reasonable choice of school for parents of every social class, and equal educational facilities for all, unhampered by disabilities on the grounds of religion' (*Declaration of the English Hierarchy 1928*).

The re-ordering of the Oratory Schools had also necessitated another reshuffle in premises and it was now that the boys moved into the Stewart's Grove buildings that had been occupied by the girls' school; Stewart's Grove would remain the school's home for almost 50 years. The connection with Stewart's Grove goes back to 1860, when the Girls and Infants Schools (which were at that time run by the Sisters of Compassion) moved into the premises under the trusteeship of the Oratory Fathers.

The Central School 'was to provide a first class education for those children who for one reason or another, were unable to gain admission to the secondary schools, but who were, all the same, worthy in every way of the best that could be given them' (Dr Ballard, LCC Inspector, 1924). The school proved very popular and parents applied from across London to secure a place. By 1924 there were nearly 300 applicants for the 80 places available. Places were awarded to pupils from over 30 different Catholic parishes who were successful in the LCC Scholarship examination and nominated by the managers of their primary school. Boys travelled from as far afield as Battersea, Balham, Kensal Rise and Tooting to take up places in the school.

The growth and success of the Oratory Central Schools (the girls' Central School was flourishing alongside the boys') increased the pressure to expand and improve the accommodation and facilities in Stewart's Grove. Parish Appeals were made to raise funds. £5,000 was needed for the necessary building work but progress in raising the money was slow. Parish notices reminded the congregation that unless the schools could better accommodate the pupils who sought places these children would be denied a Catholic

3 / The Inter-War Years

Pages from the souvenir programme for the 1933 fundraising Bazaar.

education, and the money eventually began to come in. Even when the building work began, however, all was not plain sailing. Industrial action in the building trade in the summer of 1924 meant work was halted for a while, and the pressure was on to have the refurbished school ready to open to the pupils returning after the summer holidays. Instead, as the new academic year opened, 'the delicate task of education at Stewart's Grove … carried on in sadly dislocated premises, and in an atmosphere of bricks and mortar and dust, to say nothing of the noise' (PM, iv, p632).

It would be over a year before work was completed and the new buildings were opened by Cardinal Bourne, Archbishop of Westminster. This was a special day for the school, marked with speeches and ceremonies applauding the achievement of the Oratory Central Schools. In addressing the assembly the Cardinal expressed his gratitude to the Fathers of the Oratory for the invaluable support they gave in providing a Catholic education to boys and girls from all over London. 'The more the Catholics of London were brought together when they were boys and girls the stronger would be the force of their influence in manhood and womanhood.'

Despite the growth in applications and more new pupils at the school, not to mention the strong endorsement from the Cardinal, not all parents were recognising the value of an education beyond compulsory age, and in these early years of the Central School many pupils failed to stay for the full five-year course. It would be a few years yet before parents were convinced of the benefits. A recurring theme in extant speeches and notices from this time is the need for parents to play their part in allowing their children to continue longer at school and to provide them with the necessary conditions to do homework – a new concept for many of the families from which the pupils of the Oratory Central Schools were drawn.

Another recurring theme was the ongoing appeal for funds. The arrival of the Central Schools had brought the abolition of the fees which had been paid for the Middle School, although for a few years some parents continued to pay a voluntary fee. The LCC funded the regular expenses of the school but it was necessary to address the question of funding for the building and maintenance work; this fell to the Church to provide, and new fundraising ventures became part of parish life.

A big event in the 1926 Parish Calendar was the Bazaar, a three-day fundraising extravaganza in aid of the Central Schools. On the first day His Eminence, Cardinal Bourne opened the Bazaar and expressed his pleasure at initiating such a unique event, 'that the Oratory should have a Sale of Work' was he remarked 'a new thing – it marked a fresh step in the history of the Church of this country, even as the Central Schools mark a new step. The duty of everyone was to bring all the money they could with them – and to leave it all behind' instructed Cardinal Bourne. The second day of the Bazaar was opened by Hilaire Belloc, the well-known Catholic writer, who had been educated at the Oratory School in Birmingham.

The Oratory Fete is no ordinary event to this day, and the 1926 Bazaar showed that from the very beginning the parishioners of the Oratory were able to put the full force of their talent and influence behind an array of extraordinary stalls. There was Mrs Dasent selling 'objects of piety of all kinds, and beautiful ones too', while from Mrs Dale-Taggart 'every variety of lovely cake seemed procurable.' Lady William Neville and the Honourable Mrs Tatton Bower 'provided provisions in great profusion'. Mrs Wolfe Ritchie and Miss Perks had a 'perfumery stall adorned with wonderful coloured and gilded poppies', and the Children of Mary 'persuaded many to buy their pretty clothes'. As

27

the whole enterprise was for the Schools it would have been incomplete without a contribution from those for whose benefit the event had been organised. They did not disappoint. The children of the girls' school and of the boys' school each had their own stall – 'with all kinds of goods, from woollies to umbrella-stands – not omitting the wooden figures of St Philip – of special interest when we remember that they were all or nearly all, the productions of the girls and boys themselves'. The posters for the event were also produced in the School Art Room – an early sign of the creative talent of Oratory boys and girls – and the 'cauldron' from which raffle tickets were drawn was a product of the handicraft room. The Grand Draw winners were presented with a wonderful selection of prizes, though perhaps Mr D Flory and Miss Rose Allsop might have preferred a swap, given that he won the pink silk cushion and she received the pipe rack. No doubt good fun was had by all, however, and the Bazaar raised the Grand Total of £1,130 13s 8d, all towards the School Fund.

With money coming in building improvements continued, and the installation of electric light throughout the school in 1927 meant that boys would now 'look back with pleasurable regret upon our memories of perpetually breaking gas-mantles and globes, and to the accompaniment of violent "pops" which were wont to punctuate the most interesting lessons' (PM, vii, p174).

In 1928 the Parish launched another appeal for funds as once again it was evident that there was a need for serious building work in order to accommodate the constant demand for places at the Oratory Central Schools. New building work had been authorised to proceed on the strength of borrowed money which would need to be repaid. In advertising the appeal the Fathers stated that since the Oratory Central School was opened in 1921 it 'has been attended by almost embarrassing success' and 'it has become necessary to make extensive additions to the school premises'. These works were to start straight away, meaning the incursion of a large debt. Within a year £5,377 towards the required £17,500 had been raised, but it would require many more appeals, stiff talking and donations to meet the target. In 1929 readers of the parish magazine were informed that donations to the fund were diminishing, and consequently received this stern address:

> After all the advertising, all the talking, the writing, the propaganda of the last twelve months the collection is less than the year before … hardly a

3 / *The Inter-War Years*

Above: A group of staff and pupils from the 1930s, possibly those involved in a fundraising play.

Right: The school badge is still visible today in the 1930s ornamental ironwork on a window at the Royal Marsden Hospital.

Left: The new extension at Stewart's Grove, designed by Christian Barman.

Left below: Pupils from the Girls Central School on the rooftop area, *c*.1925.

matter for congratulation is it? It seems to us that those who come to our church have in any case some obligation in honour to support the Oratory and its works: either they live in the parish, and all the Oratory undertakings are their own (or should be); or they live outside the parish, and then they should do something to repay the Oratory for the convenience of a fine church and a 12 o'clock Mass with something rather more than the usual penny in the plate.

Over the next few years the parish magazine regularly advertised fundraising events such as dances in Chelsea Town Hall. In 1932 the debt remained large, with the annual interest alone placing a heavy burden on Church finances. A new drive for funds was made with the introduction of 'a number of attractive boxes for all those willing to take one and keep it in some prominent place in their home and to invite friends and visitors to drop an occasional coin into them' (PM, xii, p32). Within just a few months this new venture had returned 'the very satisfactory' sum of £14 2s 1d. Parents were asked to take a box for their homes and along with this boys had cards on which parents noted the sum donated and sent the money into school with their son. Unfortunately suspicions that not all such monies were reaching the Fund were raised when the Headmaster asked the question 'has the very significant decrease in the amount subscribed to the School Buildings Fund lately, any connection with the extraordinary number of Yo-Yos which have recently appeared in the playground?' There were, however, some families for whom the request for a regular sum towards the Building Fund was beyond their means and although never forced to pay, life could be uncomfortable for those who did not. One former pupil recalls handing over his bus fare to his form master rather than explain that his parents could not afford to meet the voluntary subscription, and then having to walk eight miles home!

The reason for such vigorous fundraising was that this time round the builders were to be engaged for something more ambitious than the reordering and renovation entailed by previous projects; a major extension was to be built on the Stewart's Grove site. The architect commissioned with the task, Christian Barman, was to draw acclaim for the aesthetic and practical designs for the boys' and girls' schools, with *The Architectural Review 1930* detailing some of the fine work that went into design and construction of the new extension. As the old school buildings were already on the site the brief was 'to interpose a new block between

29

The London Oratory School – *Part I: Foundation to Seagrave Road, 1863–1969*

Left: Following the new extension to the school in 1930 architect Christian Barman was commissioned to design a dining room on the site of the boys' upper playground. The room shown here in 1933 provided 'pleasant, even aesthetic surroundings' in which the boys would eat their meals – surroundings which Dr Summerbell remarked 'cannot but have a lasting effect on a boy's character'.

Below left: The rare provision of 'separate, individual wash basins' was commented upon in *The Architectural Review*, 1930.

these two existing blocks designed, regardless of each other, by different architects. And the new block had not only to fit neatly into these old ones, but also to be capable of linking up with any future extensions.' In executing this task the idea that functionality should never override beauty in the construction of a place of learning was well understood, as was the appreciation of the subliminal effect of surroundings on the child's development. The 'gracious proportions', colour and form of the vestibule were remarked upon by Mr J Compton, Director of Education for Barking, as he observed that, 'Boys and girls passing daily through this vestibule will be influenced to a spiritual quickening and preparedness for intellectual enterprises.' He went on to comment, 'I have visited many new schools, among them the interesting and imposing ones in Hamburg and Charlottenburg; but standing in the vestibule of the Oratory Schools I experienced a mental excitement, a sharpened expectation, beyond anything I had felt in the others.' Practical needs were catered for too, even the provision of separate wash basins rather than the less expensive 'trough', showed the desire to set a standard and apply the belief that the pupils were worthy of decent facilities and accommodation. The importance of physical sustenance was recognised in the introduction of the dining hall – a long-anticipated improvement to life at Stewart's Grove.

When the Cardinal of Westminster came to open the building on 5 February 1930 he spoke to the assembled Fathers, teachers, pupils and parishioners and reminded them all of the association of the Fathers of the Oratory in London with education, acknowledging that the school 'was doing a work for the whole of London, north and south of the river'. Tours of the new buildings followed; one particular attraction was the new rooftop playground for the boys, with reports that on a good day it was possible to see as far as Hampstead.

The Dining Room, first conceived of in the 1929 extension, was improved in 1931 as it was noted by staff that boys travelling from all across London needed a decent meal to provide midday nourishment since they were not working as efficiently in the afternoons. 'Nothing can really take the place of a good hot meal for a growing boy', said the school authorities. Demand for dinners was growing as well, and the mothers of these 'growing boys' received the following message in the school newsletter:

> *When you have done a hard day's work and have then to set to and prepare your husband's dinner, think of us with sympathy, for do you know that your boy if he stays to dinner helps to eat per week: 160lbs of fresh meat, 75lbs of fish, 150lbs of greens, 336lbs of potatoes, 2 bushels of fresh fruit and 56lbs of dried fruit, 10lbs of lard and margarine, 14lbs of jam, 24lbs of biscuits, 70lbs of flour and pounds and pounds of other groceries… But this is only part of the tale; so when you turn over that chop in the evening, think of us!*

School dinners remain an integral part of life at The London Oratory School, and although custom dictates that boys in any school will not always appreciate the fare before them, visitors are invariably impressed with an Oratory dinner. When Technology Inspector Mr Beresford Ingram visited the school in June 1932 to inspect the kitchens and dining arrangements he ate the same dinner as the boys and expressed himself as being 'extremely pleased with everything'. The school prided itself on providing the best school dinners in London.

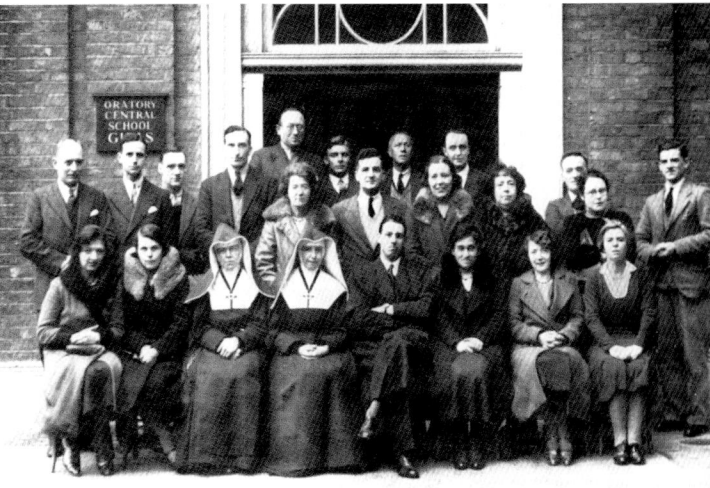

By this time the school had a new Headmaster, Dr Summerbell. Mr Duffy had retired in 1930 after a long and distinguished career over 43 years in Oratory schools. On his last day at the school all the boys gathered in St Philip's Hall, where one of them made a speech on behalf of all. Addressing Mr Duffy he said, 'We wish to thank you for all you have done for us; your help and example in our holy religion; your help in our work; and at its end your care and anxiety for us that we should make a good start in the world [for teaching us to] take our knocks and come up smiling again'. From the boys Mr Duffy was presented with a photograph album of each of the classes and of the staff, along with a four-valve, room-to-room portable wireless set. The staff presented him with 'a leather Revelation suitcase'. There were further presentations when on the evening of 8 May 1930 'a large appreciative and representative assembly' gathered to pay tribute and present Mr Duffy with £200, a gold watch and chain and the diploma of the papal order, the cross '*pro Ecclesia et Pontifice*'. Mr Cosgrave, in the role of Chairman of the J M Duffy Testimonial Fund, gave a résumé of Mr Duffy's career, drawing attention to his contribution to the academic success of his boys and remarking that his interest in sport meant 'he was always worth an extra man on the field'. In the spirit of great schoolmasters Mr Duffy also kept up an interest in the progress of his pupils after they left the school, and it was remarked that in this way he continued to assist their development beyond their schooldays. As witness to his influence in shaping Catholics for the future the impressive number of vocations to the priesthood amongst his 'old boys' was cited.

Above right: The staff of the two Central Schools in 1933.

Below: The first edition of *The Oratorian*, the school newsletter.

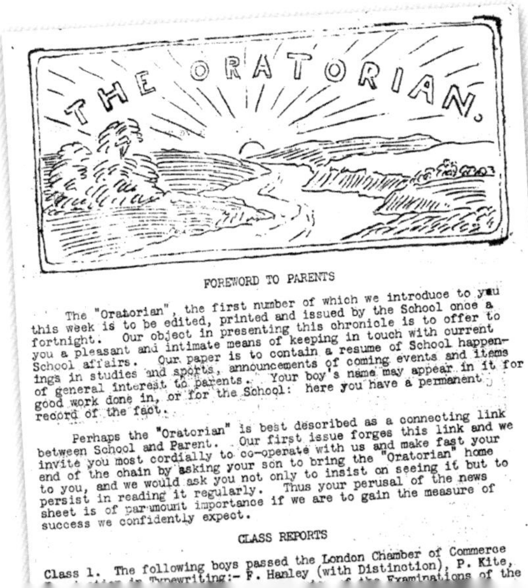

THE ORATORIAN.

FOREWORD TO PARENTS

The "Oratorian", the first number of which we introduce to you this week is to be edited, printed and issued by the School once a fortnight. Our object in presenting this chronicle is to offer to you a pleasant and intimate means of keeping in touch with current School affairs. Our paper is to contain a resume of School happenings in studies and sports, announcements of coming events and items of general interest to parents. Your boy's name may appear in it for good work done in, or for the School: here you have a permanent record of the fact.

Perhaps the "Oratorian" is best described as a connecting link between School and Parent. Our first issue forges this link and we invite you most cordially to co-operate with us and make fast your end of the chain by asking your son to bring the "Oratorian" home to you, and we would ask you not only to insist on seeing it but to persist in reading it regularly. Thus your perusal of the news sheet is of paramount importance if we are to gain the measure of success we confidently expect.

CLASS REPORTS

Class 1. The following boys passed the London Chamber of Commerce ... in Typewriting:- F. Hanley (with Distinction), P. Kite, ... of the Examinations of the

News of old boys is always of interest to their former schools. The Oratory was no exception, and visits of successful alumni are recorded with pride. With the publication of the first *Oratorian* a means of noting news of this kind was established, with many references to visits and contact from boys wanting to keep in touch with their alma mater. In this era *The Oratorian* was not quite the bumper read it has come to be, but in its infancy as *The Oratory Central Magazine*, first issued in 1927, there were some features which survive in its later version, for example publication of pupils' writing, including both poetry and prose contributions. In 1931 the first *Oratorian* in the form of a newsletter was sent home to parents, encouraging them to make sure they got their copy and read it as 'your boy's name may appear' and 'here you have a permanent record of the fact'. To this day *The Oratorian* remains the best record of a boy's Oratory career.

Another development in the early years of Dr Summerbell's leadership was the move to school uniform. Parents had been encouraged to buy their sons a suit of dark grey, with long trousers or shorts in the school pattern, obtainable from the Bradford Textile Company of Victoria Street, but as demand from parents for 'distinctive school suits at a moderate cost' grew, an official uniform followed in 1932: a single-breasted suit jacket, along with a school cap. Parents could purchase from the Bradford Textile Company 'coat, vest and trousers' for between £28 6s and £40 6s. For some families this cost would be prohibitive. Edmund 'Ted' O'Sullivan was a pupil at the school in these years. He recalled turning up to school in 'a cheap, royal blue blazer, donated by one of my cousins, and silver grey trousers, and he felt conscious of 'a class distinction caused by poverty' (Edmund O'Sullivan, *All My Brothers*, 2007, p81). The majority of parents did, it seems, make the journey to Victoria Street to get their sons suitably clothed, ensuring they set off to school looking smart each day, although there was a small minority to whom the Headmaster addressed a stern rebuke:

if parents would only realise that our cap is known and recognised throughout the length and breadth of London, and that boys must each day come … into contact with prospective employers, they will understand that in the matter of dress they have a duty not only to their own boys, but also to the School… An untidy and slovenly boy not only forfeits the respect of others but the psychological effect on his character is serious and he quickly loses his own self respect and confidence.

The importance of preparing boys for that all-important interview with a prospective employer was at stake if good habits and a neat and tidy appearance were not well established. And indeed the school was building a strong reputation with employers across London.

Throughout the 1920s and 1930s the Oratory Central School could boast many former pupils in successful employment. A good number were in clerical work, with business and commercial interests well represented, while others were finding engagements with technical firms, and some entered civil service training or found work with legal firms. A steady number of boys were also entering the Armed Forces. The significant number electing to enter the RAF may be a direct result of the enthusiasm with which 50 Oratorians attended a talk in 1935 given by CMA Scott on 'the most thrilling and inspiring' experience of winning the England-to-Australia air race. Those less ambitious for adventure found good positions nearer to home, and it

Top left: John Dennis Patrick Hogan, who attended the school 1929–34, wearing his new school uniform.

Right: Programme from 'a memorable day for the school,' 8 June 1935.

CMA Scott gave 'a most thrilling and inspiring talk' at the school in 1935 and may have inspired boys to construct the airfix model of his plane.

is interesting to note the practice of old boys returning to the school with the offer of a place in their own firms for other Oratory boys. One former pupil, so grateful for the education and opportunity provided for him by the school, was moved to send a letter of thanks and to 'enclose my first week's salary as a contribution to the School Building Fund as a small token of my gratitude for the kindness I received at the Oratory'. Not all the boys left with such happy memories. Ted O'Sullivan would look back with mixed feelings on his Oratory career, recalling teachers such as J C Burns, Siddie Kerr, Mr Blight, Mr Todd, Mr Kelly and Mr Murray as good men 'who taught because they liked their subjects, both those they taught and those they were teaching', whereas Dr Summerbell and Mr O'Neill were viewed as harsh men, who took satisfaction from inflicting brutal punishment on boys. The fear instilled by such teachers would cast a long shadow over Ted's schooling and colour his memories of those days.

Meanwhile the pattern of life at the school went on with the annual round of school events, punctuated here and there with some special moments. In the spring of 1934 the school was granted the honour of providing 20 boys to act as Official Stewards when the Queen came to open the new wing of the neighbouring Cancer Hospital. On 7 December that same year school history was made when for the first time Mass was celebrated within the school building at the newly built altar in St Philip's Hall. Another encounter with royalty came in 1935. 'We will all remember the 8th June 1935': with these words the school recorded the experience of a group of masters and boys who had lined up to see their Majesties King George V and Queen Mary on their Jubilee Drive through London. The school party had taken up position on the King's Road and secured an excellent view. Little did they know that only months later the country would be in mourning following the death of the King. The Old Boys' Dinner 1936 was postponed as a mark of respect.

Looking over the records of the school in the 1930s it is possible to see a line of continuity with the present. Expectation and opportunity were prominent in the philosophy of education and in the practical experience of the pupils. In 1935 an exciting opportunity was taken up by 18 boys and masters who sailed from Tilbury docks on a fortnight's Baltic cruise. They recorded a visit to Kiel: 'we could not help but notice Krupp's Yards with torpedo boats and submarines on the stocks and battleships in the harbour with Hitler's beautiful armed yacht. We said goodbye to the Nazis, the Hitler Youth and the Marinschule, and lazed gently through the Kiel Canal'. How poignant to think that for some on that cruise the next encounter with Germany would be as enemies at war.

The coming of war in 1939 was to bring another chapter in the history of the school and some interesting changes at Stewart's Grove.

THE SECOND WORLD WAR

Opposite: Tonypandy today. The pupils of the Oratory Central School were evacuated to Tonypandy in South Wales during the Second World War.

Below: Tonypandy in the 1940s was a new experience for the boys from the school, after life in London.

With war looming parents were advised to send their children to the country, as it was expected from the outset that London would suffer from German bombing campaigns. Some of the boys of the Oratory Central School were first sent to Herefordshire or Clacton, and then the Central School children moved to Tonypandy in South Wales, where the Oratory Boys and Girls Central Schools were to continue as separate schools, providing a full-time education for the pupils. Father Dale-Roberts of the Oratory accompanied the party and provided for their spiritual needs, reporting back to the Parish that all was going well, the children were in good health and the locals were very kind to all.

Although evacuation was encouraged a significant number of parents chose to keep their sons at home. The school register for 1939 shows 115 boys were taken off the school roll on 1 September 1939 as they were 'not evacuated'. Of these some of the older ones would soon be volunteering for war service. Forty-five Old Oratorians were to lose their lives in the Second World War. Oratory boys in more recent years may have looked over at the Memorial in the School Chapel, read those names and wondered about the achievement and sacrifice behind each one. What did these young men do in the war? The young men of the Oratory did a great deal. From London to France, in Norway, in Italy and in Germany, Egypt, Thailand and Iraq, on land and sea and in the air, Old Oratorians were making the ultimate sacrifice.

When young Derek Aust left school in April 1939, he was 17 years old and about to start his first job. Aust had done well at the Oratory – within a year of starting he was awarded a prize for his essay on the Canonisation of the English Martyrs Thomas More and John Fisher. Unlike some of his contemporaries Derek had stayed at school for the full six years. His father earned his living as an artist and he and his wife Christina, while not particularly well off, were living comfortably enough and bringing up their son in a strong faith and with a good work ethic. Throughout Derek's childhood the family lived at 29 Haldon Road in Wandsworth. Derek was a member of the local scout group and in time became a Scout Leader. When the war started he wanted to 'do his bit' and he volunteered as a

Dewinton Street, Tonypandy.

PART I : FOUNDATION TO SEAGRAVE ROAD, 1863–1969

Despatch Rider in the Auxiliary Fire Service at Wandworth's West Hill Fire Station, just a short walk from home. As a Despatch Rider Derek was charged with taking messages and instructions around the district by motorcycle, and so to assist in coordinating fire fighting and rescue services. He would report to the Fire Station at the start of each duty and be on standby until the call came to attend a fire or a bomb site. On the night of Saturday 16 November 1940, Derek, with five other members of the AFS, was in the recreation room awaiting instructions when the station took a direct hit from a high explosive bomb; all six men were killed in an instant.

Another young volunteer was John Wright; he and Derek Aust had started school on the same day in 1933, and both died in November 1940. John was on duty with the Home Guard. Just three years earlier *The Oratory Parish Magazine* had announced John Wright's success as Great British Champion in the National Schoolboys' Boxing Championships.

Both Derek Aust and John Wright were buried in Streatham Cemetery, where there is a section devoted to fire-fighters who died in the Second World War.

Derek Aust and John Wright were not the only Old Oratorian casualties of 1940. On 15 June Sergeant Colin Burran of the RAF was on a reconnaissance flight from the RAF base in the Shetlands to the Norwegian harbour at Trondheim when his plane was shot down. The bodies of the airmen were buried in a marsh at the crash site, but after the war were reinterred in the Military Cemetery at Trondheim. Wreckage from the crash is still in evidence at the site today.

After the initial stages of the war casualties were not so intense in 1941, but there was still news of losses, sometimes from tragic accidents. Peter Lynch was on a flight which took off from its base in Lincoln on a mission to lay mines off the Frisian Islands. A short time after take-off the plane crashed into the staff residences of a nearby girls' school. All on the plane and one teacher from the school were killed. From mid 1942 to 1945 there was a steady stream of bad news as the war opened up on many fronts, and all three services were to find themselves in the front line.

The Africa Campaign got underway in 1942 and Old Oratorian Corporal Thomas Blackley of the Queen's Own Royal West Kent lost his life in the fight for El Alamein in September. Two months later fellow old boy Leslie Wallington, with the Royal Corps of Signals, died in Algeria shortly after the allied invasion began in November.

Pages from the school register show that some parents chose to keep their sons in London in September 1939. Those who were 'not evacuated' are removed from the school roll at this date.

In Memory of six members
of the London Auxiliary Fire Service
who died on this site as a result of enemy action
on the night of 16th/17th November 1940
when the old Wandsworth Fire Station received
a direct hit from a high-explosive bomb.

Fm Cecil Robert Andreazzi
Fm William George Brum
Fm Leslie Walter Isaacs
Fm Albert Arthur Turner
Despatch Rider Derek Edward Aust
Company Officer AFS William Beard

Above: West Hill Fire Station as it was before it was destroyed in the bombing of 16 November 1940. A plaque on the rebuilt station commemorates those who lost their lives that night, including recent school leaver Derek Aust.

Right: The wreckage of the plane in which former pupil Peter Lynch died in 1941.

Of the 45 Old Oratorians whose names are engraved on the school War Memorial, 21 were in the RAF. At least six of these are commemorated on the RAF Memorial at Runnymede where the names of over 20,000 aircrew are recorded. In May 1942 John Rocks survived when his plane crash landed at RAF Cottesmore, but less than one month later he lost his life when his Halifax bomber came down in the English Channel. In June of 1942 Sergeant Gilbert Murphy of the RAFVR, having left his position with the National Bank where he had worked since leaving school in 1937, was reported missing after a flight from the airbase at Abingdon. Three months later Pilot Officer Desmond Downer was reported missing in action when his plane crashed off the coast of Holland. He had been with 106 Squadron under the Command of Guy Gibson.

Flying Officer James Edward Wootton had been working for an advertising agency before joining up and was flying with 25 Squadron until his death in June 1943. That same month James Carr was on a night-time mission to attack fuel dumps in northern France. Huge damage was inflicted on the target, but in the course of the attack the Lancaster in which Sergeant Carr was Flight Engineer was hit and brought down, with all lives lost. The sixth Old Oratorian commemorated at Runnymede is Flight Sergeant Wilfrid Witty, aged 21, whose plane disappeared without trace after taking off from the RAF base at Little Staughton in Bedfordshire on a mission to mark gun positions on the Belgian coast. After the war Wilfrid Witty's father donated the altar rails for the school altar in memory of his son.

Another flyer was Daniel Patrick O'Keefe (known as Pat). He was not yet 16 when his schooldays came to an end, as he left school in September 1939. Once he was eligible he joined the Royal Air Force Volunteer Reserve and was on active service in Germany in the latter stages of the war. On the evening of 7/8 March 1945, he was involved in an attack on Harburg, with the aim of destroying crucial enemy oil supplies. It was deemed a 'successful mission', with photographic evidence showing extensive damage inflicted on the refinery, but a heavy price was paid. Sergeant O'Keefe was in one of the Lancasters of 5 Group, 49 Squadron. He was the bomb aimer in the plane and had accomplished his mission when his Pilot F/O Elkington was hit in the leg by shrapnel. The pilot managed nonetheless to get the plane back to base but Sergeant O'Keefe was reported missing; his helmet was still in the plane and there was blood on his oxygen mask. His chute was gone but hopes that he had managed to bale out and survive were in vain. His body was later recovered and was buried in Becklingen Military Cemetery in Germany.

The names of at least six Old Oratorians are engraved on the Air Forces Memorial at Runnymede.

Richard Drago was also with the RAFVR. He died in a plane crash on a training exercise in Yorkshire in 1943 at the age of 22. Another RAFVR casualty was 20-year-old Wilfred Shirley, serving as a bomber until his death in May 1943. Anthony Fuge was a navigator with the RAFVR. Shot down over France in April 1943, he was imprisoned first by the Gestapo in the infamous prison at Fresnes and later transferred to a POW camp. Although he survived the war he died at home in December 1946. He rests in St Mary's cemetery in Kensal Green, along with two other Old Oratorians, Aubrey Leslie Mayo, who was in the RAF, and George Fennell. Parts of the wreckage of the plane in which George Fennell was killed are still being unearthed to this day in a field in Gloucestershire. He was Navigator on a practice flight before the D-Day landings when the Dakota in which he was flying was in a collision with another plane returning to the airfield at Down Ampney.

As the war moved on into 1944 the RAF was active over Germany, and Flight Sergeant Ronald Dudley of 5 Group 97 Squadron was to win the Distinguished Flying Medal and pay with his life for his service in the air. He had proved his mettle after surviving 'Black Thursday', 16 December 1943. On this day 97 Squadron, as part of the Battle of Berlin, were involved in bombing raids on the city. Returning from their mission they encountered dreadful weather conditions at their home station, RAF Bourn. The station staff realised that the 21 Lancaster crews due to land were going to have to be rapidly diverted, but the technical systems were not up to it and five crews lost their lives in crashes as they came in to land – and one had already been brought down over Berlin. Ronald Dudley survived that night. Five weeks later, however, Flight Sergeant Dudley and his fellow crew members were on a mission over Magdeburg. The attack was deemed successful and 19 Lancasters flew safely back to RAF Bourn. Just one aircraft failed to return; that was the plane in which Ronald Dudley was a crew member. They had been shot down over Berlin. The *London Evening Gazette* of 11 February announced the award of the Distinguished Flying Medal to Flight Sergeant Ronald Dudley.

1939–1945

AUST · D · E	GOLDSMITH · H · R	PRENDERGAST · J
BLACKLEY · T · C	HARRIS · D	PRYTHERGEH · F · J
BRITTAIN · G · A	HEALEY · J	ROCKS · J · G
BRITTAIN · W · P	KIRBY · T	ROOTS · P · H
BURRAN · C · A	LAVIS · J · E	SCOTT · J · A
CANN · B · L	LYNCH · P · J	SHIRLEY · W
CARR · J · B	MASEK · S	STAFFORD · D · H
COLLINS · P · J	MAYO · A · L	TAYLOR · A · E
CONDON · P · R	MORGAN · C · F	WALLINGTON · L · J
DOWNER · D · J	MURPHY · F	WILKES · J · F
DRAGO · R · E	MURPHY · G	WITHERS · W
DUDLEY · R	O'KEEFE · D · P	WITTY · W · T
FAIRWEATHER · S · G	PAWLEY · E · W	WOOTTON · J · E
FENNELL · G · T	PICKERING · J · F	WRIGHT · J
FUGE · A · J	POOLER · G	WHIFFEN · R · C

REQUIESCANT · IN · PACE

Casualties of the Second World War recorded on the War Memorial in the school Chapel.

Terence Kirby was still at school when war broke out but by 1944 he was serving with 166 squadron of the RAFVR until his life was cut tragically short; he was just 19 when his plane came down over Belgium.

Boys from The London Oratory School who have visited Krakow on school journeys were probably not aware that a former pupil lies buried in the Krakow Rakowicki Military Cemetery. Peter Roots was in the RAF and was with 148 Squadron assigned to the Special Operations Executive. As one veteran expressed it, 'the life expectancy in the 148 Squadron was one month. Most of them weren't coming back.' Peter Roots was part of a mission on Special Duty Operations to bring supplies to Warsaw during the uprising of 1944. Churchill, unhappy at the lack of support from Russia for the Poles in their resistance to the Nazis, ordered the RAF to organise a special mission to take in supplies and munitions to the struggling Poles. RAF 148 Squadron, based in Italy, was selected for the task. Peter Roots was in one of the planes bringing supplies when it crashed on Redutowa Street in the Wola district of Warsaw on 15 August 1944. In 1935 an entry in the school newsletter recorded that a 12-year-old Peter Roots had spent his summer holiday in Italy where he had seen 'the man of the moment, Mussolini'. Who could have foreseen how events would bring Peter back to Italy and from there to his death in Poland aged just 21? John Lavis, Royal Artillery, was also sent to Italy and now lies buried in the Caserta Military Cemetery. He had come a long way from the Lewis Buildings, West Kensington, where he grew up. Another Old Oratorian who lost his life in Italy was Arthur James Scott, a one-time stalwart of Oratory school drama productions.

The London Oratory School may have drawn its early pupils from the Irish Catholics of London, and these remained prominent over the years, but it has long been a characteristic of the school that many nationalities are represented among the boys. Stanley (Stanislav) Masek may have felt an obligation to his Czech roots when he joined the RAF 310 Czech Squadron. He completed a number of successful missions over France and Belgium and is recorded as having two confirmed victories over enemy aircraft before he lost his life. Another Old Oratorian who proved he was capable of a tough mission was Bernard Cann, serving with 45 Commando of the Royal Marines, who died on active service in Germany as the battle was fought for the capture of Berlin towards the end of the War in Europe. One week before Bernard Cann's death Ronald Charles Whiffen (known to his family as Charlie) had lost his life in western Germany. After a school career in which he had made a noteworthy contribution to the football team, he volunteered for the army in 1940, serving with the 4th County of London Yeomanry. He had survived the conflict for almost five years before tragically losing his life in the final stages of the Allied Victory.

Even after VE Day the Oratory was hit by news of casualties as the war continued in the Far East, where Old Oratorians had been serving. Edward Pawley, a gunner with the Royal Artillery, had died in a Japanese POW camp in Thailand in 1943. In 1945, with the war continuing for the 'forgotten army', Flight Sergeant Patrick Ronald Condon, flying on a mission with the Chindit Air Supply, was killed when his plane crashed while trying to avoid low cloud. How innocent the days of 1934, when 'Condon won the slow bicycle race' at Sports Day, must have seemed compared to the conditions of war in the jungle. Even in June 1945 the Oratory Roll of Honour was not yet complete

The London Oratory School – Part I: Foundation to Seagrave Road, 1863–1969

as James Wilkes, Flight Sergeant with the RAF in Basra, was killed on active service in August 1945. He lies buried in Iraq. As Old Oratorians of more recent years have also served in Iraq, the contribution of Oratory boys in the armed services all over the globe continues.

There were understandably fewer recruits to the Navy from amongst Oratorians, although Patrick Collins of Chelsea died on HMS *Springbank* when it was struck by a U boat in 1941, and Henry Goldsmith was Mentioned in Despatches after he died in an explosion on board ship at Naples.

These testimonials record the service of those who paid with their lives in the Second World War, although of course many other Old Oratorians, staff and pupils, were in the forces and engaged in civilian services during the war. Ted O'Sullivan (1930–4), who served with the London Irish Rifles, lived through the war and later wrote a memoir of his childhood, his family, and his army experience. He fought in Italy and recounts the hard-fought campaign in which he and others like him were engaged. Another Old Oratorian and member of the London Irish was Sergeant John Madigan, who was awarded the Military Medal in North Africa. Other Old Oratorians decorated for their action against the enemy include Flying Officer Frank Henry and Squadron Leader Rodney Roche, who were awarded the Distinguished Flying Cross and Lieutenant L Wells, who received the Distinguished Conduct Medal.

On Remembrance Day, November 1933, Father Holland of the Oratory had addressed the boys of the school on 'the horrors and the evil of war', but at the same time reminded them 'that it is the duty of a good Catholic to come to the aid of his country when he may be required to do so.' Many of his audience were subsequently required to do so and, as these examples show, they did so.

There is another chapter to the Oratory's War, and that is the story of what was happening at the Stewart's Grove buildings, as even the school building itself was to play a part in the war effort. When the war started the War Office took over the school and turned it into an internment camp, Brompton Oratory School Internment Centre, 001, where foreign aliens and suspected spies would be held and interrogated. For some foreign nationals they were held there simply on account of the fact that they were of the nationality of an enemy country, while other residents were more of a threat to national security.

At a meeting in the Prime Minister's Rooms in the House of Commons on 3 April 1941 Winston Churchill and fellow members of the War Cabinet considered the case of Prince Friedrich of Prussia, who was at that time

Above: Prince Friedrich of Prussia was interned in the Oratory School, Stewart's Grove.

Left: Old Oratorian Colour Sergeant Ted O'Sullivan, photographed at the Spanish Steps in Rome, was one of a small group of the Irish Brigade to be received by the Pope in 1944.

interned in the Oratory School. He had been a student at Cambridge University when the war started and was first arrested in May 1940. He was sent to a camp in Canada but had been brought back under consideration for release as he was regarded as being of no threat to security; indeed he was stated to be anti Nazi. While the matter was being deliberated he was kept in Camp 001. The Cabinet decided that he should be released but kept under surveillance.

Not all those held at Stewart's Grove were of such high status. One pupil of Italian extraction found himself temporarily back in the school in 1940 interned as 'an enemy alien.' He came back again in the 1950s as a teacher and his pupils were fascinated one day to hear him explain that the brass buttons on the floor of Form 3A's classroom were a legacy of the fact that the room had been the Recreation Room of the Internment Camp and the brass studs marked the toe line for darts. Another former internee who later found himself associated with The London Oratory School was the artist Eduardo Paolozzi. Being of Italian origin he was interned in Scotland during the war but was at one point brought to Stewart's Grove. Over 50 years later he found himself once again linked to The London Oratory School, now at Seagrave Road, as a patron of the Arts Centre, which he visited on a number of occasions.

Others who were held for interrogation at the Oratory include a double agent identified as Josef, alias Rhubarb. He was a Polish sailor who had become a Communist and had been involved in spying for the Russians against Britain. While he was being detained at Stewart's Grove he encountered the Japanese internee and former Embassy Press Attaché, Mr Matsumota, and agreed to convey some letters to a relative of Mr Matsumota's in the Japanese Embassy in Lisbon. In fact Josef had agreed to work for MI5 and would be reporting back to the British any information he could obtain. He would also pass false or exaggerated information to the Japanese. Josef was never quite trusted in his role as double agent, and a complex second layer of intelligence was woven around him. At one stage the novelist Graham Greene was involved in working with Rhubarb on a secret mission in Lisbon, which involved the intriguing character described by Greene as 'the fireman who sold canaries'.

Another Japanese internee was Matusomoto, the Japanese Cultural Attaché who was under suspicion of using influential contacts in high society, secured through his position as Attaché, to gain information useful to the enemy. It was never clear whether he was actually a spy but he was held from 1941 to 1943 before being repatriated.

Suspected German spies were also held and questioned at the Oratory School Internment Camp. One of these, Hubert Kurt Sachsel of Cromwell Road, had business interests in the British Glycerine Manufacturers Limited until giving notice in the High Court in March 1939 that the business was to be wound up. He then seems to have gone back to his native land, and on returning to London in July 1940 was promptly arrested and held at Camp 001 along with another suspect, German spy Georg Wurstle. As well as detaining enemy spies and aliens the authorities were also alert to spies from lands occupied by Germany. When the Norwegian Knut Jorgen Broderson, who worked as an agent for the Germans, was rumoured to be on his way to England, an alert was sent to all ports advising that should he land he was to be apprehended and 'sent to Oratory School, London, for interrogation'. Records indicate that Duncan Scott-Ford, who became the first Briton to be hanged under the terms of the 1940 Treachery Act, was questioned by Special Branch Officers at Stewart's Grove in August 1942. He was charged with selling information to the enemy, tried at the Old Bailey and subsequently hanged in Wandsworth Prison.

No doubt the Oratory schoolboys would have revelled in, and perhaps even embellished, stories of the school during the war had they known of what was happening in those familiar buildings, but much would remain secret while they continued to study miles away in Wales. Even when the school returned to London later in the war they could not reoccupy their old premises, having to function on the site of Bousfield School and taking some rooms in the Oratory House. Brian Cheesman joined the school in 1944 and remembers attending the Bousfield site: 'the excitement of travelling by underground to Gloucester Road Station, finding one's way through to Old Brompton Road, climbing flights of stairs to one of the top classrooms in this old Victorian building was a new sensation'. It would not be until 1946 that the War Office moved out and the Stewart's Grove buildings were returned to school use. Pupils in later years observed the prison-style bars on some of their windows, one of the visible legacies of the school's wartime occupants.

Poster advertising the Junior House programme of wartime songs and sketches, a performance in which entertaining songs were interspersed with historical sketches and reflective readings.

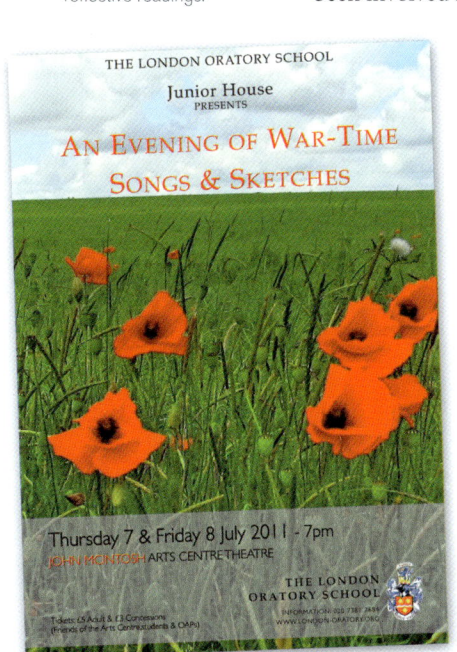

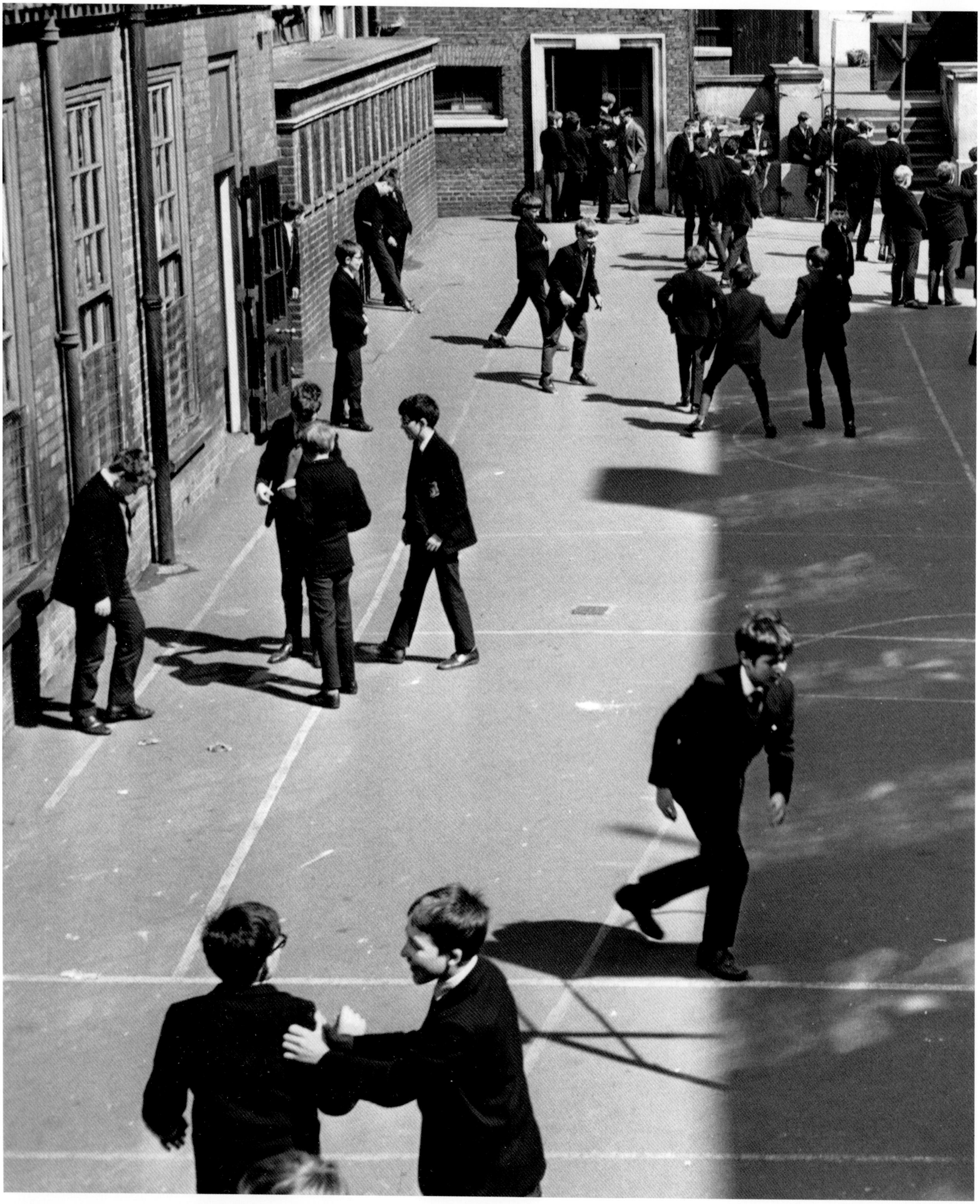

The Post-War Years, 1945–69

When the school was handed back to the Oratory after its wartime occupation by the War Office the buildings were not fit for immediate occupation and a programme of redecoration was soon underway, with much of the work being done by the boys themselves. There would be changes when the school resumed life in the old premises, not least the fact that only four of the pre-war staff returned to their posts after the war, and as ever in the world of education more change was on the way.

The Education Act of 1944 had caused considerable concern in Catholic circles, with threats to the independent religious character of schools. The Oratory Fathers had been directly involved in discussions to ensure the distinctive nature of their schools would be preserved. After a period of uncertainty the new legislation came into force, with the Church schools now receiving government funding and consequently coming more closely under state control but designated as Voluntary Aided Schools, which left the religious authority in charge of part of the funding. They were also able to determine the nature of religious instruction for their pupils. The Oratory Boys Central School was to continue to provide a secondary education from the age of 11 for boys from across London with admission by scholarship examination. The Oratory Fathers also continued to run the parish schools for primary- and secondary-age children; these had formerly been known as the elementary or free schools. By 1948 the Oratory Parish Secondary Free School was joined with two neighbouring parish schools: one run by the Servite Fathers and the other associated with St Mary's Cadogan Street. The combined schools moved into premises that were previously the site of the first Oratory Parish School in the Marlborough School Buildings on Draycott Avenue. The newly amalgamated schools would be a mixed secondary modern school initially known as the Oratory Secondary Modern, but soon renamed St Thomas More School.

Opposite: Boys on the playground of the old school in the late 1960s.

Below: In March 1949 the school name officially became The London Oratory School.

Right: Dr Laurence Summerbell, Headmaster 1930–57.

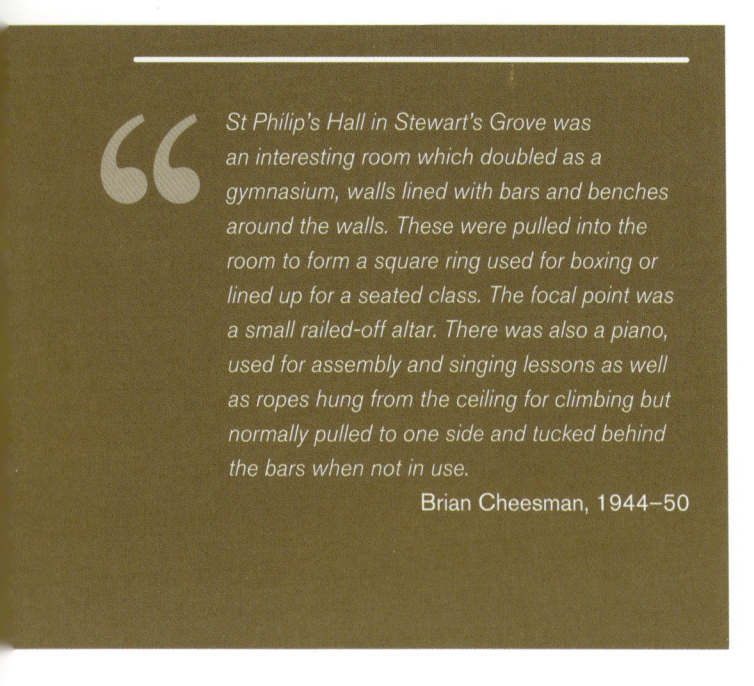

> *St Philip's Hall in Stewart's Grove was an interesting room which doubled as a gymnasium, walls lined with bars and benches around the walls. These were pulled into the room to form a square ring used for boxing or lined up for a seated class. The focal point was a small railed-off altar. There was also a piano, used for assembly and singing lessons as well as ropes hung from the ceiling for climbing but normally pulled to one side and tucked behind the bars when not in use.*
>
> Brian Cheesman, 1944–50

The Oratory Boys Central School also underwent a name change following the re-designation of schools after the 1944 Act, and in March 1949 it was announced that the official name of the school was The London Oratory School.

At this time of change news reached the school that John Menzies Duffy, Headmaster 1888–1930, had died in December 1948. An appreciation published shortly afterwards described him as 'strong in mind and character, yet gentle and helpful. His knowledge of men and boys was immense, his diagnosis of character and ability almost instantaneous… He was the perfect teacher … [and] his greatest attribute was as a Catholic educator' (PM, xxviii, p614).

Mr Duffy's successor as Headmaster, Dr Laurence Summerbell, had by now held the position for nearly 20 years. In 1955 the school marked his Silver Jubilee with a special Mass in St Philip's Hall. Amongst the guests was Mr Kelly, who had recently left the school staff to take up an appointment as headmaster of St Bernard's School. Mr Kelly, as a long-serving colleague, paid tribute to Dr Summerbell, citing the 'ever growing scholastic awards and attainments' of pupils at the school as testimony to the Doctor's achievement in his time in office. The Papal Award of the Cross Pro Ecclesia and Pontifice was to be conferred on Dr Summerbell in recognition of his work. The whole school applauded their Headmaster and Father Munster got a special cheer for the granting of a holiday to mark the occasion.

There was undoubtedly genuine appreciation by many pupils for the work of Dr Summerbell in advancing the academic ambition of the boys, setting standards and encouraging the best from his pupils. He had high expectations and a clear vision of what he wanted the school to be. It was Dr Summerbell's belief that a Central School boy could do as well as a Grammar School boy. It has been said of The London Oratory School in a more recent time 'those the school suits, it suits well' (*The Good Schools Guide*), and it seems this would be apposite for the Summerbell years. Many past pupils have happy memories of an institution where they flourished within an atmosphere of healthy, scholarly endeavour within a strong Catholic framework. For those who did not quite fit the Dr Summerbell mould, however, memories are not all so happy.

One of these was Brian Duffy. He had started at the school in May 1946 and was in his third year when his Oratory schooldays were brought to an end after an unfortunate encounter with the School Captain, one J Jenkinson. On his way home after school one day Brian became caught up in a fight between fellow pupils. The School Captain came by and told the younger boys to stop, whereupon Brian Duffy told the school's most senior pupil to leave off interfering, for which young Brian was reported to the Headmaster. When told by his Headmaster that he would be required to make an apology to the School Captain in front of the whole school Brian refused, after which the situation escalated with the result that Brian was in effect forced to leave. He moved school and then later went to Central St Martin's College of Art. He became internationally renowned, along with David Bailey and Terence Donovan, as one of the three great fashion photographers of the 1960s. He later moved into film production, *Oh, What a Lovely War* being one of his best-known films. To Brian Duffy Dr Summerbell seemed a 'vindictive' man with little natural sympathy for many of the boys in his charge. He would probably have been surprised to know that alongside the entry in the school records noting Brian's departure the Headmaster has added the testimonial, 'not a bad lad'. David Bailey once said 'aggravation and Duffy go together like a gin and tonic'. Maybe this helps us see why the young Brian Duffy and Dr Summerbell were not going to get along, though maybe it could be said that without that difference Duffy would not have gone on to realise his creative talent. When the time came for the two boys next to Brian Duffy on the school register to leave school, one went to work in

5 / The Post-War Years, 1945–69

Above: Brian Duffy, photographer and filmmaker, attended the school 1946–9.

insurance and the other took up a clerical post. This was not the world of Duffy.

Other former pupils remember Dr Summerbell as 'putting the fear of God into everyone', but at the same time 'highly respected and underneath it all liked' (David Wailen, 1949–56). Edward Forbes Jones remembers the day when a boy from a local school had arrived to deliver a message and he joined the end of a line of waiting boys. This was still in the days before all the boys wore school uniform and the visitor had unknowingly joined the punishment line. With no questions asked or explanations allowed he was caned by Dr Summerbell along with the miscreants. Brian Duffy's younger brother Michael, who was in the first form when his brother left the school, recalls that many boys were in awe and not a little afraid of Dr Summerbell. He was tall and elegant in bearing but bore 'battle scars' on his face. None of the boys knew whether these were war wounds, but of course there was speculation about the Headmaster's experiences during the Great War and the rumour was that he had worked for MI5 or MI6. Maybe for the boys this explained the fear of being interrogated by the Headmaster! In fact Dr Summerbell, who had a PhD in chemistry, had done war service in the north east of England as an Instructor in an Anti Gas school, until discharged on medical grounds.

Michael Duffy recalls other strong teachers – Mr Monaghan ('Dr Summerbell's right hand man'), Mr Kelly, Mr Elliot and Mr Greenwood – who were all tough on discipline; these men had all been in the army. Not that this was necessarily bad for their young charges. Many of the boys lacked discipline at home, as their fathers had been away during the war, and for many their earlier years had been spent playing on bomb sites. The Oratory brought new opportunities to these young boys. For some long dinner breaks were spent visiting the museums of South Kensington or wandering around Harrods. The school dinners were excellent, the sporting and musical opportunities were wide and competition abounded. Academic potential was realised in most of the boys. For those who fell short of expectation, however, there was little sympathy. Nor did the Headmaster have any compunction in exposing their 'shame', invariably attributing failure to idleness. Not that a public drumming always produced the desired effect; on one occasion, after heaping derision on the boy who had been placed last in the academic ranking, the Headmaster was not amused when the school gave a rousing cheer for the pupil in question, who happened to be one of the most popular boys in the school.

It was at this time that the first steps towards the establishment of a sixth form were being taken, and pupils such as Bernard Liengme, who in 1957 won an open scholarship to read science at Imperial College, London,

> *It was a short walk down Stewart's Grove, then a turn down a very narrow walkway to the large, foreboding, black wooden school gates. The playground was very small, sandwiched between the walls of two hospitals, the Marsden and the Chelsea Women's Hospital and the two-storey building of the school. Entry to the school was through a pair of large doors at the top of a set of stairs. At the top of these stairs Dr Summerbell would stand and observe the goings on in the playground. Uniforms, ties, caps and shoes were checked for standards of dress.*
>
> *The interior of the building was clean; corridors had notice boards giving information as to what was going on in the school for the week. Basic wooden benches and chairs were laid out in rows with a dais for the teacher to work from.*
>
> Kevin Haughton, 1951–5

The London Oratory School – *Part I: Foundation to Seagrave Road, 1863–1969*

was helping to dispel any idea that London Oratory School boys should not win places at university. Bernard Liengme went on to an academic career, becoming Professor, Dean and Registrar of St Francis Xavier University, Canada, the country's only university affiliated to the Catholic Church, where he worked for 36 years. Had it not been for his Headmaster's insistence that young Bernard stay in sixth form to prepare for a university scholarship life might have been very different. He looks back with gratitude to the influence of Dr Summerbell, who 'had the aura of a tyrant but was a kind and just man. He needed "armour" to keep us boys in order.' When Bernard Liengme was subject to a one-day suspension for antagonising Mr O'Shea, the mathematics master, Dr Summerbell on issuing the sanction advised Bernard not to go straight home as that would alarm his mother. Instead he should 'stay for lunch and then visit the museums or have a walk in Hyde Park. Go home at normal time and then tell your mother about it while you help her clear up after your evening meal.' This benevolence does not quite fit with the image of the stern Dr Summerbell. Maybe on this occasion he had some sympathy with the miscreant, whose offence had been to wear a rose in his lapel for St George's Day. When the Irishman Michael O'Shea challenged this, Bernard had retorted that it seemed fair enough as on St Patrick's Day the Irish contingent wore (and here came the offence as the young boy floundered in recalling the correct word) 'watercress'. This insult to his nation was too much for Mr O'Shea.

With Bernard Liengme and his contemporaries winning their places at university Dr Summerbell had seen his vision of The London Oratory School as a place of scholarship and academic reward come to fruition. After 27 years as Headmaster the time had now come for Dr Summerbell to announce his retirement. He had suffered an injury in a fall

Above: The whole school, 1957.

Left: Bernard Liengme (top right) messing about with pals on the rooftop playground.

5 / *The Post-War Years, 1945–69*

Sixth formers in 1963. The girls were allowed to select a new uniform in 1961 and after a visit to Derry and Toms department store in Kensington they settled on grey box pleat skirts, powder blue blouses with Peter Pan collars and the clip-on bow ties which can be seen in the photograph.

on the steps at the front of the school and was not in the best of health when he said his farewells on 16 December 1957 in a special gathering at Chelsea Town Hall. There were presentations and an appreciation from Mr Monaghan, Deputy Headmaster.

There was a brief interregnum after Dr Sumerbell's resignation, with Mr Monaghan serving as Acting Headmaster. It was he who was in charge for the next interesting step in the evolution of The London Oratory School, as the separate boys' and girls' schools were amalgamated into one mixed school. This was an exciting time for the girls who had until now been educated 'to be ladies and to make good wives and mothers' (Scarlett Trafford née Johnstone, former Head Girl), but now felt they were being regarded as academically worthy. It seemed their teachers were not accorded quite the same status, with most senior positions in the combined school going automatically to the men. The men wore their academic gowns apparently to emphasise their status, so the female staff did the same and some relished the discovery that in comparing their academic credentials, a fair few of the female staff outstripped the men. With the amalgamation settled Mr Monaghan retired in August 1958. Mr J P O'Friel, who had been Deputy Headmaster, was appointed Headmaster of the combined school. Within a year, however, he too had resigned on the grounds of ill health, and in 1960 Mr Martin Campbell was appointed Headmaster. Mr Campbell had studied history at King's College London and after Army service in India and Burma had become a teacher. He came to The London Oratory School after four years as deputy headmaster at St Aloysius' School in Highgate. After the changes in management and status over the past few years it now seemed the school was on a sure footing.

This view was reinforced with a successful Speech Day on 11 November 1961. The talents and achievements of the boys and the girls of the school were in evidence, and Mr Campbell delivered a speech on 'a new ugly word – teenager', a word which in common usage seemed to imply an association with an arrogant and selfish sub-culture, lacking values and character, but often on account of neglect by those who have responsibility for forming the young. He hoped, however, 'that my report has shown that a high proportion of teenagers are people who still work hard and play hard, practise some of the Christian virtues, and are people in whose hands the future is reasonably safe'.

The audience may also have felt reassured that their own children were 'in safe hands' under Mr Campbell's direction. Who would have known that 12 months later some of these same people would be gathered together for Mr Campbell's funeral in November 1962? A war wound had already resulted in the amputation of an arm. Cancer was to be the cause of his untimely death aged 43.

When the school gathered for Speech Day the following year Mrs Taylor, Deputy Headmaster, paid tribute to Mr Campbell, who had been Headmaster for such a short time; but in that time the final amalgamation of the two schools was completed, the sixth form had grown, the prefect system had developed, *The Oratorian* had become the annual school magazine and the frequency of school Masses had increased.

These years had witnessed an unsettled period in the history of the school, and in addition to the changes of Headmaster, the Daughters of the Cross who had been so important in educating the girls in Oratory schools for the past 100 years withdrew from the school when Sister Mary Aidan retired as Deputy Head in 1962. Yet amidst all this change and uncertainty for the hundreds of boys and girls from all over London who continued to pass through the doors at Stewart's Grove every day, life went on with the daily round of lessons, sports, music, visits, services and everyday dramas that make up 'the days of your life'. There were, however, some who were taking advantage of the changes in management and allowing standards to drop. In seeking a new Headmaster the Governors were keen to appoint a man who would have the courage of his convictions in restoring and extending the reputation of The London Oratory School as, in the words of Father Napier, Chairman of Governors, 'a truly Catholic school with high standards of academic achievement', a Headmaster able to run 'a civilised school ... with discipline restored among the pupils with a proper respect for rules', someone with the capacity to encourage pupils 'to take pride in the uniform they wore'. The man selected for this mission was Mr Ian Gaffney. He came to London from Coatbridge in Scotland, where he had been head of mathematics at St Patrick's School. When in 1970 the *Daily Telegraph Magazine* carried a feature entitled 'Six of the Best', profiling six headmasters from around the country, Ian Gaffney of The London Oratory School was one of them. He found himself on the pages of a national publication alongside the headmasters of schools such as Eton and Manchester Grammar, institutions which he jokingly dismissed as 'provincial' compared to his own. He had initially been reluctant to give up the time for the news reporter compiling the article, but afterwards he was proud that what he was accomplishing at the school should be recognised in this way. The idea that the boys of the Oratory were as good and as deserving of the best education as those in the most famous of public schools was, and still is, deeply felt, and Mr Gaffney did not mind the readers of the national press knowing it.

When Ian Gaffney took up office as Headmaster in 1963 he did so at the same time that the school was recognised as a Grammar School, and there were plans to move the school to a new site as a school for boys only. The decision to phase out the girls was based on the fact that there was considerable provision for the education of girls in selective schools across the Westminster Diocese but a lack of places in schools for boys. The decision, however, came as a surprise to Ian Gaffney. He had been interviewed for the post of Headmaster of a mixed school, yet by the time he was assuming the position the school was to be for boys only. He had not been consulted on the change and when he heard it suggested that the girls would be expected to leave with immediate effect he insisted that at the very least they must be phased out, feeling it would not be right to abandon the girls who had already started their education at the school. In the event the school would never lose its girls altogether because when, five years later, it came to the last girls in the school reaching the sixth form it was agreed that the school would continue to admit girls into the sixth form. Mr John Griffin, looking back over his career when he retired from

Ian Gaffney, Headmaster 1963–77.

The ventilation panels on the old school building in Stewart's Grove are now visible on the Royal Marsden Hospital Education Wing.

the school in 1976, commented on the era when the school was mixed, saying, 'I think the girls really did raise the tone of the school'.

When he began his reign as Headmaster Mr Gaffney knew there would be challenges ahead. The move from Stewart's Grove had become entangled in diocesan concerns and government policies, regarding restructuring and reorganisation in education. A no-nonsense Scotsman, Mr Gaffney was ready for the battles that ensued – this was, after all, a man who as a Major with the Royal Artillery had seen action in France and whose war service had earned him the Croix de Guerre from the French government. After three years of meetings, discussions and wrangling the Headmaster notified parents and pupils that 'The Department of Education and Science has made it clear that money would not be available for building new schools which did not fit into the department's plans for new schools. Faced, therefore, with the loss of our present building the Governors' choice was virtually between a comprehensive school or no school at all.' The Headmaster pointed out that while there were merits in the comprehensive system and evident benefits to a grammar education, the debate was not going to be a factor in the decision, which was now a foregone conclusion.

The 'loss of our present building' was consequent upon the take-over of the Stewart's Grove site for development by the Royal Marsden Hospital. The proximity of the school to the hospital is recalled in many memories of the school in these years. Former pupils remember how the boys would enter the school through a gate next to the entrance to the hospital morgue, and would sometimes see hearses pass by. This necessitated the removal of school caps as a mark of respect, followed by the convenient forgetting to replace the unpopular cap on the head afterwards. On Thursdays, when the hospital used its incinerator, a sweet-smelling odour could be caught on the air and school windows would be closed. Imaginative boys spread gruesome tales of burning bodies.

Looking back to their time in the 'Old Building', pupils recall a warren of staircases and connecting corridors, changes in floor levels and on top of the building the rooftop yard. Visitors to the Royal Marsden Hospital today will struggle to find much of a legacy of the old school, but a careful look will pay dividends. A top storey of newer build than the floors below fits snugly up against a stone balustrade which once formed part of the roof terrace wall. On the exterior of the Royal Marsden Education Wing are the ventilation panels modelled by Laurence Bradshaw in 1930 and cast in Sweden. In 2012 a new meeting room was opened in the Education Wing. A name was needed for the room and a number of names were put before the deciding committee. It was a source of great pleasure to learn that the room was to be known as the Oratory Room, and so the legacy of the school remains in evidence. The satisfaction at this is heightened by the knowledge that the name was up against some strong competition when put to the vote, as in keeping with that year's celebrations one of the proposed titles was the Jubilee Room.

The building may have had its architectural merit and curiosity, but for many years the school had struggled to manage in the Stewart's Grove accommodation. As the school intake increased architects were consulted and various schemes proposed for a fourth wing to be added at Stewart's Grove, but it was becoming increasingly impossible to comply with legal and safety regulations. The site in Seagrave Road which belonged to the Ministry of Health was identified as a potential site for a new school building, so an exchange was worked out whereby the Royal Marsden would take over the old school and the school would rebuild on Seagrave Road.

In September 1970 the pupils of The London Oratory School made their way for the first time down Seagrave Road and through the gates of the new school. They probably knew little of the wrangling, negotiation, frustration and politics that lay behind the move from Stewart's Grove, but they were most likely aware that they were part of a new chapter in the history of The London Oratory School. For the first time since 1863 the boys of the Oratory would not be educated in Chelsea. Fulham was to be the daily destination from now on.

49

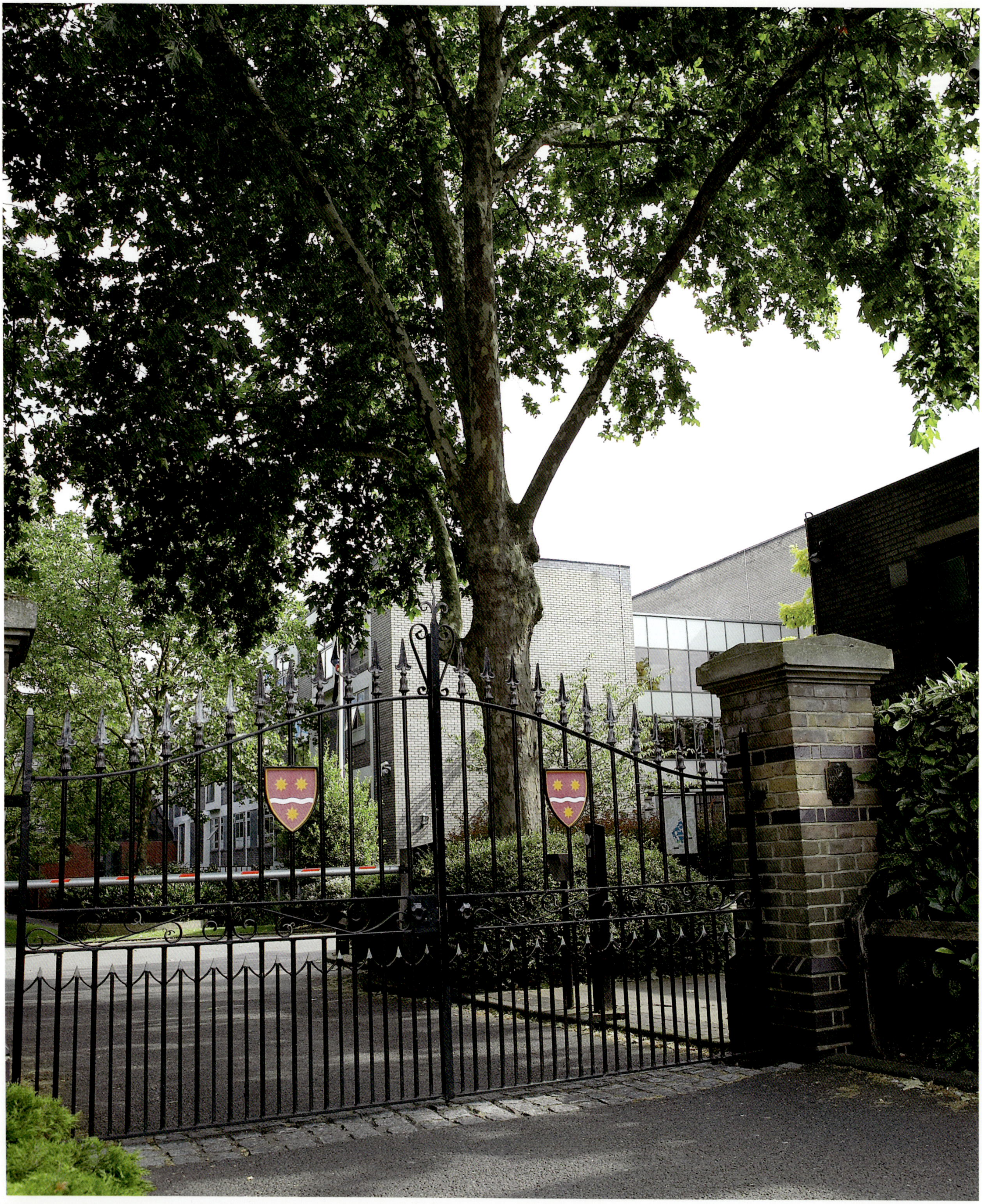

6

1970 TO THE PRESENT DAY

'The area on the far side of the playground is where they buried the bodies.' With these words the teacher explained to his pupils the layout of their 'new school.' What prompted this macabre reference was the fact that the building the boys now occupied was constructed on the site of the Western Fever Hospital, built in 1876 to accommodate patients with smallpox. In fact the school is situated on the extension to the original hospital, added in 1891, by which time the hospital was no longer dealing with smallpox cases but was primarily a hospital for infectious diseases. The suggestion of bodies under the playground perhaps emanated from the fact that the hospital mortuary was part of the 1891 extension, or maybe from the fertile imagination of the teacher.

Pupils who walked down Seagrave Road in the 1970s will recall a coal yard near the top of the road and then the old hospital buildings, standing on the land which is now Brompton Park Crescent. The wall which hundreds of pupils walk past each day is a relic of the hospital which finally closed in 1979. One building adjacent to the school and recently converted into a private dwelling is all that remains of the original hospital.

One of the reasons why a smallpox hospital was constructed on Seagrave Road was the need to house these cases in a secluded area; accommodating victims of such a dangerous and infectious disease in residential areas was likely to cause alarm in the neighbourhood. There may be those who have similar feelings about a school, but they would concede that the latter is not such a concern when comparing the relative health threats! Both the hospital and the school benefited from being on an enclosed site in what has been described as 'an oasis of calm' at the end of Seagrave Road. The fact that they were literally 'down a dead end' was, however, a source of concern to some of the teachers as they swapped the buzz of South Kensington for 'out of the way' Fulham. To add to the disappointment the buildings which awaited them at the 'new school' were

Opposite: The school gates, Seagrave Road.

Right: Exterior and interior of the Western Fever Hospital, Fulham.

PART II : SEAGRAVE ROAD, FROM 1970 ONWARDS

Left: The building of the school in 1969. The floodlights of Stamford Bridge can be seen in the background in the top photograph and in the bottom picture the layout of the main building with the swimming pool under construction.

Above: The entrance to the 'new school', 1970.

not even finished when they started the term in September 1970. The new accommodation was intended to bring greater comfort and educational opportunity but there were problems with a building of reinforced concrete erected somewhat hastily, and there followed years of wrangling with builders to effect remedial work. There wasn't even a playground for the first few months, as a pile of rubble filled the designated area. Mr Hartigan, who began teaching at the school in 1969 and was Head of Mathematics at this time, remembers observing Mr Duckham, Deputy Headmaster, throwing bricks at the rats on the would-be playground. Mr Hartigan also recalls that the main ground floor corridor consisted of rubble and exposed pipe work, and that the swimming pool was just a huge hole in the ground.

Nor was the move as well organised from an administrative point of view as might have been desired. The neatly packed and labelled tea chests which should have been awaiting teachers in the appropriate rooms of the new school did not arrive at their specific destinations as expected. Instead teachers found in the centre of the school hall a huge pyramid of tea chests from which staff had to unearth their own boxes. When all of the chests were claimed it was apparent that what had made it from Chelsea to Fulham did not quite equate to what had been packed

6 / 1970 to the Present Day

Cardinal Heenan meets pupils as he tours the new building, 1970.

and despatched from the old school, and consequently much by way of valuable records and documents was at this point lost for ever.

Despite the upheaval and troubles that would continue behind the scenes for some time, the pattern of school life was soon established, and on Monday 30 November 1970 His Eminence John Cardinal Heenan, Cardinal Archbishop of Westminster, came to bless and officially open the school.

The first decade in the new school saw the loss of a number of teachers of the 'Old Guard', who after long service at Stewart's Grove left the school a few years after it was established in its new home. Mr J Sullivan (popularly known as Snowy on account of his white hair) was one of these, retiring in 1975 after 25 years. He taught geography and introduced geology to the curriculum. 'His collection of weird and wonderful rock specimens intrigued all', wrote Mr Frizelle in *The Oratorian*, 1975, but he is probably best remembered as the Housemaster of More House. The original four houses had been reduced to three by this time and rededicated after the move to Seagrave Road. In Fisher House there was Jack O'Neill (Jacko), looking forward to retirement after 29 years at the school when he died unexpectedly. Roger Knight (1956–62) recalls his old maths teacher fondly: 'whereas a few teachers would make you look an idiot in front of the class if you got something wrong … Jack O' Neill was a real exception … shouted a lot but was a really good chap.' Others remember well the distinct Irish accent as he gave out the instruction 'will you fellas get into your ranks'. George Canty retired after 20 years teaching English. Few forgot an encounter with Mr Canty: 'one of the real characters of the teaching profession … and probably the wittiest person in the school', said sixth former Vincent O'Brien in a tribute in the 1975 school magazine.

In 1976 John Griffin retired after 16 years at the school. He had something of a fierce reputation, but individual pupils found out that beneath that forbidding exterior there was a kind nature, and 'a gentleman, a good bloke' (Roger Knight). When he was interviewed for the school magazine

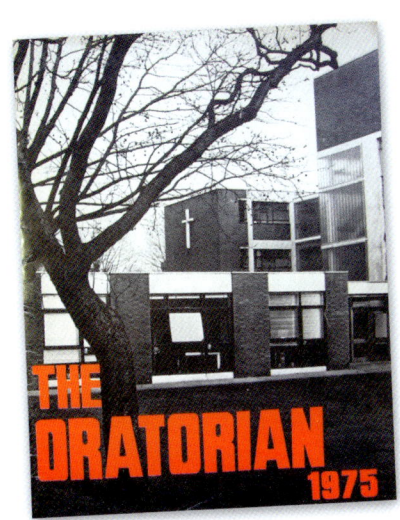

> *There is still the necessity to inculcate the basic skill of writing, grammar, spelling and punctuation. The Modernists might put Creativity first. Maybe they are right. In an American zoo gorillas' creativity was developed by providing them with paint, brush and paper. For a time their creative faculties were highly praised but within the last week all this had to cease – they ate the paint. Maybe there's a lesson somewhere here.*
>
> George Canty, writing in 1976

before his retirement Mr Griffin was asked what he thought makes a good school, to which he responded, 'the primary ingredient, in my opinion, in making a successful school is a headmaster who has the interest of his pupils at heart, who knows what he wants and gets it'. These are words that would have applied very nicely to his own Headmaster at that time.

Mr Gaffney as Headmaster had seen the school settled in the new building and had stood firm in the face of the difficulties of establishing the school in its new location. He had faced challenges in ensuring that the Oratory character had survived intact – there had been those who feared a move from Chelsea to Fulham and from Grammar to Comprehensive would dilute the essence of the school – and had seen the coming and going of a significant number of the teaching staff. He had assumed charge of the school at a time of great change and had to deal with entrenched interests both within and beyond the school, but this was what he was good at. He was a formidable man to many of the pupils: 'he really did put the fear of God into people' (Gerry Power, 1973–80); he was 'the only teacher I know who could walk into the playground and everybody would stop' (Antonino Santi, 1970–4).

There are still former pupils who give a little shiver at the name of Mr Gaffney as they recall being sent to the Headmaster's office to be caned for such seemingly innocuous offences as 'playing basketball with a rolled up apron' or even for 'looking at a cat in the tree'. Mr Isaaks, former pupil and now Assistant Headmaster at the school, recalls the day a boy had come down to the office to deliver a note from his teacher. Arriving at the office to carry out his mission he heard the familiar Scottish accent of Mr Gaffney intoning, 'come here that boy', and following the Headmaster the boy found himself receiving a caning for being out of class. No one in that class ever volunteered to deliver a note again. His reputation as a disciplinarian is often the first comment made by those who attended the school under Mr Gaffney, but it is invariably followed by fond recollections, as behind the tough exterior many of the boys realised there lay a dedicated teacher and a man of dry wit.

In typical style Mr Gaffney once warned parents of the need to address a 'certain lack of self discipline' in the young: 'the sort of boy who spends his evenings on a scooter and in coffee bars is unlikely to make a success of a GCE course' (PM, xlv, Dec. 1966, p2). Even teachers were not to escape the sharp rebuke, and quotes from Mr Gaffney are still repeated, complete with Scottish accent, in the Staff Common Room, such as that of the geography master who was not meeting expectations and who was known to frequent a certain hostelry at the top of Seagrave Road: 'If he were to spend as much time looking in an atlas as he spent drinking in The Atlas then maybe his classes would know a little more geography'. Eamonn Malone, Head of School 1972, recalls that 'Jock', as Mr Gaffney was

Above: Mr Gaffney with award winners and prefects, 1977.

Far right: John McIntosh, Headmaster 1977–2006.

known amongst the boys, had a fearsome reputation but was 'a fantastic teacher' who would put himself out for the boys he taught. Vincent O'Brien, School Captain in 1976, remembers Mr Gaffney as 'a disciplined man, but when I became Head Boy I realised such an honourable, decent and good humoured man'.

By the time he announced his retirement in 1977 the first boys to have walked down Seagrave Road as first formers were walking up the road for the final time as they came to the end of sixth form.

As Mr Gaffney retired so too did the 'most scholarly' Mr Frizelle, who had taught at the school since 1949. Years later the actor Simon Callow (1961–7) recalled Nic Frizelle as the teacher who really inspired him: 'an exceptional man, he was interested in engaging pupils and having a proper intellectual exchange' (TES, Teaching Resources, 2007). 'Cultured, sophisticated and very civilised … taught us about the finer things in life' is how David Wailen (1949–56) remembers Mr Frizelle.

> I consider that a pupil will respect a teacher who respects himself; that the pupil will respect a teacher who tries to do his work properly; that the pupil basically wants to work and that if a teacher makes a pupil work, I think that a bond of good relationship will be established between teacher and pupil.
>
> John Griffin, writing in 1976

With so many changes amongst the staff it now fell to a new, younger generation of teachers to shape the school, and chief amongst these was a young teacher by the name of John McIntosh, who had joined the staff in 1967. At that time the school had two Staff Common Rooms, one for seniors and another designated for the female teachers. As a new recruit Mr McIntosh was not deemed to be ready for admission to the Senior Common Room, and he spent his early years under the formidable direction of Miss Molloy, Head of History and, as Mr McIntosh recalls, 'Queen of the female Common Room'. He was made welcome, however, so long as he minded to sit where he was told and allow himself to be mothered. After so long of this he decided the time had come to face the Senior Common Room. With a degree of trepidation he entered the domain of the old guard and after a few moments was relieved to see Mr Canty, stalwart of the English department, look up and say 'Good for you.' Ten years on, after continuing to rise through the ranks, John McIntosh was appointed Headmaster. This could be regarded as a risky appointment; he was just 31 years old, young for a Headmaster, but he had cut his teeth at The London Oratory School and had worked alongside Mr Gaffney as the school moved to Fulham and took shape on the new site. John McIntosh would be his own man but he shared his predecessor's tenacity and commitment to excellence, qualities which would be needed as he moved the school through new challenges.

The McIntosh years were eventful. There were challenges to face which if not resisted would alter the character and status of the school. These years also saw significant changes in the curriculum and in examinations, with John McIntosh involved in advising and planning at a national level, as a National Curriculum was introduced to schools for the first time. In addition there were building works to manage, and alongside the large-scale developments there was the steady, ongoing evolution of a school that had by this time been educating Catholic boys from across London for over a century.

This is not the place to recount the precise details of the politics and people who were shaping and influencing what was happening in schools in the last quarter of the 20th century, but suffice it to say change, or the threat of it, was never far away. Under John McIntosh the school stood firm and maintained its character and standards in the face of shifting education policy and legal constraints. In 1989 the school moved to grant maintained status, and with the receipt of direct funding the opportunity arose for new developments. One of the lasting legacies of this period was the Arts Centre, which was inaugurated by then Prime Minister John Major, who along with his wife Norma visited the school in 1991. They toured the school meeting staff and pupils, including Mark Thomas, who was the Head of School that year.

John Major was not the only Prime Minister to visit the school. In national politics the 'Blair Years' refer to the Labour governments of 1997–2007, but at The London Oratory School the Blair Years cover the period from 1995 to 2006 when first Euan, followed by Nicky and Kathryn Blair, attended the school. Having the Prime Minister's children at the school did add a few extra security considerations. Perhaps it is as well that pupils were not aware of the red telephone at the reception desk just in case the temptation to lift the receiver became too great. The unfortunate electrician who accidentally cut through the wiring while working at the school during the summer

> *One of my fondest memories of my school years must be when I was Head of School and was asked to return early from a biology field trip in Wales to accompany the then Prime Minister, John Major, and his wife Norma around the school for the inauguration of the new Arts Centre. I vividly remember waiting for their arrival outside the main school entrance. Of course I was a little nervous and Mr Bamford was doing his best to put me at ease, saying, 'he is only human like the rest of us'.*
>
> *As the tour moved on through the different parts of the school I spent a lot of time chatting away with the very charming Norma, talking about her two children. By this time most of the nerves were gone and I was able to enjoy every minute. We moved into the school hall to sit down for a brief musical performance. Mr McIntosh asked if I wanted to sit next to the Prime Minister but I, of course, allowed the Headmaster to take that position.*
>
> *It was simply one of my best days at the school, and I remember sitting down that evening to see the BBC News which because of other events that day was showing a lot of footage of the Prime Minister, and there I was proud as punch!*
>
> Mark Thomas, 1985–92

Prime Minister John Major and Mrs Major on their visit to the school in 1991.

Above: Mr and Mrs Blair are met by the Headmaster and the Guard of Honour as they arrive for the Patronal Festival celebrations at the Oratory Church in 2002.

Right: Mr Blair presenting the awards to sixth formers after the Patronal Festival Mass.

holiday got a surprise when within minutes the whole school was surrounded by armed police. When in 2002 Mr Blair presented the Awards on the Patronal Festival at the Oratory Church a sweep of the Church by sniffer dogs was an unusual addition to the preparations for the annual celebration of the school feast.

Cardinal Basil Hume, Archbishop of Westminster, visited the school on a number of occasions, coming in 1992 to bless and dedicate the new school Chapel on the Feast of St Edward the Confessor. When the 'new' school building was erected in 1969–70 the Chapel had been positioned on the west side of the main block, abutting the playground. Pupils in recent years will not have realised that the 'sticking out bit' half-way down the playground was once the wall of the Chapel sanctuary. The old Chapel was a place of calm within the school, with the stained-glass windows designed by Patrick Reyntiens casting a burst of colour over the sanctuary on a sunny day, but it was small for a school of this size and tucked away between classrooms and corridors. Now the school was to have a free-standing Chapel at the heart of the school.

The Cardinal returned for the opening, blessing and dedication of the Junior House in 1996. The Junior House was the realisation of a vision: John McIntosh's idea for a specialist musical education for boys from the age of seven, matching that of the cathedral schools but offered at a Catholic day school within the state sector. The boys would be trained in choral and instrumental music to a standard that would enable them to go on to music colleges and scholarships and to offer their musical talents in their own parishes. From the start some of the boys in Junior House were to be trained as choral scholars, and the Schola was

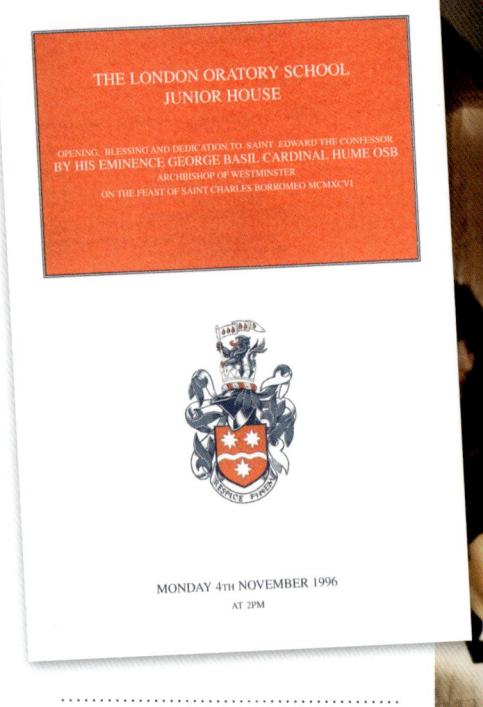

The London Oratory School – *Part II: Seagrave Road, from 1970 onwards*

Cardinal Basil Hume blessed and dedicated the Junior House on the Feast of St Charles Borromeo, 4 November 1996.

formed as a specialist Catholic choir, singing at the Saturday evening Vigil Mass in the Oratory Church.

The sight of seven-year-olds in their distinct maroon blazers was at first a novelty for the senior pupils, but it was not long before the juniors were well established. There cannot be many schools where a boy can make the journey to school for the first time at the age of seven and with the same journey 11 years later finish his school days, nor eat his first school dinner at the age of seven in Fisher Houseroom and his last at 18 in the same room. When the Oratory Middle School began in the 19th century it was hoped a boy would see his education through for four years; who at that time would have envisaged an 11-year school career?

Looking back over a London Oratory School career former pupils have many different memories and experiences, but any reminiscences soon come round to 'which House were you in?' The subsidiary question of 'and who was your Housemaster?' might prompt the reply Mr Gestra, Mr Matthews or Mr McCarthy, who for many years held sway respectively in Campion, Fisher and More. The House system had come a long way over the years. There was still the competitive element with the various House Sports events, but the House system also fulfilled an important pastoral role and Housemasters held, and still hold, a significant place in the career of an Oratorian. To get a mention in the House Notes in the school magazine was the aspiration of many. The Houses were restructured in 1992 when Campion, Fisher and More were joined by Howard, Owen and Southwell. In time Messrs Gestra, Matthews and McCarthy all finished their careers at the school, having made a huge impression on many hundreds of young Oratorians. One way in which they all did this was by engaging their pupils and by taking an interest in the lives and progress of their charges: Mr Gestra regaling his pupils with tales of his life as a young boy in Mussolini's Italy; Mr McCarthy's history lessons brought to life with extraordinary stories (and jokes); and Mr Matthews with his fascinating travel experiences and his involvement in and encouragement of sport.

Other 'great names' of this era include Deputy Headmasters: Mr Harrington, with a reputation as a disciplinarian but as many came to discover a real interest and sympathy for pupils as individuals; Mr Hartigan, in charge of the sixth form for much of his career, where his soft Irish tones stirred many a reluctant pupil to action, also to be heard on the rugby pitch or touchline; Mr Bamford,

6 / 1970 to the Present Day

with his dulcet Welsh tones and benevolent interest in all at the school; Mr McGeeney, who worked assiduously for the school during the grant maintained years; and Mr Griffiths, who influenced many with his quiet scholarship, charm and most equable temperament. More recently Mr White and Miss Devereux, both of whom joined the school as new teachers in 1987, have served as Deputy Headmasters. When Mr White left to assume a headmaster post in 2011 there was disappointment from many at the loss of a great teacher and excellent leader. Fortunately a strong successor was installed in the office in the shape of former pupil Mr Rooney.

John McIntosh continued, as energetic and influential as ever, until in 2006 he announced his plans to retire as Headmaster. He would not, however, be headed for the golf course, the seaside or the fireside; Mr McIntosh would continue to be very busy in matters educational, though no longer at The London Oratory School. This was indeed the end of an era and was marked by a fitting round of concerts, parties and receptions. Amongst the presentations was the manuscript of the Bach complete organ works, a reflection of the great influence of John McIntosh on music at the school. His indefatigable dedication to maintaining The London Oratory School as a school for Catholic boys from

Above: Senior Staff, photographed in the mid 1980s.

Right: The original Junior House intake, September 1996.

59

across London, his insistence on high expectations and standards from all who had a part to play in the school, be they pupils, teachers, parents, support staff or contractors, ensured a sound legacy. His unflinching belief that no child or parent should be patronised when it comes to schooling, but that all deserve an excellent, broad and rounded education, is realised in The London Oratory School.

It will come as little surprise that John McIntosh's successor was a former pupil. As a boy David McFadden made the transfer to Seagrave Road after one year in the old Stewart's Grove School. In 1982, as many others have done, before and since, he came back to teach at his old school. After four years in the biology department he moved to Australia to take up a post at Aquinas College, Perth, and from there went on to become headmaster of the Christian Brothers College, Freemantle. After almost 20 years in Australia Mr McFadden came back to Seagrave Road and once more through the familiar gates, but now as Headmaster. He would find much changed in the buildings and people he encountered on his return, but also much the same.

Nearly all of The London Oratory School pupils in the 150th anniversary year will have been through the school under Mr McFadden's leadership. In this time there have been, as with each Headmaster, some new dimensions added to the experience of an Oratory education, both in physical and in educational terms. Not for the first time in the history of the school on Seagrave Road did a new building arise in a space where most people had never appreciated that there was a space, as the Newman Wing was constructed in 2008 to provide five new classrooms, offices and flexible space for meetings. At the same time the old multi-gym was transformed into a large, well-equipped Fitness Centre.

The school under Mr McFadden remains true to the philosophy of putting developments in the world of education to the test of how any change will benefit the pupils. In an Oratory education any new idea or approach which can stretch a pupil, present new challenges and improve the mind is to be considered; aim high, expect the best and learn from disappointment.

The teaching staff 2002 and the Long Service Notice Board which hangs in the Staff Common Room.

THE SCHOOL UNIFORM

There are arguments for having a school uniform and there are arguments for not, but there is no argument for something in between. It is on this philosophy that The London Oratory School regulations insist on school uniform properly worn. Boys and girls who attended the school over almost the past 100 years will be familiar with this approach. Ever since there has been a school uniform, expressions relating to 'top buttons, socks, caps and ties' have been part of school vocabulary.

Uniform did not exist before the Central School was established, and at first it was optional. The first blazer appears to have been navy blue, rather than the black blazer with which current pupils are familiar. All the boys wore caps and in 1931 this could be bought with a metal badge which could be transferred from cap to cap, as up to that point it was a cloth badge. There was an expectation by the 1930s that all boys would wear uniform but boys were not punished for failing to do so. Instead their parents were warned by Dr Summerbell that they were 'not honouring the pledge given when their sons were admitted' because they were 'not sending their boys to school in school uniform but in "fancy dress" looking like "imitation bruisers" in training for goodness knows what'. This is not the only occasion on which Dr Summerbell reminded parents that the question of uniform was a matter of honour.

The school uniform was supplied by the Bradford Textile Company of Victoria Street, and parents could either make their purchases from the shop or take advantage of selected times when company representatives would visit the school to measure boys for uniform. By the 1950s the school outfitter was the Scotch House, Knightsbridge.

It is not only in recent times that boys and girls might find themselves checked, as they leave school, travel through the station or stand at the bus stop, to see whether their uniform is as it should be. Michael Sheehan (1957–62) recalls that in his time caps were still compulsory from first to fourth form, and prefects and masters were placed near the bus stops and tube stations in South Kensington to ensure they were worn.

The rules might still be strict, but apart from in the Junior House it is a good many years since a cap has graced the head of an Oratory boy.

School uniform serves many purposes, but the sense of identity, belonging and community that it engenders is one of the strongest arguments for it. The uniform was deemed most useful in character forming for the boys of the Central School as it began the process of corporate belonging and loyalty which would help to form men who would be successful in business. As Dr Summerbell reminded the wearers of the uniform, they were each 'a member of the Oratory Central School, an Oratorian'. Today's school has changed somewhat from the Central School days and the pupils may be destined for different things in life, but the wearers of the uniform are still, as they ever were, 'Oratorians'.

The London Oratory School – *Part II: Seagrave Road, from 1970 onwards*

THE SCHOOL BADGE

The badge that adorned the early uniform was the old school badge which depicted the three eight-pointed stars, which is the crest of St Philip Neri's family, within an oval shield and crowned by a priest's hat, with tassels. At one time this was contained within another oval (the double rings) because the black hat would not have showed up on the black blazer without the second ring to provide a border to the badge. This was then surrounded by a shield. Many former pupils recall a certain ignominy felt at wearing a badge that 'looked like a girl's face with pigtails'. When Bernard Liengme was in sixth form in 1954 he and some fellow pupils asked Dr Summerbell whether there might be some dispensation for sixth form with regard to uniform and to their relief found a sympathetic ear. By the following term the cap no longer had to be worn by the more senior years and the sixth form had a new badge based on the crossed keys. Today's sixth formers wear a version of the same badge as the rest of the school, but with the addition of the school coat of arms, along with their own ties. The girls have their distinctive striped blazers. The boys from first to fifth form now wear the three stars arranged two above and one below the wavy line from the London crest, and highlighting the school colours, as on the tie, of red and black. The Junior House pupils' badge is adapted from the school arms, and ties and blazers are in the Junior House colour of burgundy and black.

Pupils wearing school blazer with badge.

The schoolkeeping team.

High expectations do, as the achievements of pupils over the years prove, yield success, and pupils, parents and staff have the opportunity to acknowledge and reward achievement in the Annual Awards Evening which was added to the school calendar by Mr McFadden in 2009. There had for many years been an Annual Sports Awards Evening at the school, and each year fifth and sixth formers are presented with Awards at the Patronal Festival at the Oratory Church, and now younger pupils have their achievements and victories acknowledged publicly. The finale of the Awards Evening in the school theatre is the presentation of the Gaffney Cup, awarded to the House which has accumulated the highest points in four categories: Sport, Arts, Academic and Leadership. Mr Kelly was delighted to be the first Housemaster to receive the Award, for Owen House in 2009.

6 / 1970 to the Present Day

Clockwise from top: Junior House boys enjoying a game during break; senior pupils catching up on their Latin vocabulary; pupils of More House tucking into a hearty meal.

The designation of Leadership as a category for House points reflects the emphasis on encouraging pupils to take responsibility and through example and service grow in their faith as they move towards their adult lives. Recent years have seen a more structured Catholic Community Service programme running throughout the whole school, providing opportunities for pupils to benefit from making a difference for others.

The influence of an Old Oratorian Headmaster, perhaps along with the zeitgeist as the school approaches a significant anniversary, has brought about a resurgence in the activity of the Old Oratorian Association. The Association offers former pupils a chance to meet up with old friends, to exchange news, to compete in sports fixtures and quizzes, and to revisit the scenes of their youth, as well as a chance to reconnect and reminisce with former teachers, especially those whose service spans many years. When Miss Delap, Head of Learning Support, retired in 2011 after 39 years at the school, many amusing tales were told and heartfelt tributes made to a most dedicated

The London Oratory School – Part II: Seagrave Road, from 1970 onwards

THE HOUSES

One of the innovations introduced when the Central School was established was a House system. Originally there were four Houses: Philip, Wilfrid, Sebastian and Edward, with Sebastian later being replaced by Francis. The Houses existed mainly for competitive reasons and served the purpose of introducing healthy rivalry between the boys in the different sporting challenges. From the very beginnings of the House system the boys entered enthusiastically into the competitive spirit, something that remains the case today, although the House patrons have changed and the House system involves a much wider spectrum of school life. When the school moved to Seagrave Road three Houses were established, named after three of the English martyrs: St Edmund Campion, St John Fisher and St Thomas More. From this point the Houses were also an indicator of which form group a boy belonged to, with two form groups in each House, labelled as North and South forms. These appellations were linked to which end of the House block the form was based in: North was the end nearer Seagrave Road, South nearer the railway line end. Housemasters were now appointed with pastoral responsibility for the boys in their House. Mr Griffin was in charge in Campion, Mr O'Neill in Fisher and Mr Sullivan in More. House identity became much stronger over these years, with the scope for inter-House competition expanding beyond sport. Under long-serving Housemasters such as Mr Gestra in Campion, Mr Matthews in Fisher and Mr McCarthy in More, the Houses took on distinct characteristics. In 1992 the three Houses expanded to six as St Philip Howard, St Nicholas Owen and St Robert Southwell were added as House patrons. The green of Campion House, red of Fisher and light blue of More now competed alongside the dark blue of Howard, maroon of Owen and yellow of Southwell; the pin badges, with which every boy was issued to inaugurate the six houses, are now something of a collector's item.

Above: House badges, 'a collector's item'.

Left: Mr Mantio and pupils of Howard House celebrate winning the House Cup.

Above: The art department is always busy.

Right: Heading home on a rainy afternoon.

and tireless teacher. On a sadder note the death of Rory Tierney in 2012, whose association with the school went back to 1974, prompted many former pupils to express their gratitude for the interest and encouragement they had received from one who was ever the pupil's friend. Former pupils now take the opportunity to put something back into their old school, having established a support fund to assist current pupils.

After 150 years the mission of the Oratory Fathers to educate the Catholic boys of London remains grounded in Oratorian tradition. The London Oratory School continues to turn out young men and women equipped for modern society after an education that embodies scholarship and service – an education that extends far beyond the classroom and continues, consciously or not, far beyond and long after passing out of the school gates.

THE YOUTH CLUB

In 1972 a youth wing was opened in the school, on the site of what later became the Library. This had come about after protracted discussions between the ILEA (Inner London Education Authority), the school and the parish of St Thomas of Canterbury. At the time of construction of the school on Seagrave Road the possibility that St Thomas would get a Parish Hall as part of the build was included in the planning. After the school was established, however, agreement could not be reached as to exactly how any shared use would be organised, and the different parties all had different hopes for the site. In the event John McIntosh, who was Deputy Headmaster at the time, suggested that a Youth Centre with ILEA backing be established and this is what happened, with Mr McIntosh in charge under the title Tutor Warden. Mr Gaffney was keen on the idea and gave it full support. The Youth Centre was open three evenings each week and on each of those evenings full use was made of the school facilities with 12 different activities on offer, ranging from basketball to craftwork to sub-aqua diving. The centre was well attended and proved successful and popular with many of the boys from the school. All members had to participate in an activity on each visit before they were allowed to avail themselves of the more social aspects of the centre.

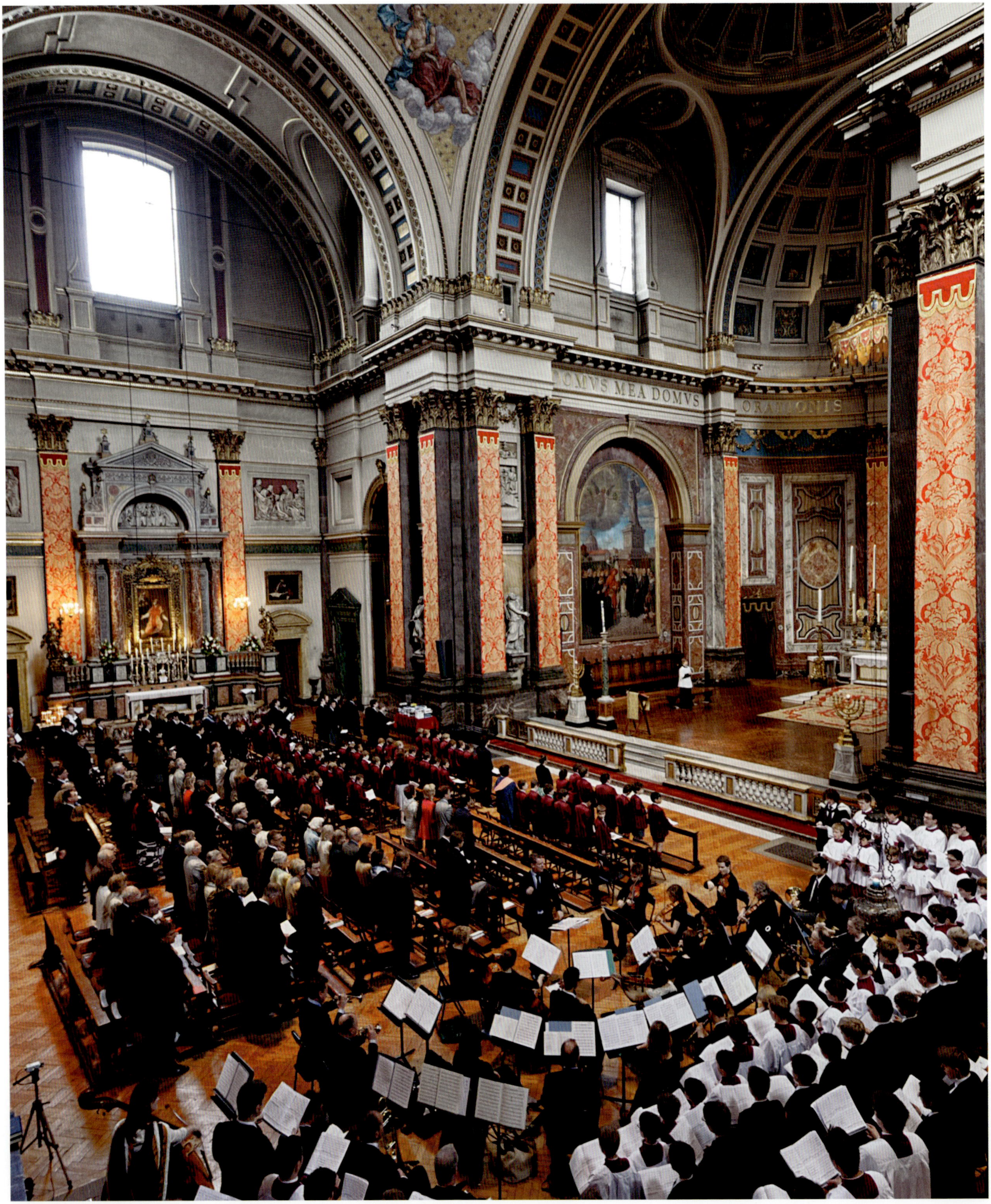
DOMVS MEA DOMVS
ORATIONIS

7

Religious Life

From the beginning of the Oratory Schools in London it was the Fathers' Mission to provide the means for a Catholic education through academic and spiritual teaching. The link between school and church was established from the start and to this day the Oratory Church plays a significant part in the life of The London Oratory School pupils.

When the school opened in Chelsea the Fathers visited regularly to check on the quality of religious education and to test the boys' knowledge, sometimes with mixed results.

Opposite: The Patronal Festival.

Below: Religious Inspection report, 1906.

The Archdiocese also sent Religious Education Inspectors to the school. In 1902 the RE Inspector, visiting shortly before the Archbishop Cardinal Vaughan himself paid a visit to the school, had rated 'the repetition of the prayers' by the boys in Division B as 'very imperfect'. At least Division D was rated 'very good' on 'The Life of Our Lord'. By the 1920s, however, Inspectors were confidently reporting that RE was very good in the school, and this has been the trend ever since. Another strong feature of religious life in the early days and today is the singing of Church music: 'the Church music was extremely well sung' (Inspector's Report 1931).

In the formative years of the school it was the Oratory Fathers themselves who were instructing and testing the children. In time formal instruction and teaching moved to the schoolteachers, and RE has long been part of the academic curriculum. Brian Cheesman (1944–50) tells how his friend Peter, a non-Catholic, did not attend Religious Instruction, which was timetabled between 11.30 and 12.20 each day. Instead Peter was sent to assist the ladies laying up the tables for lunch. Service was slow, however, and soon Brian was enlisted to help in the lunch preparations: 'it being felt that as I was a choirboy, my religious education was not so important!' God works in mysterious ways, however, as Brian was to develop a love of catering which was to influence his future direction in life.

As the years went on the Fathers' role in the school became more specifically directed to working as Chaplains helping to form the pupils in the Faith and to administer the Sacraments. There have been many Fathers associated with the school over the years and former pupils recall the influence of the priests. Michael Duffy, who attended the school in the 1950s, valued the association. He explains that in the Oratory Fathers he encountered a form of Catholicism that gave him something different from what he was used to from his own Irish heritage. To him 'they were the good guys'. They provided something to look up to. He remembers them coming into school each day for about half an hour, most particularly 'a titled priest, very English'. This encounter with something different is often what strikes pupils on their first visit to the Oratory Church, but soon they recognise the familiar as well, and the liturgical forms and traditions of the Oratory become a part of their own practice of the Faith.

It has always been the case that few of the pupils from the school reside in the Oratory parish, and the Oratory Church is therefore only known to them through the school. It was reported on more than one occasion in the parish magazine during the 1920s that regulars at Sunday Mass passed comment on how few of the children of the Central Schools were in attendance, and the reply given was (as is true of the school today) that only a small number of the children of the Central Schools resided in the Oratory Parish. In 1938 of 600 in the Central Schools only about 12 lived in the parish. The school has always drawn its pupils from many different parishes across London, and it is in these churches that they attend Sunday Mass. It has been remarked, however, that for the pupils of the school the Oratory Church is 'a second parish', and they are linked through this with a tradition to which they can feel a lifelong association. Former pupils recall the occasions on which they visited the Oratory Church for Mass or the Annual Carol Service, and the 'walk back', as the whole school processes from South Kensington to Fulham, still causes the cameras of passing tourists to flash as they are impressed by the sight of hundreds of boys in school uniform making their way through south west London. Even before the school was in Fulham there was the tradition of the Oratory walk, as once a month the boys would set out from Stewart's Grove in a crocodile to Church for Mass. By the time they arrived at Church a few would be lost but these would miraculously reappear after Mass! Lola Louca (née Epiphaniou) attended the girls' school between 1951 and 1956. She recalls how when the boys and girls attended services together at the Oratory Church the boys were walked there along one side of the road and the girls on the other.

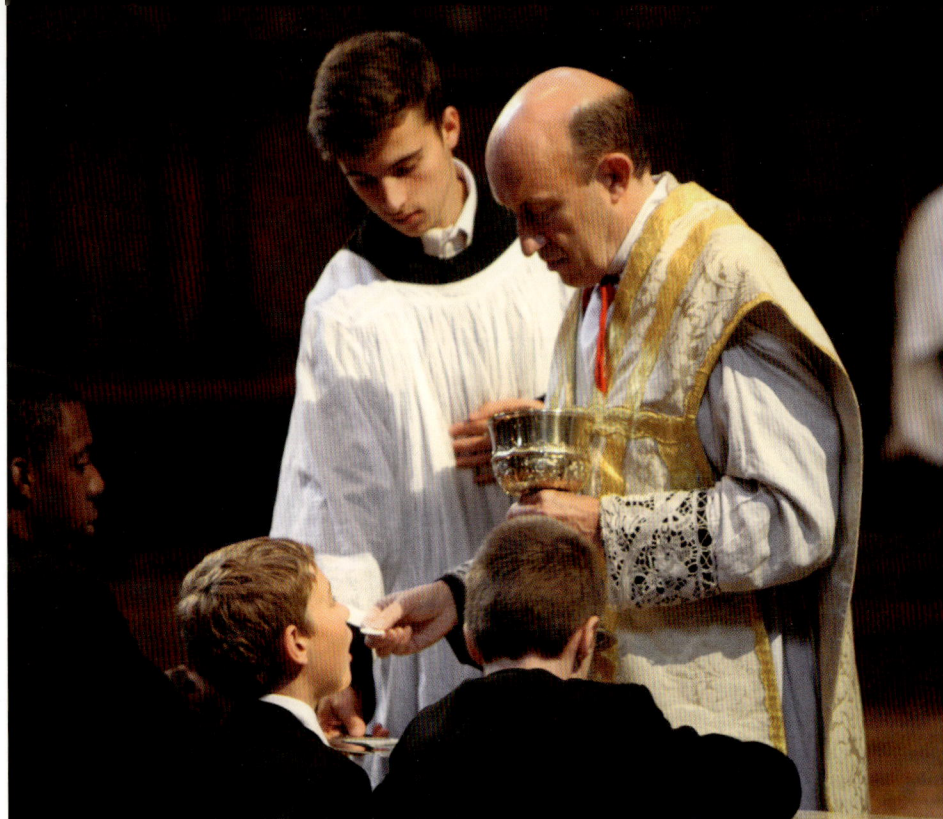

The building in which thousands of pupils have looked about them during Mass over the years was designed by Herbert Gribble, a local and relatively unknown architect when the Oratory Fathers decided to entrust him with the commission for their new church. The Congregation had, since arriving in Brompton Road, operated from a temporary church, but now were set upon something more fitting to the Oratorians, their mission and their origins.

Above: Mass at the Oratory Church.

Left: The 'walk back' from the Oratory Church.

7 / Religious Life

Herbert Gribble produced designs for an imposing building which would dominate the surrounding area. This was at a time when the Gothic Revival, exemplified by men such as Augustus Pugin and J J Scholes, was seeing a return to the splendid, soaring architecture of the Middle Ages, reviving and adapting the styles of medieval imagery, tracery and colour. The Oratory Fathers deliberately rejected this English style, insisting instead on an Italianate design as befitted the congregation of St Philip Neri and its Roman origins. Gribble died at an early age before the project was completed and it fell to George Sherrin to complete the dome of the Church. Gribble lies buried in the graveyard of St Thomas's Church, Rylston Road, Fulham, a church designed by Pugin and, coincidentally, the parish within which the school is now situated.

While attending Masses at the Church pupils no doubt do look about them and survey the impressive architecture, the vast space and the hidden corners of the quiet church. How many pupils realise, though, that there was a time when those were the very features appreciated by Soviet spies working in London? In 1991 the Oratory Church was named by Oleg Gordievsky, a Soviet defector who had been head of the KGB's British operations, as the safest place in London to pass material from one intelligence officer to another. He revealed that a 'dead letter box' had been situated behind a marble column in the Chapel of St Patrick in the Oratory Church and was used in the 1980s to leave small containers and papers to be passed between spies. If any pupils attending Mass on the Feast of All Saints in 1991 observed a 'suspicious character' near the War Memorial in St Patrick's Chapel this was not a Soviet spy but a *Sunday Times* reporter testing out the undercover post box. At 9.45am the reporter left a 35mm film container containing a £20 note and wrapped in a page of the *Financial Times* in the alleged hiding place. It was reported in the Sunday paper that he returned seven hours later and retrieved the packet intact. When presented with the story Father Napier, the Provost of the Oratory, conceded that the large church with its shadowy corners might well give scope for foreign agents, adding that maybe it also showed that 'our cleaning is not up to standard'.

Of all the occasions on which the pupils attend the Church the Annual Carol Service and the Patronal Festival are the two that remain longest in memories. At the former the singing of the final Carol followed by the dismissal from the Church marks the start of the holiday after the long Michaelmas term. The relief with which the Housemasters on duty at the bus stops and the station wish a Happy Christmas to one and all echoes the cheery greetings of the departing pupils. For the boys it is home to start the holiday, and for many of the staff it is across the road to The Bunch of Grapes to do the same.

While the end of the Michaelmas term is often dark and cold, Patronal Festival memories are of the brighter days of late spring, as each year the school gathers on the Friday nearest to the Feast of St Philip Neri, which falls on 26 May. The tradition of marking St Philip's Day was inaugurated in 1936 when, according to the school magazine, 'St Philip's

Right: First Communicants, c.1900.

Far right: First Communicants, 2000.

The London Oratory School – *Part III: An Oratory Education*

Above: The school Chapel today.

Left: The first Chapel at Seagrave Road.

Day was celebrated in a manner which will leave a lasting impression on every boy in the school'. The hymns were 'lustily sung', including one entitled 'St Philip's Death'. A special dinner of lamb cutlets, fresh garden peas, chipped potatoes, jelly, blancmange, ice cream and chocolate was served. The afternoon treat was a cinema talkie programme, Charlie Chaplin in *Easy Street*. The whole celebration was recorded as 'another happy memory in school history'. There have been many more memorable Patronal Festival Days since then and traditions have evolved and continue to this day. The Church is filled with boys and girls gathered for Mass, teachers wear their academic gowns and hoods, guests are ushered to their seats, cadets form a guard of honour and the music begins with a stirring anthem as the Procession enters from the back of the Church. After Mass Awards are presented, usually by that year's distinguished guest; the final award goes to the outgoing Head of School, and in a custom of more recent years he then presents ties and badges to the incoming prefects for the year ahead. For sixth formers, and indeed for any teachers in their final year at the school, the rounding off of Patronal Festival with the School Song is a moment to remember.

Visits to the Oratory Church for Mass are reserved for special occasions in the school year. When the school was situated in Chelsea and the numbers on roll were smaller the Church was more accessible, and the Convent Chapel was close by. There was, nonetheless, a desire to have Mass for the boys in their own school building, and it was with great delight that this happened on 7 December 1934, when for the first time Mass was held in St Philip's Hall in the Stewart's Grove building. The altar was built by the boys themselves.

Today the School Chapel is the centre of the daily liturgy at the school. House Assemblies for Morning Prayer, class Masses in RE lessons, voluntary Mass on a Friday morning, Rosary on a Thursday and Benediction on a Friday form the regular cycle of worship, but there are many more occasions when the Chapel is in use, as well as the quiet times when individual staff or pupils may seek a moment away from the bustle of school life. The Chapel is situated at the heart of the school and replaced the smaller original Chapel which had served the community since the school moved from Stewart's Grove. That first Chapel had been included in the Seagrave Road Building as a gift from the Oratory Fathers. In 1970 Father Napier, the Chairman of Governors, had explained that 'it has always been the wish of the Fathers of the Oratory that the school should include a Chapel where the Blessed Sacrament would be reserved and which would act as the spiritual centre of the whole building'. In addition to the £7,500 which the Fathers donated for the essential design and construction, an appeal was launched to raise the additional costs to furnish and decorate the Chapel.

7 / Religious Life

Above: Cardinal Hume at the Blessing and Dedication of the Chapel.

Left: The tabernacle from the Oratory Fathers' house in Sydenham.

Far left: The dedication plaque.

In 1992, under the auspices of John McIntosh as Headmaster, the plan for a new and larger Chapel was devised and implemented. The architect was Richard Hazell and he worked closely with the Headmaster, who took a very direct role in the design. The simple ecclesiastical style with its exposed wooden beams in the high roof space provided the school with a natural, functional and spiritual building which fitted perfectly into the designated site and happily allowed for the altar at the east end of the Church. Within the Chapel the specially commissioned altar rails are from the workshop of David Kindersley. Each of the six was engraved in distinct Kindersley script with the names of one of the six House Saints. The Stations of the Cross were also from the Kindersley workshop, and the sanctuary lamp was the work of silversmith Simon Beer. These special commissions all contribute to making the Chapel a very special place within the school. A particularly wonderful gift was the tabernacle from the Oratory Fathers. It had been brought from the Oratory Church store, a rounded tabernacle covered in a cream-painted plaster, but underneath this was a very special piece, as this tabernacle was from the Fathers' House in Sydenham, once the country retreat of the early Oratorians. The coating was removed and after a good clean and polish there emerged the tabernacle which is now in the Chapel, and before which Cardinal Newman himself would have celebrated Mass. Its presence in the school Chapel provides us with a wonderful link to Blessed John Henry Newman. The Oratory Fathers have also given three splendid paintings to the school for the Chapel: the one of St Philip is a copy of a painting that hangs in the house of the Roman Oratory and is believed to have been painted before he was canonised; that of the Madonna and Child is a copy of the painting in the private Chapel of the Fathers in the Oratory House; and the one of Cardinal Newman is a copy of the portrait by Sir John Everett Millais and was presented to the school on the occasion of the Beatification of Newman in September 2010.

The London Oratory School – Part III: An Oratory Education

Oratory servers with Pope Benedict at the Beatification Mass of John Henry Newman.

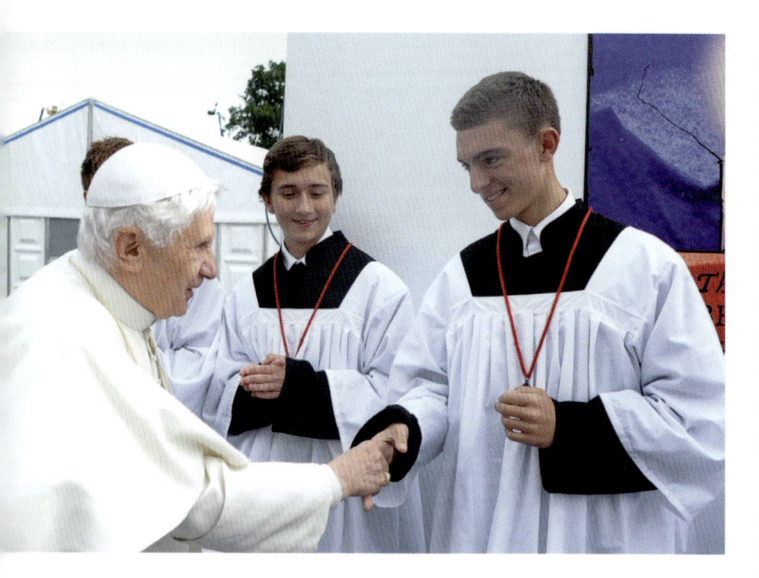

The Beatification was of particular significance for the school, as it was Cardinal Newman who brought the Oratorians to England. On account of the close link with the Oratory the Schola were honoured to sing at the Beatification Mass in Birmingham, where Lee Ward, Director of Music, was the organist and two sixth formers served at the Mass. Paul McGee Renedo and John-Joseph Tyldesley recall the great anticipation and trepidation with which they travelled to Birmingham's Cofton Park. Before Mass they had 'the unforgettable experience of meeting Pope Benedict, a simple shake of his hand, something that will always stay with us'. The two pupils carried out their duties without a hitch, apart from a minor panic when the candles they were bearing blew out just before going out for the procession to the altar. Looking back on the whole occasion they reflected 'it was a true honour to serve His Holiness at the Beatification Mass of a theologian who has special import to those of us associated with the Oratory. In addition both Pope Benedict XVI and Cardinal Newman are men of great learning who both stress that a true faith is an informed faith; this relevance to the mission undertaken at our own school was not lost on us.'

Many London Oratory pupils took part in services or events associated with the Pope's visit; some contributed to the music at the meeting for school children at St Mary's, Strawberry Hill, while others gathered at the Vigil in Hyde Park. All appreciated that they were part of an historic and spiritual experience.

The opportunity for spiritual development is a vital part of education at The London Oratory School and retreats have over many years offered pupils the chance to take time away from the everyday routines of school. In 1936 many of the boys and girls from the Central Schools joined in a Childrens' Retreat to Walsingham. The party gathered at King's Cross Station and after an address from Cardinal Hinsley and the singing of a verse of 'Hail Queen of Heaven' the party boarded the train and headed off for a rainy day of prayer, hymns, Benediction and tea. In later years the school introduced residential retreats, and the opportunity for boys to spend time away in a spiritual atmosphere opened up the possibility for personal growth, for prayer and reflection, and for the attempts at some collective rule breaking as wily boys tried to exploit the innocence of their religious directors; but those leaders probably knew a lot more than they revealed.

Another destination for many young Oratorians was Allington Castle, where the Carmelite Friars provided the hospitality and some of the spiritual direction for the retreat. David Gray on retreat in 1976 recorded the contest between the two minibus drivers, Mr Quinlan in charge of the boys and Mr Brunwin driving the girls. No matter what wiles Mr Quinlan and his passengers adopted it was Mr Brunwin's vehicle that was always first back to the car park. This retreat included a heated discussion on 'morality', with Shaun Mackle and Perry Sykes presiding. The latter was destined for the priesthood; perhaps the Allington Castle experience helped in his formation.

While it is often the resident religious who direct residential retreats, there are times when the Oratory Fathers, in particular the school Chaplain, take the lead. Edward Forbes-Jones, who attended the school from 1949 to 1952, remembers a retreat at Manresa College led by Father Barrett-Lennard which began at a graveside, as Father Barrett-Lennard had first to conduct a burial service before commencing the retreat with the boys. Father Hugh's retreats have been described as 'hilarious events with midnight processions through gorse bushes and other such obstacles' (Peter Lloyd, *An appreciation of Father Hugh Barrett-Lennard*, 2007).

Outdoor night exercises were also included in retreats at the SPEC Centre in London Colney, the destination for fourth formers in the 1990s. Here over three days boys took part in collective and individual prayer, talks and challenges, including the aforementioned night-time orienteering task. The team-building obstacle course was for many the highlight of the retreat. Sixth formers in more recent times have forged their memories at Downside, where pupils get an insight into monastic life, take time for prayer, discussion and reflection, walk barefoot up Glastonbury Tor and learn card games, with rules invented by Father George.

Sixth formers on retreat with the Brothers of The Communauté St Jean.

At Downside the pupils are exposed to the Benedictine way of life, and this is also the case for all fifth formers who spend a day at Douai Abbey in Berkshire. The one-day retreat or Day of Recollection has been in the school calendar in different formats over many years. From the First Form Pilgrimage to the Leavers' Retreat the focus is varied to suit the age and direction of the recipients. Whereas in the 1950s the Leavers' Retreat was directed towards preparing the boys for married life, which it was envisaged would soon be upon them, today's leavers give more thought to how they will continue to grow as Catholics and the contribution they will make in the world as they move on to life beyond school.

At the other end of the school the First Form Pilgrimage was over many decades an annual treat and an opportunity for sharing a day away at the end of the academic year. Boys boarded the coach in Seagrave Road and headed out of London to venues such as Oxford, Arundel or Aylesford, the latter a favoured Oratorian destination since the 1960s. One teacher recalls a pilgrimage to Aylesford in the late 1980s, when Peter Cooke, esteemed Head of the RE Department, exercised his prerogative of assigning duties for the day, and so it followed that while the new, eager-to-please, and less-experienced teachers were given the tasks of supervising 180 boys eating packed lunches, playing football and visiting the gift shop, Mr Cooke took a gentle stroll in the Rosary Walk.

The area had been designated out of bounds but it was, he explained, just possible that first formers might abandon lunch, football or shop and wander that way. The day was rounded off with Mass in the outdoor Chapel of the Priory before it was back on the coach for London.

Aylesford, Oxford and Arundel are all within reach for a day trip but a more ambitious destination was introduced, with characteristic enthusiasm, one year in the late 1980s by Mr Patrick Moran of the RE department. This 'retreat' comprised a three-hour journey to Worcestershire to see the priest holes of Harvington Hall, a quick packed lunch in the rain with no time for Mass as it was time to leave and a very long journey home. The historic interest of the Hall with its priest holes designed by House Saint Nicholas Owen is not to be doubted, but Mr Moran's enthusiasm was thereafter checked and that particular destination disappeared from the RE department journey list.

As well as organising pilgrimages to places of religious significance in and around London and the south east, the RE department have taken boys on pilgrimages overseas, most often to Rome, although Miss Delap did lead an enterprising expedition to Sicily.

Pupils of recent years who have stood on the steps in front of the basilica after attending Mass at St Peter's are unlikely to experience a chance encounter quite like that described by an Old Oratorian on those very steps in

September 1944. Sergeant McElroy, an Old Oratorian on war service in Italy had just left St Peter's after High Mass when 'as though drawn by a magnet to a point on the steps outside St Peter's, I met seven Old Oratorians, none of whom knew the others were coming, and all within a space of five minutes' (PM, xxiv, Sept 1944, p100). Maybe it is literally true that for Oratorians at least, all roads do lead to Rome.

In addition to religious journeys, participation in collective worship and practising individual prayer and reflection, the pupils of The London Oratory School are active in bearing witness to their faith through community and charitable works. From the first form to the sixth form through voluntary service activities boys and girls are busy enjoying the chance to help others.

Every year during Advent and Lent the House Collections promote particular causes and give scope for imaginative fundraising. Oratory pupils were no strangers to charitable fundraising in the past, for example in the 1930s by donating to the Crusade of Rescue the school's pupils assisted Father Craven in the cause of 'helping Catholic waifs and strays', but the House Collections which take place in Lent and Advent open up the scope and nature of giving. Sometimes individual Houses adopt a charity, and links which last over many years are forged. From the 1960s pupils collected for the Catholic Blind Asylum in Liverpool and in due course Campion House took up this mantle, with pupils on one occasion making a visit to deliver a cheque in person. For Mr McCarthy's More House the Across Trust, which runs the Jumbulances (specially adapted vehicles to take sick and disabled travellers to Lourdes and other destinations), was a favourite for a number of years, and another More House cause was the Sisters of the Little Way, who support overseas missionary work. For Fisher House, under Mr Matthews, the Elizabeth Fitzroy Houses for disabled children were for many years the beneficiaries of the collections. Junior House adopted the Catholic Children's Society as their main charity, but they also participate in the Love in a Box event each Christmas, preparing gifts to send to underprivileged children overseas.

As well as the individual Houses directing funds to their own causes the school also organises whole-school collections, with the competition between the Houses increasing the incentive to give to good causes. An interesting element has been introduced by CAFOD, with form periods being given over to classes discussing whether they wish to fund a goat or perhaps a water well, or maybe a pig or some educational resources. No doubt the notion that they know exactly what their money is

Above: The Dom Bosco Institute in Rwanda, twinned with The London Oratory School.

Left: Sixth formers on a fundraising walk for CAFOD.

ORATORY PIE FOR 100 (WITH A LITTLE HELP FROM ICELAND!)

Ingredients
10 kilos fresh best minced beef
4 bags frozen prepared onions
4 bags frozen prepared Mediterranean vegetables/peppers
6 bags frozen peas
12 bags frozen sliced crispy potatoes
2 tubes of tomato puree
10 cubes Knorr beef stock
8 bags grated cheddar
Oil for frying off the mince
A baby's handful of pepper
A child's handful of oregano
A carefree teenager's idea of a dash of Soy sauce

The night before
Heat the oil in two very large saucepans.
Then stir in the mince to 'seal' it, adding handfuls of fresh mince at a time.
Once it is all more or less brown, add onions and peppers.
Cook for 15 minutes before adding the stock cubes dissolved in two pints of hot water, along with tomato puree and the seasoning.
Cook over low heat for 30 minutes.
Take off the heat and allow to cool and marinate overnight.

The next morning at The Passage
Spread the meat mixture in five baking trays and cover with frozen potato slices.
Top with grated cheese and bake for 45 minutes at 180°C.
Put peas in boiling water and bring back to full boil with lid on.
Simmer for five minutes.
Cut the pie into generous slices and serve with peas.

supplying increases the interest and involvement of pupils in fundraising. Nowhere has this been more in evidence than in the raising of funds for the Oratory's sister school in Rwanda. This link, forged by Father George as Chaplain, has brought pupils from The London Oratory School into direct contact with the Dom Bosco Institute in Kabarondo, Rwanda. The LOS Community has now contributed to sports equipment, a library, computers, new washing facilities and a bio-gas water heating system at the Rwandan school, and former pupils on gap years spend time working voluntarily at the Institute. The link has been two-way, with the insight and satisfaction derived from direct involvement with another culture and the sharing of experiences with the young pupils in the African School opening up new ideas to the pupils of London. The needy nearer home are not overlooked either, and Advent Collections have been directed to providing money to purchase shoes and other goods for the homeless who visit The Passage Centre for the Homeless in Westminster.

Oratory pupils are capable of great generosity. In addition it should never be overlooked that there is not much boys will not contribute to if there is a cake sale involved; and cake sales there certainly are, along with quizzes, and sponsored runs, and swims, and games tournaments, and beat the goalkeeper (and when the goalkeeper is your form teacher, the attraction increases), all of which brings added excitement to the act of giving.

Giving of time is another sign of the community work of the pupils in the school. Every week sixth formers visit the elderly in the local Farm Lane Care Home, listen to children read in Fulham Primary School, work with autistic children in the nearby Snowflake School and once a month spend Friday evening and Saturday morning at The Passage Centre. This is where the famous Oratory Pie is prepared. No account of the recent history of the school would be complete without recording the recipe; there is no secret in terms of ingredients, but something special obviously goes into the making of it, as it is reputedly a particular favourite with visitors to the Centre.

In the 1960s sixth formers who wished to collectively demonstrate their faith joined the Young Christian Students (YCS). The aims of the group were to 'to encourage a better student-teacher relationship, to create a more active interest in the school's religious and other activities and to help its members take a personal interest in other students', and it was also the hope that the society would 'encourage in our members a better understanding of the world and its difficulties' (Orat. 1968). How exactly they tackled this rather daunting brief, other than organise social events, remains something of a mystery, but with Father Napier as Chaplain there must have been a sound spiritual dimension. In his article in *The Oratorian* 1966, YCS Vice President Simon Callow records the turbulent period of preceding years, when the loss of representatives caused a lack of direction and some division amongst the Young Christians. There was Moira McKrill, who was appointed as Secretary, but 'when school reassembled in September 1964 Miss McKrill did not return due to an unexpected (at least to her) series of events', and shortly afterwards Anthony Bradbury resigned mid term when he left the school 'to study

Mass in the Oratory Church.

privately'. After organising the Halloween Dance, 'which took place with considerably reduced profit' though with 'a thankfully lighter casualty list,' M McGreal (Treasurer) and Albert Marshall (President) 'resigned' their posts. With more changes to follow it was still an unsettled group when the year ended, but with Michael Barry running one of two packs within the Society and James Harrington in charge of the other it was hoped that 'a measure of stability' was on its way, and it seems that the Society did prosper over the next few years. In 1971 Dermot Power (now Revd Dr Dermot Power) wrote of the work of the young Oratorians in fundraising for the Notting Hill play scheme to provide safe play areas and supervised schemes for children during the summer holidays. For Dermot Power the YCS were involved in something that was a 'matter of justice' and required a 'selfless response' from the pupils of the Oratory.

The aforementioned Dermot Power went on in time to become Spiritual Director at Allen Hall, the Diocesan Seminary in Chelsea, and is one of a significant number of Oratory pupils over the years who have gone on to the priesthood. In the 1920s and 1930s this was a regular occurrence, with maybe four or five boys leaving the Oratory each year to pursue a vocation. Usually the boy progressed to a sixth-form education at another school or to seminary. One who followed this route was Philip Harvey. Born in 1915 he was a pupil at the school until he left in 1928 having been awarded a Junior County Scholarship to Cardinal Vaughan Memorial School. After serving as priest in a number of parishes in the Westminster diocese he became involved in the diocese's welfare work, starting as Assistant Administrator to the Crusade of Rescue and later as Head of the Catholic Children's Society. In 1977 he was consecrated as Auxiliary Bishop of Westminster by Cardinal Hume. Bishop Harvey died in 2003. As the pupils of Junior House continue to raise funds for the Catholic Children's Society the boys may not have realised that they are supporting a cause that was very close to the heart of an Old Oratorian.

Throughout the 1940s and 1950s there were usually a few Old Oratorians in seminary, and in parishes around London.

Fr Paul Keane attended the school 1986–93.

In 1963, when Mr Gaffney arrived to take up his post as Headmaster, he bought a house in New Malden, and after attending Mass in his local Parish he discovered that his new priest, Father O' Sullivan, was an Old Oratorian. In 2011 the school enjoyed welcoming former pupil Father Paul Keane to celebrate the Patronal Festival Mass. Father Keane was a pupil at the school, 1986–93, before studying history at Cambridge and then pursuing his vocation with the Brentwood Diocese. He is now Chaplain at the University of Essex. David Howell, who was a Senior Prefect and Head of School in his final year, is training for the priesthood in Rome. Also training at the English College in Rome is Stefan Kaminski (1998–2003).

For those boys at the school seeking a way to serve as lay members within the Oratory community there was the Brothers of the Little Oratory, a lay organisation for young men. Fifth and sixth formers in the school could join the Brothers. Bernard Liengme and his friend Henri Glouchkow did so; they recall serving two or three Masses each Sunday, and going on outings with Father Hugh Barrett-Lennard, whose eccentricities they remember with affection. Pierre Kacary (1975–82) also forged a long-standing link, serving at the Sunday High Mass into his 30s.

Through the years pupils have attended the liturgy, joined the choir, read at Mass, learned to serve, helped with porter duties and assisted at functions at their 'second Parish', the Oratory Church.

For 150 years of life as a Catholic school in the trusteeship of the Oratory Fathers, the school has helped to form generations of Catholic boys and girls. Now with the school Chapel at the heart of the school, and with dedicated Chaplains and committed staff and pupils, religious life flourishes and the central mission remains the same as ever.

> *I did not think of becoming a priest until my last year at the school, after a few teenage years of drifting away from my faith, but in hindsight, I can see that God used my time there to prepare me to respond to his call. The firm but gentle discipline and family-like atmosphere encouraged me to engage with the studies as a search for truth rather than as a box-ticking exercise. Inspiring saints cropped up throughout history classes and Mr Belsito was disarmingly open to any question voiced during RE lessons. The rugby, choir and flute practices instilled self-discipline and broadened my horizons and Head of School duties gave a taste of shepherding a little flock. So by the lower sixth, I was ready to start again in my faith during an inspiring pilgrimage to Lourdes with Father George, which prepared me to consider the priesthood the following year. After Oxford, I went to seminary in Rome four years ago and am enjoying my training next door to the church where St Philip founded the Oratory.*
>
> David Howell, 1998–2005

David Howell as a pupil in 2005, with Housemaster Mr Ashenden.

SCHOOL CHAPLAINS

Since the school began the Oratory Fathers have supplied the school Chaplains, and there have been many over the years, some for longer periods than others and all with their own characteristic ways. Each has made a valuable and vital mark on the religious life of the school in his own distinct style. The following three long-serving Chaplains well serve to illustrate this.

Father Hugh Barrett-Lennard

Hugh Dacre Barrett-Lennard, Baronet, was born in 1917, the son of a soldier and colonial judge. He was educated at Radley College and converted to Catholicism, along with his mother, in the 1930s. He was for a short time a teacher at St Philip's prep school before joining up at the outbreak of the Second World War. He had by this time been intending to join the Oratory but war service came first. The tales he later told of his war years fascinated the young Oratory pupils whom he encountered. These recollections included: finding that the orderly carrying his bags on arrival in brigade headquarters in France was a waiter who had been sacked from the Dorchester after spilling soup on one of Father Hugh's guests; being struck by a grenade in Holland, which left a piece of shrapnel in his head for the rest of his life; advancing after the D-Day landings and announcing to the mayor of a small town in Normandy '*Je suis l'Armée Britannique*' as he drove his jeep into town with the retreating Germans still in sight, after which his driver reported back 'Lieutenant Barrett-Lennard is bonkers.' Maybe he was, but he was fearless too, and certainly unconventional. He finished the war as Captain in the Second Battalion of the Essex Regiment and earned a Mention in Despatches for his exploits.

After the war he studied for the priesthood in Rome. His ordination coincided with that of a German whom he had shot in Normandy. Father Hugh joined the Oratory in 1946 and began his work ministering to the Parish and the schools. He also took a great interest in the Oratory Cadet Corps. As school Chaplain he drew the pupils to him with a charisma and eccentricity which seemed to reflect that of St Philip Neri. He was equally at home in the drawing rooms of his Knightsbridge parishioners as in the rough and tumble of the school playground. It was not unusual to see Father Hugh shuffling along in odd shoes, with the remnants of dinner on his cassock. His retreats were legendary and unforgettable to those who took part; somewhere in the programme there was guaranteed to be lively and robust singing, rambles and recitations, and admiration for this apparently innocent but actually very wise priest. He died in 2007, after 60 years as an Oratorian.

Father Michael Napier

Pupils or visitors attending a meeting at The London Oratory School might find themselves sitting around the table in the Napier Room, but have they wondered why the room is so named? Father Michael Napier was a Governor from 1966, serving as Chairman from 1977 to 1981. He was school Chaplain for many years until his sudden death from a heart attack in August 1996.

Born in 1929, Michael Napier was from a military background, a direct descendant of Charles Napier of Peninsular War fame, whose statue stands in Trafalgar Square. His own father, Major-General Charles Napier, served in India and played an important role in the operation of the D-Day landings. He was not a Catholic, and his son was baptised into the Church of Scotland, educated at Wellington College and at Trinity Hall, Cambridge, where he studied architecture. It was at Cambridge that Michael Napier took instruction to be a Catholic under Monsignor Alfred Gilbey and was received into the Church in 1952. He joined the Oratory one year later, and over the ensuing years became Parish Priest, Provost and Apostolic Visitor for Rome to the 63 Oratories around the world, as well as serving The London Oratory School as governor and chaplain.

Above: Fr Hugh Barrett-Lennard.

Left: Fr Michael Napier with sacristans.

Fr George with London Oratory School pilgrims on World Youth Day in Madrid, 2011.

At the Oratory Church Father Napier did invaluable work in showing how tradition could be maintained alongside the changes of Vatican II. The music and forms for which the Oratory is well known were preserved, and the importance of ritual, order and beauty permeated worship at the Church. These values were passed on to pupils. As Chairman of Governors he steered the school through political and educational challenges which threatened to alter the character of the school, but he held firm. With his background in architecture he had an interest in the aesthetic influence on Church and school. He was responsible for ensuring that the new school, on moving to Seagrave Road, had its own Chapel, and later took great pleasure in the design and building of the current Chapel. Father Napier was a meticulous man and he resisted any decline in standards or expectations, insisting on correct turnout at all times, with no slouching allowed. The boys who served Mass for him well remember the order 'keep those hands up, boy' if prayerful hands began to slide from an upright position. Although he appeared to some to be a stern and rather distant man, those who knew him recognised a dedicated priest with a great interest in the work and value of the school and its pupils.

Father George Bowen

Father George, the current school Chaplain, might appear to get results where others do not; somehow the late submission of a form or the double booking of a minibus do not throw a spanner in the works for him as they would for anyone else. Whatever the reason for this apparent immunity to the obstacles that thwart others, it is a benefit to the pupils, as Father George must be one of the most active Chaplains the school has known. Journeys, debates, charitable works and many a new enterprise have been added to the liturgical and counselling roles associated with the Chaplain's post while he has been in office. He assumed the position of Chaplain in 1996 and in the years since hundreds of pupils have benefited from Father George's labours.

John Bowen (Father George) was educated at Downside and has maintained strong links with his alma mater, establishing the annual retreat for London Oratory sixth formers at the Somerset school and engaging in Model United Nations (MUN) meetings with Downside and other prestigious schools. The MUN was introduced to the school by Father George and is now a thriving part of senior school life. Father George led the way in linking the CCF with the Irish Guards. It is Father George who established the link with the Dom Bosco Institute in Rwanda and arranges the gap year programme for Oratory sixth formers. Father George associated the school with The Passage, the centre for the homeless in Westminster, and oversees the Saturday morning volunteers. In the spirit of Oratorian Chaplains before him Father George has organised memorable retreats and pilgrimages but has also widely expanded the programmes offered to the pupils in this sphere. Father George has definitely earned a place in school history.

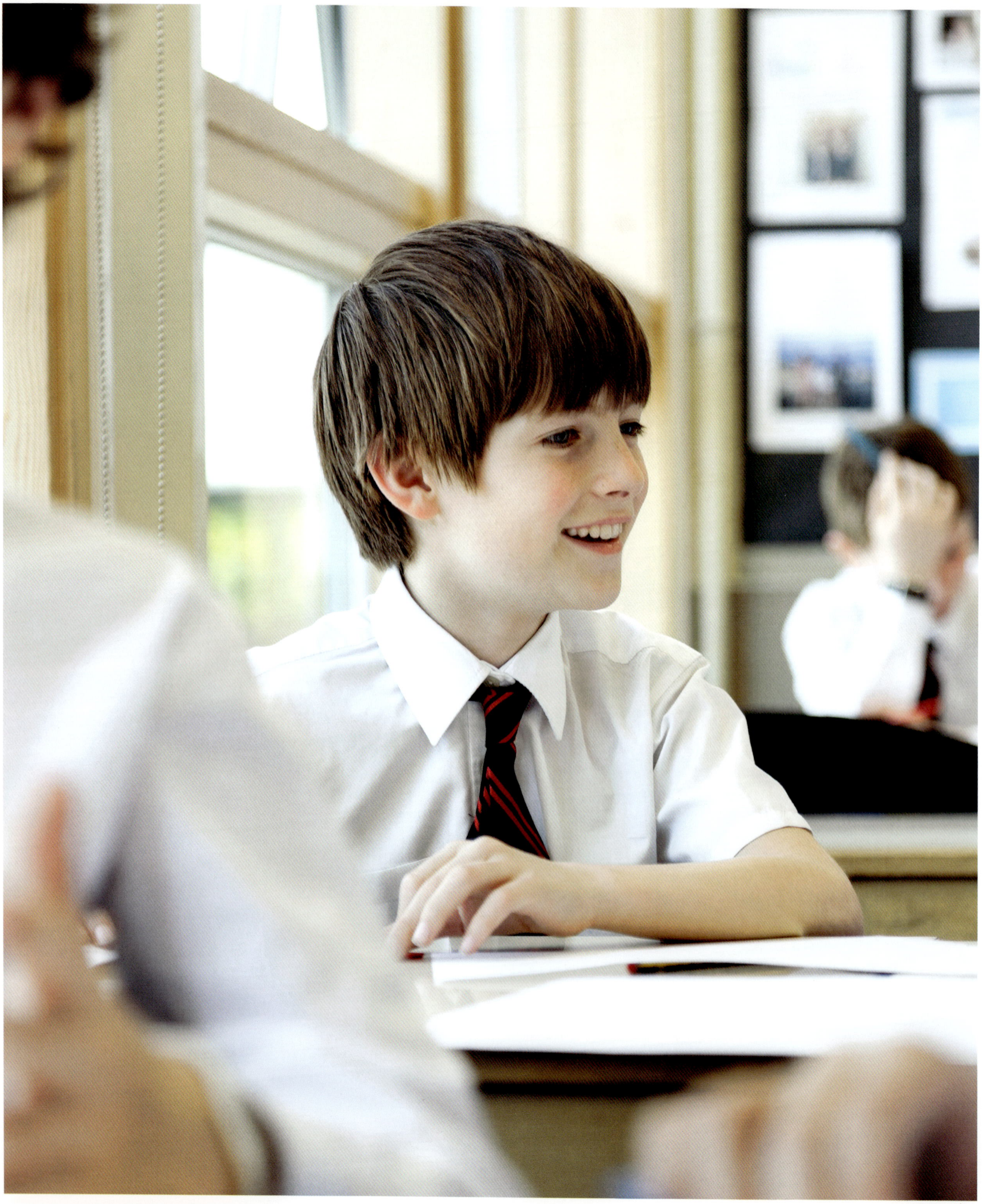

8

Academic Life

When the Fathers of the Oratory first established their school a primary concern was the need to ensure a Catholic education for the children in their schools and to equip them to take their place in society. In determining what would be taught in the school, managers were aware that many of their pupils came from poorly educated backgrounds and would have little scholarly ambition. The school curriculum was designed to instil essential skills and training within the Catholic context.

Secondary education was not compulsory when the school was founded and there was certainly no statutory curriculum. There were, however, core subjects to be taught and examined and School Inspectors would visit to judge the quality of provision. Nineteenth-century Inspection reports consisted of, at most, a one-page summary of findings and recommendations. The surviving reports from the Middle School show that the following subjects were studied and judged by the Inspectors: reading, spelling, handwriting, composition, recitation, arithmetic, geography and history. Oratory boys were also being taught French and Latin, evidence of the desire to extend the curriculum beyond the minimum. The inspection report of 1890 records that the singing in the school was very good. It seems this was a regular part of an Oratory education from the start, although it seems singing was the limit of the musical education on offer. By 1891 the school was putting forward candidates for a drawing examination for the first time. As this was done under the combined auspices of the science and art departments perhaps botanical drawing was required. Shorthand was also taught as a necessary skill for any young man seeking worthy employment in the business or commercial world.

Although endeavouring to provide a good education for life the school was, in the early years of the 20th century, strongly inclined towards preparing boys for work, perhaps to the detriment of more cultural pursuits. The 1914 Inspection report comments 'The School is very successful in its chief aim to prepare the boys for commercial life. On leaving school many of them obtain good places in offices', but went on to say

> *a more liberal treatment might be adopted such as would entail no sacrifice of vocational utility and would lead to ultimate issues of high educational value … more care is needed to foster a love of good literature … in history too much attention is given to*

Opposite: Pupils in class.

Right: A classroom in the Middle School. The text on the board reads 'An island is a portion of land surrounded entirely by water' and is dated 17 July 1900.

military and legal affairs and very little to the social life of the people … in arithmetic the predominance of artificial and mechanical, and the absence of practical exercises, is very conspicuous.

By the time the school was moving to becoming a Central School the aim of fitting boys for the world of commerce, business and trade was the main focus of the curriculum. As Dr Ballard, the London Education Council District Inspector explained at the school Exhibition Day in 1925, the Central Schools had been established for those children who either did not get a secondary school scholarship or whose parents could not pay the fees. All the children in a Central School are admitted solely on their abilities. 'There are no duffers in a Central School', he said, 'a statement received with deafening applause by the assembled boys' (PM, v, p15). When comparing the Central School curriculum to that of the other secondary schools Dr Ballard observed that the only difference was that in a Central School they did not teach Latin. It would be some years before Latin was reintroduced at the Oratory School in the 1940s, and today the fact that the boys do study Latin is one aspect that distinguishes the school from so many others.

For some pupils the challenge of learning Latin can be a tough one. Bernard Liengme (1949–57), who went on to a distinguished scientific career, recalls being given his Latin examination result and being told he had come 31st in class. When he enquired 'but Sir, how can I be 31st in a class of 30?' Mr Hooper replied, 'because I do not want to insult the boy who came ahead of you'. This sharp-tongued Latin teacher is also the author of the words enshrined in '*Quam bonum est*', known to pupils past and present as 'the School Song'. In more recent times Magister Sullivan has ensured the ancient languages remain strong, attracting a steady number of disciples with a good number going on to study Classics at prestigious universities.

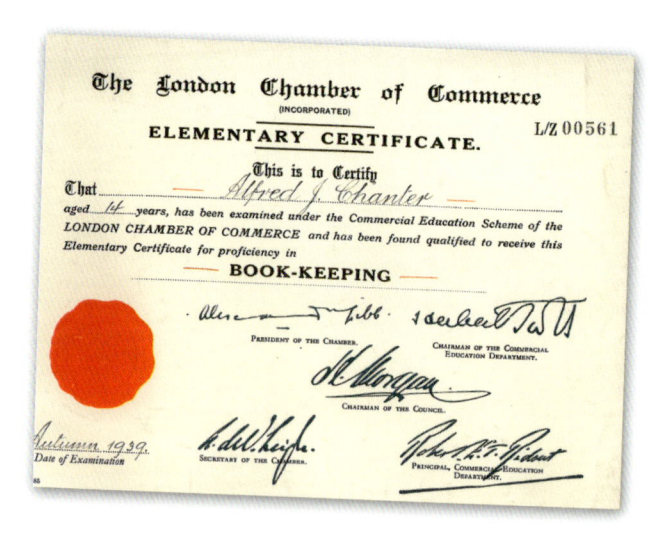

Brian Cheesman, who attended the school from 1944 to 1950, recalls how the boys were divided into the Academic or Commercial stream. He was moved to the Commercial stream after an arm injury affected his studies, and 'this opened up a new exciting world of practical skills, typing, shorthand, book-keeping and woodworking in which I thrived. Starting to type at an early age was a life-long skill – chanting a-s-d-f-g-space as we typed under the eagle eye of Mr McCowatt'. The school newsletter and the parish magazine regularly listed successes in commercial examinations. For woodwork lessons the boys were taken to premises further down Fulham Road where, as Brian Cheesman records, 'a practical, taciturn, brown-overalled craftsman would guide us through the use of saw, hammer, planes, the mysteries of French polishing and set us to making cigarette boxes for our parents to give at Christmas'. It was much to Mr Cheesman's disappointment that he excelled in the practical subjects as he was subsequently transferred back to the Academic Stream, although this did spark a lifelong love of history due to the teaching of 'Georgie' Walman.

Often it was the teacher and not the subject that sparked the young Oratorian's desire to learn, and once the spark was lit then the subject could take hold. For some it was maths, with the 'ebullient and provocative' Mr O'Shea (David Wailen, 1949–56), or with Jacko (aka Mr O'Neill),

Above: Commercial subjects were taught to some of the boys.

Left: Bernard Liengme (second from right) in class in the 1950s.

Above: Chemistry today.

Left: Science with Mr Montgomery and the chemistry laboratory in 1956.

or with Mr Gaffney, the Headmaster. Some of those who learned their algebra and arithmetic from Mr Hartigan find their own sons now doing the same. For others a love of the French language was born with the sophisticated Mr Frizelle or Mr Griffin, or a lifelong interest in history started with the 'very inspiring' Mr Crosby (Ted Forbes-Jones, 1949–52), or with Mr Quinlan, or with Mr McCarthy, a great storyteller. These latter two gave invaluable help to Vincent O'Brien, charting new territory as he prepared for entrance to Oxford University in 1976. An appreciation of good literature and grammatical rigour came to many from Mr Monaghan, the monocled Mr Bell, or Mr Canty. Fifty years after leaving school Roger Knight (1956–62) observes that to this day when he sees an example of poor grammar he is transported back to an Oratory classroom in the 1950s and can hear his teacher's voice saying, 'You do not follow a comma with the word "and", boy!' Vincent O'Brien acknowledges that he did not realise it until much later in life but the encouragement of Mr Wilson for pupils to read outside the syllabus and to appreciate literature was planting the seeds of something that would grow into a deep appreciation of English. More recent pupils have been inspired by the fascinating Mr McKenna.

In the sciences Mr Montgomery ('Jam') was an inspiration, '*very* quiet, but a great teacher', encouraging a love of science that would lead Bernard Liengme to university and an academic career in chemistry. When Mr Montgomery retired in 1966 even Simon Callow, writing in *The Oratorian*, and with little love of science, had to concede, 'as one who admittedly did not always shine at the subject of physics, but at least from insistent inculcation knows all the Laws and Principles from Ohm's to Archimedes; damned useless they are too, but quite unforgettable,' that 'Mr Montgomery's teaching is an insidious poison which aims at total destruction of a tendency towards the Arts; to resist it requires a supreme failure of exam'.

More questionable but certainly no less memorable experiences were to be found with the eccentric teachers whose methods for dealing with forgetful or recalcitrant boys belong to a former age. Brian Cheesman remembers the geography teacher 'who would have one running around the playground with outstretched arms carrying a heavy satchel for forgetting where the Outer Antilles were situated'. Then there was the woodwork teacher who Roger Knight recalls 'would occasionally throw a mallet or chisel at you for misbehaving but would let you have a cigarette around the fire on a winter's day'. Flying objects, more usually pieces of chalk, were also a memory of Kevin Haughton's lessons (1951–5). Today's pupils, should they transgress, need fear no missiles launched by teachers, nor do they need to dread the cane. The distinction of being the last entry for corporal punishment in The London Oratory Punishment Book goes to DaSilva of 1CN, who received two strokes on 1 July 1985 for 'charging around on the playground after the bell'. The punishment was 'inflicted' by Mr Matthews and signed off by Mr McIntosh. DaSilva will no doubt hold the distinction in perpetuity, as no matter what education 'reforms' any government might inflict on our schools we can be pretty certain that a return to corporal punishment will not be on the agenda. Today's pupil will be in detention or doing extra work or community service, he might be brought up before the Headmaster or forced to come into school on a Saturday, but the days of a quick slap or the short sharp shock of the cane are gone. Those who received these more physical punishments look back with mixed views. For some it was a brutal approach which stifled learning, for others it was the 'way it was done then' and preferable to getting lines or detention.

A visitor from the Stewart's Grove days or from the first years at Seagrave Road would be struck by the more collaborative yet still rigorous nature of teaching today. He might see differences in the content and approach to work for current pupils, but he would see also that the familiar core subjects remain on the timetable, although with a few shifts; handicraft, woodwork and technical drawing are out, design technology is in. ICT and Computing are entirely new and sixth formers have the opportunity to study such things as economics, politics and critical thinking. The Awards for Speech Days and Patronal Festivals of past years provide clues as to what was once offered in the sixth form curriculum. In 1977, for example, awards were presented for such unfamiliar subjects to today's pupils as zoology, British Constitution and sociology.

Modern technology has significantly altered both teaching and study over the past decade or so, but the school has never shunned new technological advances. In the 1930s lantern lectures, such as that on 'Paris' given by Mr Murray, were greeted with excitement as boys gathered to see images including the Hall of Mirrors at Versailles. In June 1934 the school newsletter reports that the Weather Station is almost complete and will soon be operating with a new barograph and 'the self recording rain-gauge made by boys of the technical class'. In 1936 the purchase of a Beck Micro Projector opened up new possibilities in science classes as magnified images could be projected onto a screen, which proved useful in chemistry 'for the rapid examination of crystals'. Today classrooms are equipped with computers, internet access and interactive whiteboards. Films can be viewed on a large screen in every classroom, but at one time the arrival of a series of educational films was a cause of great excitement in the school. 'One of the best educational sound films we have yet seen was shown to several classes this past week' announced the school newsletter in March 1936. What had earned this high praise? A film entitled *Filter*, dealing with the purification of water. The same week films were also shown on *Canals* and *Sheep Rearing*. To later Oratorians these might sound dull entertainments, but the excitement at the opportunity for an audio-visual presentation of material otherwise far beyond the experience of London boys was real. Most often it was scientific and industrial processes which were filmed, or demonstrations of the natural world.

Today the way lessons and homework are conducted and presented is changing, but what is good of the old can be preserved and incorporated into the new to ensure the academic success of the pupils. In the Library (still pleasing to note a 'library' and not a 'learning hub') books line the shelves, but in addition computers and new technology allow for access to wider resources and for new methods of research and writing. The science laboratories have modernised since the bottle-lined shelves fascinated the boys of Stewart's Grove, but bunsen burners and ticker tape

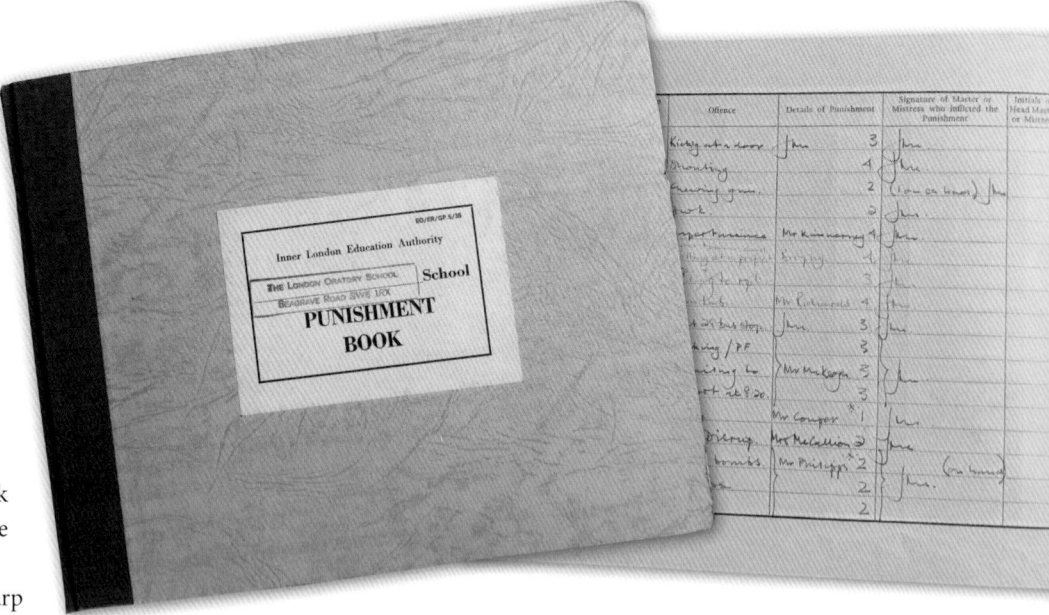

The use of the cane was recorded in the official Punishment Book.

Pupils at work in design technology.

are still going strong. Debates and investigations feature in history lessons but medieval crop rotation is still on the syllabus. The ropes and vaulting horses in the gym have been replaced by weights and rowing machines in the Fitness Centre but boys still run laps of the playground.

Whether at Stewart's Grove or Seagrave Road, whether in 1930 or today, the end of year report has always been a matter for great rejoicing or dread. In the 1930s Oratory boys took home a record book in which form teachers recorded the year's work and effort 'without fear or favour; as nearly truthful as is possible, to indicate to the parent, where the boy is going wrong, whether he is really making an effort or whether he is deserving of praise'. The philosophy has not changed much over the years, but the format has expanded and the parent of today receives a lot more detail and data than his 1930s counterpart. Test results are recorded and ups and downs are clear to see.

Inevitably examinations loom large in a pupil's school career, and from the earliest days boys were prepared for examinations as a means of equipping them for life beyond school. Initially tests in commercial subjects formed the culmination of school life, but it was with considerable pride that it was announced in 1932 that boys would be entered for the Cambridge School Certificate for the first time. This shift towards a more academic and less commercial emphasis fitted with Dr Summerbell's notion that boys in a central school might achieve as much as those in a grammar school. With this belief he encouraged parents to keep their boys in the school beyond leaving age, and when he saw the potential for higher-level study he pushed pupils accordingly. Brian Cheesman had expected to go on to further study, but when he received his School Certificate results he was greatly disappointed and very surprised to find that he had not done as well as expected. Instead of going to Loughborough College as he had hoped, he found himself taking up a post with an insurance company. About three months later, as he recalls, 'I was asked to go and see Dr Summerbell. He explained that he had been mystified by my examination results and it transpired that they had been muddled with those of a classmate and that I had not only passed my examinations but gained matriculation. It was with unbelievable joy that I decided to finish my time with the insurance company, my new exam results meaning I could apply for aircrew training with the RAF for my National Service and take up college afterwards. I often thought of my classmate who took up a position on the strength of my results, only to discover later that he was under-qualified.' In 1954 Dr Summerbell encouraged a group of pupils to stay on beyond O levels to prepare for university. This was the beginnings of the sixth form at the school. Included in this select group were Bernard Liengme, David Wailen, Henri Glouchkow, John Denton, Graham Williams, Chris Byrne, Robert (Oli) Davies and Tony Archer. After A levels Bernard Liengme stayed on for a

85

The London Oratory School – *Part III: An Oratory Education*

third year in sixth form to prepare for university scholarship exams. He won both a Royal Entrance Scholarship and State Scholarship to read chemistry at Imperial College, the first Oratory scholarship. His contemporary Henri Glouchkow went to Keele University. The two friends lost touch in the ensuing years only to reconnect after a chance encounter much later on a beach in Prince Edward Island, subsequently discovering that they both now lived in Canada. Oli Davies got a post with the Meteorological Office after graduation but was tragically killed in an air accident on a reconnaissance flight not long after starting work. David Wailen studied at the London School of Economics and there followed a career working for multi-national companies, mainly in the oil and shipping industries. He believes the 'first-rate education' he received at the Oratory made this possible. These young men of the 1950s were pioneers and set the trend for future generations of Oratorians by making university a genuine aspiration. Exactly 20 years later 27 sixth formers headed off to institutions of higher education, including the first to go to Oxford, Vincent O'Brien. In 2012, 135 pupils were awarded places at university, eight of these at Oxford or Cambridge University.

Of course many pupils did not go on to university but made their way in the world straight from school, and many did so with great success. Kevin Haughton went to train as an architectural draughtsman, and after a number of years he was working for the Inner London Education Authority, Building Surveyors Department. One of the schools he had to look after in this capacity was none other than his own alma mater, now in new premises in Seagrave Road. He recalls with pleasure this quirk of fate by which some of the skills learned at school, particularly in technical drawing classes, were now being put to use for the school.

A significant number of former pupils have found themselves working one way or another at their old school. Of the Senior Staff of the school in 2012, Mr McFadden, Headmaster, Mr Rooney, Deputy Headmaster, Mr Isaaks and Mr Marty, Assistant Headmasters, and Mr Jones, Procurator, all once wore the Oratory blazer. Who knows which of today's pupils will return to hand on an Oratory education to a new generation?

Today's pupils enjoy learning in a variety of ways.

86

8 / *Academic Life*

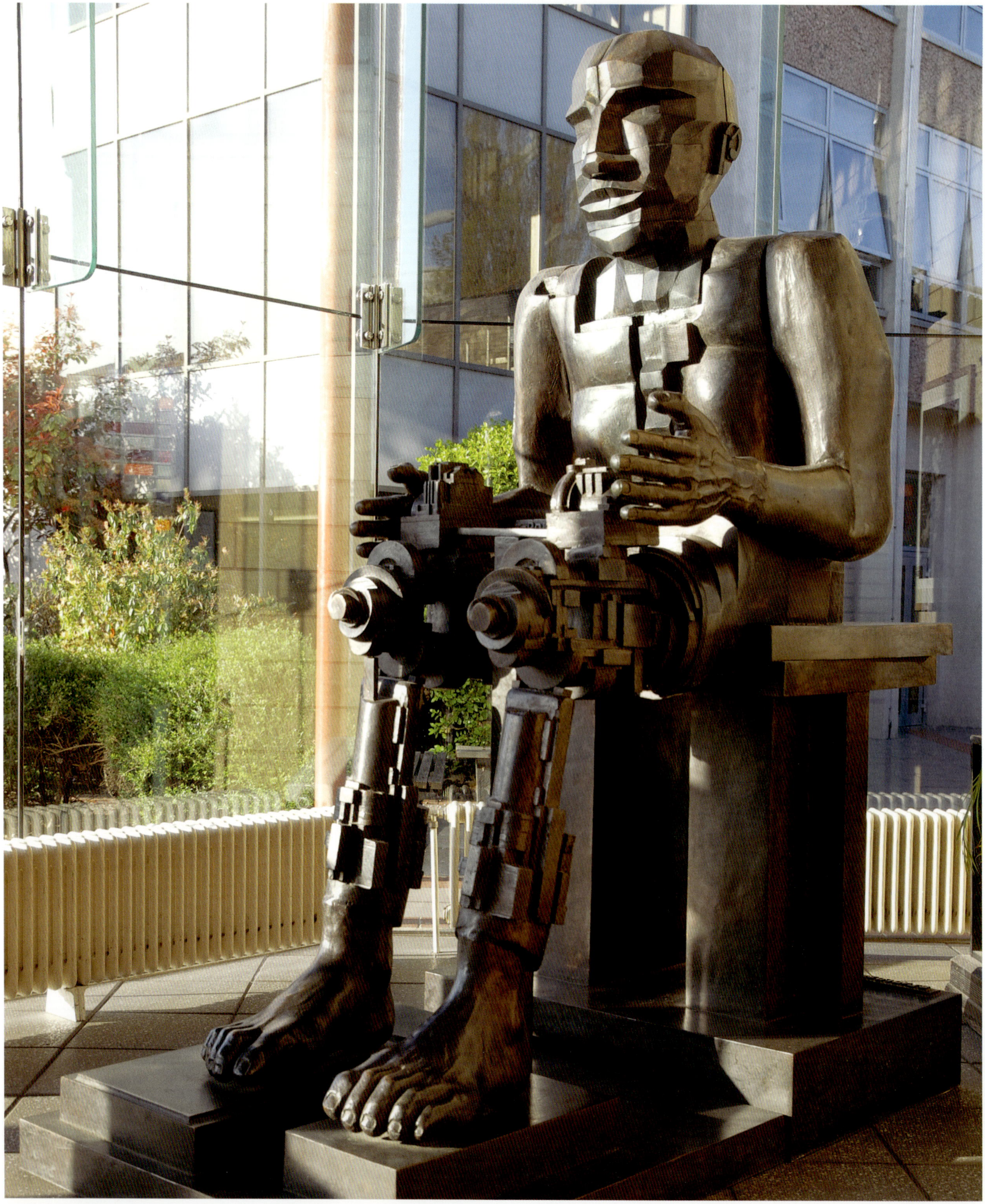

9

The Creative Arts

THE JOHN MCINTOSH ARTS CENTRE

John McIntosh, Headmaster 1977–2006, did much to promote the arts within the school. A keen musician himself he regularly played the organ at Chapel services, and in one senior school concert made his own concert debut with a performance from the Saint-Saëns *Organ Symphony*. He appointed talented professionals to teach music, art and drama and encouraged performance at all levels in music and theatre. With an interest in architecture and design he had a vision of providing a worthy setting for the pupils of the school to study, to practise, and to perform. The opportunity came with the building programme after the school moved to grant maintained status in 1989 and Mr McIntosh directed time and money to realising the idea of an Arts Centre to bring new facilities and opportunities for the arts in the school. At the heart of the building is a 300-seat theatre complete with fly tower, lighting box, set design and storage areas and a good size orchestra pit. Around the magnificent theatre are music rooms, art rooms, a pottery kiln and an exhibition space.

From its inauguration in 1991 to the present day the Arts Centre has been the scene of many memorable theatrical productions, wonderful concerts, talks and debates, awards and ceremonies. In the specialist teaching rooms the seeds of artistic and musical achievement have been sown and the Foyer and Gallery have seen presentations, unveilings and exhibitions of impressive talent, as well as many a social evening.

It was a momentous day in school history when Prime Minister John Major accepted the invitation to inaugurate the building of the Arts Centre by symbolically turning the earth on which the building was to be erected. The Prime Minister and his wife Norma toured the school and spoke to many pupils and teachers. Rory O'Connor of second form had the honour of presenting a bouquet of flowers to Mrs Major, who was impressed to hear that young Rory had sung in the production of *Tosca* at Earls Court a few weeks earlier.

As well as providing excellent facilities for the pupils of the school the Arts Centre is also the envy of many amateur dramatic societies, and over the years the theatre has been hired by companies seeking a venue for their productions.

Opposite: The statue of Athena by Eduardo Paolozzi in the foyer of the Arts Centre.

Below: The Arts Centre.

PART III : An Oratory Education

When in 2006 Mr McIntosh announced his intention to retire as Headmaster the Governors of the school considered different ways in which to mark his departure. Legacy is a somewhat over-used word these days, but in the case of John McIntosh and the Arts Centre it was clear to see that as the driving force behind it John McIntosh had created a real legacy. How better to make that explicit than to name the Arts Centre in his honour? The idea was quickly adopted and a secret plan was put into place. The commissioning of a suitable plaque, the installation of the same and the ceremonial opening of the newly named John McIntosh Arts Centre had to be carefully orchestrated. The lettering was entrusted to the Kindersley workshop and on the day before Mr McIntosh was to retire the delicate glass panels had to be brought to the school and hung in the Arts Centre Foyer, all without the Headmaster's knowledge. That afternoon, from the moment the truck delivering the panels was directed through the gates and across the playground, all those in the know had to contrive to ensure the Headmaster had neither time nor reason to walk across the playground or anywhere in the general direction of the Arts Centre. Father Ignatius, the Chairman of Governors, had arranged a dinner engagement for Mr McIntosh for the evening. Once the Headmaster had been whisked off the premises the preparations were completed and the following day to his surprise Mr McIntosh found that he had a building named after him!

Preparations for the naming of the Arts Centre.

ATHENA

The Foyer is dominated by the statue of Athena by Eduardo Paolozzi. Athena is a large bronze figure based on the Greek goddess of Wisdom. It offers a juxtaposition of the realistic and mechanistic portrayal of the human figure and combines the recognisable concept of the ancient goddess with symbolic elements of more modern origin. In Eduardo Paolozzi's own words he set out 'to create a figure that symbolises our debt to ancient learning but at the same time, describes the ambiguities of the present and can lead one to point to the future'. The statue was unveiled by Lord Renfrew, the Master of Jesus College, Cambridge, on 5 October 1993. Paolozzi was present and he remained a friend of the school over the years that followed. Since first taking her position in the Arts Centre Athena has been a source of artistic appreciation and critical discussion and will no doubt continue to intrigue and inspire for years to come.

9 / *The Creative Arts*

THE TIME CAPSULE

Underneath the huge statue of Athena in the Foyer of the John McIntosh Arts Centre there lies a steel box. This is The London Oratory Time Capsule.

Within the time capsule is a collection of items carefully selected and stored by a team of sixth formers in September 1993. After a briefing by Dr Brian Durrans, the then Deputy Keeper of the Museum of Mankind and an expert on time capsules, the pupils spent months collecting and assessing ephemera which would serve to give a future generation an interesting insight into society in the 1990s. Amongst the final selection for depositing in the box were school badges and school publications, a troll (the cult toy of the day), an Argos catalogue, a cash card, a plastic joke mask of John Major (who was then Prime Minister), a video diary of school life, an audio cassette of contemporary music, samples of pupils' work and photographs of Fulham past and present.

When in 2012 a former pupil of the school organised a loan of Athena for display at a contemporary Arts Fair a major lifting and transportation operation was required. The raising of Athena meant the time capsule was relatively accessible. After some deliberations as to whether to open the box before the designated time, even if only for a peek before replacing everything, was tantamount to bringing down the curse of Tutankhamen it was decided to risk it for this glimpse into the past. The box was opened. Inside all was at it should be and apart from taking some photographs for the school archives all was replaced after a quick look, and laugh, at the contents.

With all 1.5 tonnes of Athena back in place over the capsule who knows when the steel box will be opened again?

The installation of Athena, and Eduardo Paolozzi with pupils.

ART

The creative arts are supported and developed in many spheres at The London Oratory School and the art department is at the heart of much of this creativity. Things have come a long way since the days when Bernard Liengme (1949–57) used 'linoleum squares and potatoes to carve and make prints with'. A visitor to the art department could not fail to be impressed with the facilities, the surroundings and above all the talent in evidence. The only chance of seeing a potato now is sliced, fried, flavoured with cheese and onion, and served with drinks at a private view.

In the very early days of the school art was not given much accord on the curriculum, although by the time the Middle School was established after 1880 the young Oratory pupils were taught basic drawing skills. An Inspection Report of March 1910 noted that 'drawing is well taught', and by 1892 the school was for the first time putting forward candidates for a drawing examination. In 1921 the Oratory Central and Middle School was authorised by the education authority to engage a teacher who would specialise in teaching art, but even then the school was only allocated the funds to engage a half teacher. The drawing master would need to offer another subject to earn his pay – maybe he would also teach science, as it seems the science department had at this time some responsibility for the pupils' progress in drawing. Once the school was situated in Stewart's Grove a room had been designated as the art room and art was certainly not a neglected subject. It would still be some time, however, before any notion of mixed media was introduced to the Oratory pupils. In 1947 prospective pupils and parents visiting the school on an open day were invited to 'come and see the art – marvellous and original pictures' (PM, xxvii, p228).

The artistic talent of pupils of the 1960s is preserved in *The Oratorian* of these years. The idea of using pupils' drawings, painting and photographs to illustrate the school magazine was introduced over this period. At this time the cover of *The Oratorian* was often created by a pupil. The 1971 cover, the first issued in the new school building, showing Ewa Tompolski's stylised self portrait incorporating the title and year, is a reflection of its time (shown above).

The London Oratory School – Part III: An Oratory Education

Left: Norma Major visiting the art department; David Gifford looks on.

Below: The Annual Art Exhibition is now well established in the school calendar.

By the time the school opened at Seagrave Road art had expanded considerably. The opportunity for pupils' work to be viewed by fellow pupils and visitors to the school was afforded by regular displays in the main school entrance. There was much to admire in the work as these were years of real development in art at the school.

The appointment of David Gifford to the art department in 1974 was the beginning of an Oratory career that would last until his retirement in 2008. At first Mr Gifford worked with two colleagues, Rod Langsford and Rene Cheeseman, and was soon sharing Head of Department duties with Mr Langsford. The department had previously been managed by Mr O'Donnell, who, amongst other things, had been responsible for the Radio Club, and who, as Mr Gifford recalls, left a legacy in endless amounts of wire and bits of circuitry that fell out from every cupboard. Mr O'Donnell, like many who followed him in the department, had the knack of encouraging boys in the subject. Michael Sheehan (1957–62) says 'you just had to do well for him; he gave such insight on different techniques to try and never lost patience. My pride in winning a prize for art one year was down to him.'

At this time there were just a few boys taking O level art and A level was still to be established, nor was there any extra-curricular art. Opportunity for the latter came as the House Drama Festival was established, and more and more scenery was introduced into these productions. In these pre-Arts Centre days the sets had to be constructed and painted in the classrooms. This expansion in the scope of work undertaken within the department led Mr Langsford to develop an interest in stage design. He eventually left to take a post-graduate Theatre Design course, thereafter to become assistant to Anthony MacDonald, who designed many of the massive and spectacular outdoor sets for the Bregenz Festival. From contributing to the annual drama competition the art department became an integral part of all school productions and set design went from strength to strength. As the scale and quality of school music and drama productions grew, so did the size and scope of the sets. David Gifford reflects, 'looking back, I am amazed how we built some quite ambitious sets for productions in St Philip's Hall: *Le Malade Imaginaire*, *The Sea*, *Endgame*, *The Magic Flute* and *Noye's Fludde* spring to mind, but there were many others. Several boys became heavily involved in stage lighting, most notably Paul Josefowski, who went on to become Head of Lighting at the National Theatre, Olivier Theatre.' In addition to the design and construction of sets teachers in the art department, and in particular Miss Crompton, also took the lead in designing and making some splendid costumes for the plays which were being staged at this time.

Conditions in the art department were cramped, yet remarkable work was being achieved. A level, O level and CSE art classes became popular, and O level photography was offered as a new subject in the curriculum. There was a large electric kiln in the old art rooms, and an after-school pottery club was introduced, as well as a painting club. In 1985, with funding from the Greater London Arts Association and assistance from Riverside Studios, the school managed to create a studio space within Mr Gifford's art room, to accommodate an artist-in-residence. The first was a painter, Glenys Barton, whose large-scale works opened the pupils to new possibilities in their own pieces.

In the early 1980s the school took part in the South Bank Festival; this involved the art staff and 12 pupils taking charge of a site in Jubilee Gardens on the South Bank and creating their own jubilee garden on what was at the time a pretty bleak site. The Oratory design, incorporating life-size papier-mâché costumes, earned much praise and the venture was repeated the following year. That year also saw over 400 Oratory

9 / *The Creative Arts*

Pupils work though a variety of media in art and design technology.

pupils supplying the entire collection of works in the Fulham Secondary Schools' Biennial Art Exhibition.

In 1980 the Annual Art Exhibition of work by staff, parents, former pupils and friends of the school was established, and for two weeks the Reception area in the school was taken over by more than 100 exhibits comprising oil paintings, water colours, etchings and screen prints, drawings, photographs, ceramics, costumes and jewellery. The exhibition opened with a private view and even the sixth formers were allowed a glass of wine as exhibitors and viewers discussed the works. This was the forerunner to the Annual Art Exhibition which now continues in the Paolozzi Gallery in the John McIntosh Arts Centre. One exciting element of this annual exhibition is that it gives pupils, staff, parents and friends a chance to view works by teachers, and not just those of the art department. Mr Stobbs, Head of Modern Languages, Mr Flanagan, Assistant Headmaster, and Mr Ashenden of the English and drama department have all exhibited excellent photographs. Miss McRoberts, Development Officer, has shown stunning marble sculptures. Year on year the teachers of the art department can be relied upon for some magnificent work.

One of the strengths of the department is the range of art specialisations within the teaching staff, a characteristic of the department for many years. These include David Gifford, whose ceramic work draws acclaim in the annual exhibition; Mary Crompton, a painter of delicate and evocative watercolours; Sonia Watson, another ceramicist with a very distinctive and much admired style. Dan Deegan is an impressive and atmospheric painter. Alessandro Rigano is also a painter, caricaturist and much more, and no pupil who spent any time in the art department of The London Oratory School 1982–2001 will forget Ray Little, a ceramicist and a great teacher, as well as a charming gentleman. Until his retirement Mr Little nurtured the artistic talent in the school at every level, being equally at home with a Junior House boy forming his first tentative shapes in clay as with the sixth former completing an A level project. One of his former pupils is Dan Deegan, current Head of Art, who recalls his old art teacher. 'It is fair

The London Oratory School – *Part III: An Oratory Education*

to say that most of Ray's former pupils will remember him fondly for his kindness, dapper attire and the fantastic stories he would regularly tell, referring to us as "Captain". Always encouraging, his lessons were certainly a large factor in my pursuit of a career in teaching art and design.'

With the building of the Arts Centre in 1991 the art department entered a new period of opportunity. Not only did teachers have specialist rooms and exhibition space but there was now a dedicated pottery room and a kiln. The department also boasts a mid-19th-century block printing press that has enabled pupils to produce some truly outstanding wood and lino prints.

As Director of the Arts Centre, Mr Gifford was also responsible for managing the varied programme of events taking place in this new and exciting venue. No longer would sets need to be constructed and painted at the side of the classrooms, as the new theatre had a purpose-built scenery dock and a fantastic stage area on which to bring the creative vision of Mr Gifford to life with the help of the teachers and pupils of the art department.

As it is interesting to look back at the early writings of those whose work makes it to print in later life, or at the first performances of those who later make a career on the stage, it is a source of pleasure to look back over the early stages in the development of an artist's life. As Dan Deegan puts it, 'it is at A level where the pupils really mature as young artists, and it is always a joy to work with such budding talent. Many go on to study art and design at university after completing a foundation diploma, and it is always a pleasure to receive an invite to a former pupil's exhibition of work at the end of their foundation degree or even beyond.'

The London Oratory School has helped to nurture some very talented artists. Tom Flint (1988–91), who painted the magnificent set for *Pygmalion* (1991) whilst at school, went on to study MA printmaking at the Slade, and has become an established painter and printmaker, with exhibitions in West End galleries. His etchings of scenes of London hang in the school. Isobel Peachey (1995–7) is a successful portrait painter. In 2009 Isobel won the BP Portrait Award's travel category and her work was exhibited in the National Portrait Gallery. In 2010, she was commissioned by the Cunard shipping company to paint a portrait of Her Majesty, The Queen, which now hangs in the new cruise liner, *Queen Elizabeth*. Jessica Linares (2005–7) graduated from the University of the Arts and is now an illustrator and model maker. She worked as a model maker on the feature

Above: Former pupil Isobel Peachey meets The Queen. Isobel painted the portrait of The Queen for the Cunard liner *Queen Elizabeth*.

Far left: The set for *Pygmalion*, designed by Tom Flint when he was a sixth former at the school; he is now an established painter and printmaker.

Sixth formers continue to excel in art; exploring a variety of media in their work.

film *A Liar's Autobiography*, starring John Cleese, Michael Palin and the rest of the Monty Python team. The film was screened as part of BFI's London Film Festival at the Empire cinema in Leicester Square in 2012, before its general UK release in January 2013. The year 2006 was a bumper one for artistic talent, with 16 pupils going on to study art at foundation level and a further two to read architecture, the most art students in a single year to date, but every year yields a steady number.

Reflecting on art in the school today Dan Deegan comments that

the department is as strong as ever and with a recent lick of paint over the salmon pink walls, unchanged since the time of the Art Centre's construction some 20 years ago, the rooms are in great condition and equipped with all the mod cons you would expect from a classroom in 2013. Now, as a teacher and Head of the Art Department, I am lucky enough to occasionally meet with the teachers who inspired me as a pupil. All are very much still involved in the arts and creating their own work and they continue to be an inspiration to me through their boundless passion for the subject. I can only hope that my work at the school does the same for my pupils.

As the school looks forward after 150 years, the work and talent in evidence in the art department suggests there is little reason to doubt this will be so.

MUSIC

No account of The London Oratory School would be complete without a section on music. The early Oratorians of the 16th century established an association with music which continues in the liturgical tradition of the Oratory Church. All the boys and girls of the school enter that tradition and all are at some level affected by music while at the school.

Over a third of the pupils in the school learn a musical instrument and the range of orchestras, ensembles and choirs is impressive. Concerts are anticipated as an opportunity to show off talent and to provide a genuine musical experience for a wide audience, and not only to entertain proud parents and friends.

The role of music within and beyond the curriculum has not always been appreciated in education circles, but from the early beginnings of The London Oratory School attention has been given to music. At first this seems to have been almost entirely centred on singing. The boys learned a selection of what seem to be Victorian parlour songs, not only for communal singing in school, but we imagine in these days before widespread technology, to equip the young boys to play their part in family evenings around the piano performing their 'party pieces'.

In 1883 when Mr Campbell, the Inspector, visited the school he was welcomed with a performance of songs which included: 'Proudly as the Eagle', 'The Rovers Song', 'In the Forest Glades' and 'Hark 'tis the Indian Drum'. In 1903 the school log informs us that Standards IV and V were taught 'Gently Evening Bendeth', while Standards VI and VII were mastering 'The Sun is Sinking' and 'When the Wind Blows'. The worthy intent to present boys with what now seems like a quaint repertoire is an interesting insight into the aims of the school as borne out in the Inspector's report of 1911, where it was noted that the school was 'fulfilling its specific purpose of providing a more than liberal education.' Although just three years later the Inspector found the curriculum to be a little too weighted to 'commercial utility' and encouraged a 'more liberal treatment'.

By the 1920s folk dancing was part of musical life at the school and by the 1930s teams of Sword Dancers and Country Dancers were competing with creditable success each year in the Chelsea and Westminster Musical Festival. Folk dancing, with its historic origins and quintessential Englishness, was highly regarded by the managers of the school and by the Oratory Fathers, in particular by Father Ralph Kerr, who was for many years the Manager of the Central School and himself a folk dance enthusiast. That his encouragement and support for the pursuit was acknowledged and appreciated was shown after his death in 1932, with representatives from the school's Country Dancing and Sword Dancing Clubs attending the funeral.

Pupils in the Central Schools, the boys' school and the girls' school, were taught their folk dances by staff member Miss Vera Blake, as well as receiving weekly lessons from Miss Lett of the English Folk Dance Society. Mrs Pink provided piano accompaniment. In 1922 honour was bestowed on the boys and girls with an invite to take part in the Folk Dance Festival at the King's Theatre Hammersmith. The performance of the children from the Oratory schools was full 'of vim and jolliness' as they performed such old English delights as the Singing Games, 'Roman Soldiers' and 'Oats and Beans', the Morris Jig, 'Bacca Pipes' and the most critically acclaimed of their presentations, the energetic Sword Dance 'Flamborough'. The Oratory children 'won the hearts' of the organisers and the 'good opinion' of the spectators. They made a similar impression on parents and friends at public performances in St Philip's Hall in 1926, at which display the Boys' Orchestra under the direction of Mr Toomey accompanied the dances in a very 'spirited way'. Writing in *The Oratory Parish Magazine* one reviewer ventured to hope he 'was not being heretical if we say how much we enjoyed the strong element of mixed dancing in

The Folk Dancing group 1922, and a School Open Day programme from 1930 showing the dancing and music on offer.

the programme'. This coalition of the pupils of the boys' and girls' schools was seemingly a little daring for the time! Folk dancing and the annual display would remain an item in the performance diary of the school into the 1930s. The reputation of Oratory dancers went beyond the school and five of the boys, J Condon, R Howard, S Vince, J Rocks and P Cottrell, along with Mr Kelly, gave splendid help to the English Folk Dance and Song Society in the 1936 production of Vaughan Williams' ballet version of *A Christmas Carol*.

The orchestra that played so spiritedly alongside the folk dancers was made up of musicians from the school who once a year at the annual Prize Day took centre stage to perform a programme of pieces to the assembled pupils, staff, parents and dignitaries who gathered to hear the Headmaster's report of the school year. For many years Mr Sidney Carr was responsible for the instrumental and choral performances. The choir at this stage seems to have been made up of unbroken voices, drawn from the first two years in the school. In 1933 some older boys decided to launch a male voice choir; initial membership comprised Elkins of Form VIA with five other senior boys and three masters. The choir flourished for a time and on a number of occasions joined forces with the school choir to expand the choral repertoire open to the singers in the school.

An al fresco performance by pupils in 'The Headmaster's Garden'.

Although provision for instrumental tuition was very limited at this time the fact that the school could accompany the folk dancers does suggest there were some boys in the school who were learning musical instruments. For most of them this was arranged outside of school, but for violinists there was the opportunity to learn the instrument at school. Mr Toomey, who directed the orchestra, offered violin lessons for an hour after school every Thursday at sixpence a lesson. For boys keen to pursue this seriously there was the opportunity for parents to purchase a violin and to pay in instalments. The scheme was promoted by Headmaster Dr Summerbell, advising parents that 'the ability to play the violin is a first class social accomplishment' (Orat. vol. 2, no. 33). Each year the young violinists were examined by the National Union of School Orchestras, and those of a suitable standard were selected to appear in the annual Crystal Palace Concert arranged by the Union. The success of ten boys in earning this distinction in July 1935 was a source of pride to Dr Summerbell, who gave the announcement top billing in *The Oratorian* newsletter.

When the following year Dr Summerbell wrote to parents to inform them that after 16 years the school was no longer able to offer violin lessons, the outrage he felt is apparent in the explanation he gave for the decision: 'apathy, disinclination to practise seriously and other curses have killed the classes. Apathy seems to be one of the curses of our modern civilisation, and like a rank weed it chokes the things really worth having and living for. Our forefathers would not have called it apathy but lack of backbone and in doing so they would have been nearer the truth of the matter' (Orat. vol. 2, no. 42).

Although this was a blow to the orchestra and to instrumental music the singing continued as a regular activity at school. Even during the war years when the Oratory boys were evacuated the value of communal singing was appreciated. In 1940 the London County Council provided a piano for the evacuated school in South Wales 'so that singing practice can be kept up' (PM, xx, 1940, p20).

Through the 1940s and 1950s music continued to play a part in school life, but it was somewhat limited in terms of the experience on offer and the numbers involved. With music as with drama, this was not the most dynamic era in the school's history, although these arts were not absent altogether. There continued to be a worthy school choir and gifted singers were nurtured by Mr Myerscough and Mr Handyside of the music department. Brian Cheesman (1944–50) was encouraged by these teachers, who came to

The London Oratory School – Part III: An Oratory Education

hear him sing in his parish church and helped get Brian into the Oratory Choir. The young singer 'was reluctant at first – having to travel twice weekly for services and practices', but 'when I discovered I would be paid three pounds a month, I was overjoyed as this knocked my sixpence a week pocket money into insignificance'. In his final years at the school Brian founded a Music Appreciation Society and with 'an old gramophone, an ancient collection of school records and the encouragement of Mr Handyside' he introduced fellow pupils to a classical repertoire.

While singing was never neglected at the school, instrumental tuition was still somewhat lacking. The Recorder Group could always be relied on for the annual Speech Day concert and the violins had made a comeback by the 1960s. The audience at Speech Day in 1962 was treated to an arrangement for violin of Jeremiah Clarke's 'Trumpet Voluntary' and by the following year lessons in flute and clarinet were proving popular, with tentative moves towards the formation of a school orchestra. In this same year Dolores Parsons became the first pupil at The London Oratory School to be awarded an O level in music. She later studied at music college. Was it with girls like Dolores in mind that Mr Gaffney three years later spoke of the threat to music and drama in the school as the girls were being phased out? He advised that 'the boys must take an increasing interest in these activities if the reputation of the school is to be maintained and enhanced' (Orat. 1965).

The move to Seagrave Road would be an opportunity to expand the provision and encouragement of the arts in the school. The first House Music Festival took place in 1975 and through the 1970s choral and instrumental music was continuing to grow. Much of this was under the direction of Mr Ferguson, who had first joined the school in 1957. He went on to hold the position of Head of Music and then Director of Music from 1980, in which year the School Choir was once again established. His unexpected death in January 1982 was a sad blow to many. He had worked alongside Mr Wilson of the English department on a number of productions; these two gifted members of staff had the confidence to stage operas such as *All the King's Men* in 1976 and *Down in the Valley* in 1977.

Working alongside Mr Ferguson was Kevin Breen, who had been teaching at the school since 1977 and who was himself a former pupil (1964–72) – he had in fact been taught music by Malcolm Ferguson. Completing the music staff was Mr David Bevan, who ran the St Philip's Choir for soprano voices. Regular concerts became part of the school calendar and the number of boys learning musical instruments was growing. Ensembles also began to emerge. The Wind Band performed a number of pieces in the 1980 summer concert and in 1981 the String Orchestra made its debut. These were the forerunners of today's Concert Band and Junior Strings.

The sudden death of Malcolm Ferguson in January 1982 following a heart attack was a great shock to all who knew him, and it was testimony to the esteem in which he was held that the whole school attended his Requiem Mass at the Oratory Church in February 1982. Just a few days before this a concert had taken place at the school; it was a concert that had been planned and rehearsed by Mr Ferguson. His colleagues and pupils had decided to go ahead with the performance in his honour and memory.

At the relatively young age of 28 Kevin Breen was now appointed as Director of Music. In 1980 he had written an article in the school magazine recording the principal events of the Choir's year, in the opening line of which he had commented that 'the wind of change has blown through the music departments in schools. No longer are school choirs expected simply to provide a folk song or a madrigal at their Speech Days but they are now achieving great success on the London music scene.' Mr Breen would take The London Oratory School Choir to new heights.

As well as giving many concerts of sacred and secular music in school and singing regularly at the Oratory Church, such as at the impressive concert to mark the

Left: Mr Breen with Choir trebles, 1984.

Above: The Schola in Rome 2013.

Above right: The Chamber Choir on tour in Krakow.

Above: The Post Tour Concert each September allows parents, teachers and friends to hear the music performed by the choir on the summer tour.

100th anniversary of the Church in 1984, the Choir was performing on the public stage with concerts at venues such as the Royal Festival Hall. The Choir also provided boy singers for the English National Opera and for the Royal Opera House, Covent Garden. In 1985 two pupils, Massimo Mezzofanti and David Harte, even travelled to Los Angeles to perform on tour with the Royal Opera House. Other globetrotting singers would follow their example. In 1990 first former Rory O'Connor secured a six-week contract in Germany, while fellow pupil Stephen Falero went to Russia to sing in Verdi's *Macbeth* with the ENO.

The 1980s also saw the first of what continues to be a regular aspect of life in a choir at The London Oratory School, the Choir Tour. The first major tour was in 1982 when the Choir went to Rome, where they sang in many churches including St Peter's, St John Lateran and the church of the Roman Oratory, the Chiesa Nuova. The Choir also had a recording of their music broadcast on Vatican Radio, something the Schola have done on more than one occasion in more recent years. Tours to Switzerland in 1985 and to the US in 1991 followed. Looking back over the years it seems almost all the countries of Europe have seen an Oratory choir. In recent years the Chamber Choir and Schola Tours have included Spain, Portugal, Germany, the Czech Republic, France, Ireland, Scotland and Italy, and both Choirs have toured in the US.

With Mr Breen at the helm in the music department and David Gifford leading the art department, a talented collaboration produced some impressive musical and operatic performances. One of these, *The Beggar's Opera*, was performed on the St Philip's Hall stage in 1985. It was an accomplished performance but has gone down in school history for the more dramatic finale when, as the cast came out to take their final bow, the stage curtains caught fire. There was no time for a curtain call, as the curtains themselves began to go up in flames – the audience gasped, the alarm sounded and in very quick time the hall was evacuated!

In 1988 *The Oratorian* magazine carried a report on the School Orchestra. The different ensembles, soloists and bands that had for a number of years made up the orchestral elements of the school were now sufficient in standard and number to form an orchestra. The Concert

The London Oratory School – Part III: An Oratory Education

in which they performed in the school's 125th anniversary year was described in *The Oratorian* 1989 as 'the best ever'. The accolade may have been well deserved at the time but the following 25 years were to provide many more evenings for justified superlatives.

When in 1988 Kevin Breen took a year's sabbatical to pursue engagements in America it was left to Paul Flanagan to run the music department and he did not fail to ensure that it was a significant year for many Oratory musicians. In June 1989, 180 pupils auditioned for the large-scale production of *Carmen* being staged that summer at Earls Court – and all 180 were selected to form groups of 'urchins' who would perform on a rota over the week of performances. The production did not attract great critical acclaim but it was a successful enterprise and certainly a memorable time for the young singers, as was an appearance on *Blue Peter*, in a feature about the boys' operatic experience. For 50 of the singers something even more memorable was in store as they were selected to tour with the production to Tokyo. With José Carreras as Don José and Maria Ewing as Carmen this was an opportunity to appear alongside some famous names, and the boys managed to secure some autographs and photographs as souvenirs. There was another performance of *Tosca* at Earls Court in 1991 and on this occasion Rory O'Connor of second form had the honour of singing the solo part of the shepherd boy, something he was able to discuss with opera enthusiast Norma Major when she visited the school with her husband, the Prime Minister, to inaugurate the Arts Centre on 3 July that same year. Robert Jones, now a member of the staff at the Oratory, where he holds the position of Procurator, remembers the day of the Prime Minister's visit very well.

By 1992 as the number of pupils involved in singing continued to grow the School Choir and St Philip's Choir had developed into three choirs: the Schola, the best singers, who formed the choir at School Masses; Coro, a large-scale choir which tackled big choral compositions; and the First Form Choir.

Once the new Arts Centre was finished and the first round of performances was underway from the summer of 1993, it was evident that music and drama would be raised to even greater heights in these new surroundings. The new Allen organ in the theatre was given 'a glorious start in life' by the famous organ impresario Carlo Curley, who in an evening of 'unforgettable panache' entertained

> " *The orchestra were to play as Mr and Mrs Major entered the Hall and then the choir were to sing. We were given the nod and Paul Flanagan brought in the orchestra. They played their way through the entire piece of music, finishing with a flourish. Mr Flanagan turned around and the Majors hadn't yet arrived. What a rehearsal. Shortly after we were given another nod and this time the distinguished guests did arrive, the orchestra played and the choir sang. Being on the front row I had the privilege of meeting the Prime Minister. As he shook my hand he asked me how often we rehearsed. I could have said, 'several times a week, with early morning sectional rehearsals and then gathering again after school for lengthy full rehearsals, of course with additional practice necessary at busy times'. Instead, I replied 'Quite a lot', and Mr Major moved on.*
>
> *I was one of a group of boys who were performing at the Royal Opera House in Verdi's Attila. It just so happened that 3 July was one of those performances. We appeared on stage twice in each performance, once as refugees coming over a hill exhausted having travelled far, and later in the performance as acolytes in a Bishop's procession. As we collected bales of blankets from the props men and entered the stage of the Royal Opera House, the member of the opera chorus appointed to keep an eye on me muttered to me, 'So, what did you do today?' I imagine he expected me to say 'French, science, geography…' Instead, I replied 'oh, I met and sang for the Prime Minister, what did you do?'*
>
> Robert Jones, 1989–96

9 / *The Creative Arts*

THE LONDON ORATORY

Above: Cartoonist Matt marked the beginnings of the Schola in 1996.

Right: Ensembles perform in lunchtime concerts, as shown here on the cover of the 1995 school magazine.

an appreciative and enthusiastic audience in October 1993. The first opera to be staged in the theatre was *Orpheus in the Underworld* in the summer term 1994, with David Gifford and Kevin Breen as Directors. This was the 14th collaboration between these two and the result was an incredibly professional staging of Offenbach's comic operetta. This was to be Mr Breen's last major Oratory school production as he took up a new post after that summer. The tradition of an opera or musical performance each year has been sustained every year on the Arts Centre stage, with a mix of serious repertoire such as Purcell's *Dido and Aeneas*, light operetta including many a Gilbert and Sullivan – for example *Iolanthe* in 1990 in which Mr Paul Johnston, Head of History (1980–2001), made his Oratory stage debut – and popular musicals such as *South Pacific*. Mr Johnston is not the only teacher to take an acting and singing role alongside the pupils; the performances of Miss Dawson as Miss Baggott and Mr Niblett as Blackbob in the 1999 Junior House musical *The Little Sweep* were most impressive.

The Little Sweep was only the third musical in the history of Junior House, the House having come into being in 1996. The quality of the music in the school, the keenness of the boys to learn and perform, the link with the Oratory Church and the liturgical tradition with which the school was thereby strongly associated had all contributed to the culmination of an idea in the mind of Headmaster John McIntosh. To offer a specialist musical education to boys from the age of seven along the lines of the cathedral choir schools, but to do so within a day school and within the state sector was something of an innovative idea and a new direction for the school. This was the idea, however, and it was to become a reality. With the blessing of Cardinal Basil Hume, Archbishop of Westminster, the Junior House was opened in 1996.

With the Junior House there came a new force in Oratory music, and this was not only the arrival of Mr Lee Ward as Director of Music; this was the year the Schola was born under the direction of Michael McCarthy, then under Steven Grahl (2004–6). After this Lee Ward combined the positions of Director of Music and of the Schola until 2012. David Terry then assumed the Director of Music post and Charles Cole became Director of the Schola.

Since its foundation the Schola has sung, performed, recorded and travelled, raised spirits, enthused audiences and earned plaudits. For boys who have sung with the Choir there have been amazing opportunities and moments to remember, and constant in all of this is the regular and sustaining liturgy of the Saturday Masses and morning service in the school Chapel. Many of the boys from Schola continue to sing after leaving school and the numbers ready and able to perform in the Farewell Concert when Lee Ward left the school in 2012 shows voices are still strong.

THE ORATORIAN 1995

101

The London Oratory School – Part III: An Oratory Education

Looking back over the years of Schola highlights there is much to recall: the concert in June 2001 with Viktoria Mullova, renowned violinist and mother of Schola chorister Misha; the 2006 Tenth Anniversary Concert in St John's Smith Square; in the same year the spectacular performance of Monteverdi's *Vespers of 1610* in the Oratory Church in the presence of Schola patron HRH Princess Michael of Kent, marking the retirement of Mr McIntosh; representing the Vatican in Rome at Al Gore's Live Earth venture in 2008; singing in concert with the Priests; the 2012 Farewell Concert for Lee Ward in the Cadogan Hall. There have also been the exciting recording sessions, from high-profile ventures such as performing the music for *The Lord of the Rings* films to making their own CDs of religious music, most recently a recording of Christmas music, *The Road to Bethlehem*. Oratory boys are not new to recording. The first time an Oratory Choir made a recording, of which rare copies survive, was the 1980 LP *Beatus Vir*, sacred music directed by Kevin Breen.

The Schola is one of a number of choirs in the school today. The Chamber Choir, for many years directed by Mr Ward but since 2007 under David Terry, has flourished alongside the Schola, and with a large membership covers a wide repertoire which can be expanded by joining forces with the even bigger School Choir. In 2004 the Chamber Choir made their Proms debut in a performance of Humperdinck's *Hansel and Gretel* with the BBC Concert Orchestra, an impressive achievement by the boys, who only found out a matter of days before the performance that they were to sing it all from memory.

The girls of the sixth form have always been part of the School Choir, and today sing in the Chamber Choir. When the school was a mixed school at the Stewart's Grove site there had been a separate choir for the girls. Once

Above: The Farewell Concert in Cadogan Hall for Director of Music, Lee Ward, 2012.

Left: Schola pupils with The Priests.

Below: The London Oratory School Choir recording, 1980, with the Chapel stained glass depicted on the cover.

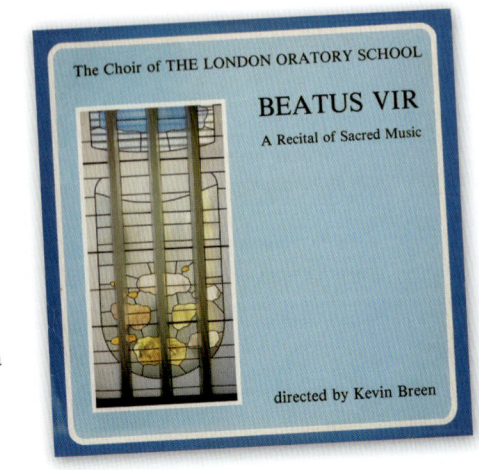

9 / *The Creative Arts*

settled at Seagrave Road and with girls in the sixth form there had been requests from some of the girls for their own choir, but until 1996 the ears of the music department were deaf to this particular call. From that date the Girls Choir has provided a distinct addition to the musical groups in the school and now and again the Girls Choir manages to oust the boys from Chapel, choir loft or stage.

As well as the traditional classical repertoire of most of the choirs, orchestras and ensembles in the school other genres have their niche. When Simon Ashenden joined the English department at the school in 1988 few of his colleagues realised that he would be hugely responsible for a new chapter in the musical life of the school. Mr Ashenden would before long reveal himself to be a jazz aficionado, and his successful jazz band The Seagrave Stompers is now established as one of the prime musical groups in the school. They were not always so named, beginning life as the Oratory Orpheans in 1989, but following a renaissance in 2003 the group re-emerged as the Seagrave Stompers and a new era had begun. In line with the change of name for the group, sixth former 'Georgetown Steptoe' (aka George Steptoe, 1996–2005) attached the title of Mr *Jazztastic* Ashenden to their revered leader.

When not on stage Mr Ashenden is teaching English. He is one of a significant number of teachers, not necessarily of the music department, who bring their musical skill to the school. Mr Stobbs, Head of Modern Foreign Languages, has played clarinet in the Orchestra and Concert Band. Miss Devaney, Head of History, plays violin with the orchestra and directs the Junior Strings, making a successful and widely anticipated conducting debut in December 2011. Mr Flanagan of the RE department (formerly of the music department) plays clarinet, and from the music department itself Mark Ward has brought a new dimension as a saxophonist. For conducting skill the School Orchestra has benefited in recent years from two principal conductors: the talented former pupil and teacher Aidan Coburn, and Miss Dawson, who draws great expression from the young players with her conducting prowess, and

Right: The Seagrave Stompers.

103

has even made an appearance on BBC television with the School Orchestra, albeit in James May's Christmas special, *My Sister's Toys,* rather than in something more highbrow on BBC4.

Over the past decades there have been many pupils from the school who have gone on to study music at university or college. One of those pupils is Nathan Mercieca, who left the school in 2009 after 11 years. At that time he looked back and commented 'as a seven year old I would have laughed if you had told me I would be singing for the rest of my life. After 11 years, thanks to three choral directors, approximately 336 sung Masses, 1,560 assemblies, and long over 2,000 hours of rehearsal I think I probably shall.' And after three years at Oxford University and one year postgraduate study he still is.

Three brothers who made an outstanding contribution to London Oratory music between 1996 and 2009 are the Melvin trio, Joseph, William and Leo. There must be a strong musical gene in this family; all three played in the National Youth Orchestra and all three continue to study and play at a very high level. Having studied at the Royal Academy of Music, Joseph enjoys a busy career as a professional double bassist. He plays regularly with all the top London orchestras, such as the London Symphony Orchestra and the Philharmonia Orchestra. William also studied at the Royal Academy of Music and is now following a career as a professional violinist, focusing particularly on chamber music. He is first violin with the Bernardel Quartet and leads the Arnold Camerata. Cellist Leo was a student at the Guildhall School of music and drama before commencing postgraduate study abroad.

Misha Mullov-Abbado, who won a music scholarship to Cambridge University in 2009, is not only a gifted horn player but also an accomplished composer. He wrote the music for a number of school productions and continues to write original music; his clarinet concerto received its world premiere with the Cambridge Symphonic Players in May 2012. With a strong interest in jazz music it looks like Misha will develop this in future compositions.

Then there are those who take a degree in another subject, continuing with music at an amateur level until the lure of the music gets too strong. One of these is Maciek O'Shea (1991–8). After a degree in history at University College London he pursued a post graduate career in music and now sings with the Choir of the Chapel Royal, and can be spotted at the great occasions, such as royal weddings in Westminster Abbey.

Even after they leave the familiar surroundings of school Oratory singers can continue singing, as the Choral Society is open to past pupils, parents and friends of the school. With weekly rehearsals and termly concerts in churches around London this is yet another example of the extent and versatility of musical life at The London Oratory School.

This section opened by drawing attention to the long tradition of music associated with the Oratory and with The London Oratory School. School life has never been entirely devoid of music but it is in the past 25 years or so that a huge expansion in range and quality has taken place. Consider the following in this regard. In the past ten years 12 pupils have won music scholarships to Oxford or Cambridge, three of these as organ scholars, and many pupils continue music within their professional life or as enthusiastic amateurs. In 2012, 720 individual music lessons were given each week in school, in a wide range of instruments. The range of instruments, beyond what might be expected in a full orchestra, seen and heard on the Arts Centre

Above: *Les Miserables*, 2012.

Below: The Choral Society, made up of parents, friends, staff and former pupils, perform a concert each term.

9 / The Creative Arts

Above: Players from the Concert Band, 2012.

Above right: David Terry, Director of Music.

stage, is certainly extensive, and includes the harp, the marimba, the piano accordion, the sousaphone, the banjo and the bagpipes. Even an anvil, weighing over 120lbs, was transported from the design technology department to the arts centre stage to ensure the Anvil Chorus from Verdi's opera *Il Trovatore* was given an authentic performance. In a school where Mr Terry, Director of Music, Oxford scholar and Fellow of the Royal College of Organists, plays the organ for High Mass at the Oratory Church one day and is happy to play a bicycle bell on stage in a Junior House performance of the theme tune from *Postman Pat* the next, it is evident that participation in music is widely encouraged and the value of music appreciated at all levels.

Music and The London Oratory School are inextricably entwined and all seems set fair for the next chapter in the history of the school.

> *The inclusive aspect as well as the opportunity to challenge all to the highest musical standards and experiences meant that there were some astonishingly good performers from all backgrounds. It was always a delight when a pupil came 'out of the woodwork', perhaps one equally committed to sport. The loyalty and hard work of such pupils was a joy to see. Chorally, the daily services and Mass on Feast Days brought much to the boys, staff and community. They might not see it that way whilst a pupil, but so many former pupils have told me over the years how much the music on these occasions meant to them and what a long lasting effect it has had upon them. Additionally, those who have gone on to pursue music have been highly regarded by those already in the profession. I am sure the LOS musicians, and particularly choral and organ pupils, will continue to make a significant contribution to the musical life of our cathedrals and churches.*
>
> Lee Ward, Director of Music 1996–2012

DRAMA

The London Oratory School has produced a number of distinguished actors of stage and screen over the course of its history.

One renowned actor who is reputed to have attended the school in its early days was Alan Mowbray, who was born in London in 1896. His real name was Ernest Allen, the name by which his teachers knew him. There is, unfortunately, no record of any acting prowess while he was at school, but from humble beginnings he was to go on to fame in Hollywood. After distinguished service in the First World War (his actions earned him the Military Medal and the Croix de Guerre) he began to work in theatre and from there moved to America, working at first as a stage actor and writer, but soon he was attracted to the burgeoning film industry. By now he had adopted the name by which he would be known to film goers, Alan Mowbray. He featured in over 100 films of the golden age of Hollywood; viewed as the archetypal Englishman he tended to get the roles where the casting directors were looking for excellent diction and 'a stiff upper lip'. He was Inspector Lestrade in *Sherlock Holmes* in 1932 and featured in two more Holmes films, *A Study in Scarlet*, 1933, and *Terror by Night* in 1946. He played Throckmorton in *Mary of Scotland*, 1936, and Sir William Hamilton in *That Hamilton Woman*, 1941. He moved into television in the 1950s, featuring in some mainstays of US prime time viewing, but he still took film roles. He played the part of Sir John Hay in the famous film version of *The King and I* in 1956.

Alan Mowbray is buried in Holy Cross Cemetery, Culver City in California. Remarkably in the same cemetery lies another Old Oratorian and star of the screen. Gene Lockhart, born in 1891, was a Canadian singer, actor and writer who starred in many films in the 1930s, 1940s and 1950s. His English wife, Kathleen, was also a film actress, as was his daughter, June Lockhart. They famously all appeared together in the film version of Dickens's *A Christmas Carol* in 1938. Gene Lockhart had lived for some of his childhood years in London, where he attended the Brompton Oratory School. In the late 1930s he was living in Beverly Hills directly across the street from Alan Mowbray. Alan Mowbray's son, also named Alan, recalls how the two actors discovered their link with the Oratory and they and their families became good friends; June Lockhart and Alan Mowbray's daughter Patricia attended school together. Gene Lockhart died in 1957 and was buried in the Holy Cross Cemetery, where 12 years later fellow Old Oratorian Alan Mowbray was also laid to rest.

Above: Members of the Junior Drama Club in the 2012 production of *Sherlock Holmes*.

Left: Actor Alan Mowbray attended the school in the early 20th century.

Below: Gene Lockhart, Old Oratorian (centre), with Bing Crosby and Barry Fitzgerald in *Going My Way*.

9 / The Creative Arts

Right: Two Oratorians in costume for a school play in the early years of the 20th century.

Below: *Tons of Money* was a popular play in the 1930s. The programme for this school production notes that the play was directed by Mr S A Carr and that 'ALL parts were played by BOYS between the ages of 12 and 16'.

While Old Oratorians were making their names in Hollywood budding actors were regularly performing in Stewart's Grove, and indeed in the earlier buildings, as records show plays were being performed from 1895. Each year the school put on a play around Christmas time and the parish magazine published effusive reviews. A particular favourite was the popular farce *Chiselling*, which was performed in 1922 and again in 1926. Maybe the explanation for the popularity of the piece lies in consideration of this extract from the 1926 review: 'D FitzGibbon in the exacting part of Trotter-Alexander, played as usual with energy and skill; the increasing horror in his voice as he listened to the fates in store for him – baked for forty-eight hours in a slow oven, thrust through with an iron rod etc – was very exhilarating' (PM, vi, p35). If they were not to have a farce it seems the Oratory audience enjoyed a bit of Victorian style theatre in a 'burlesque'. Such was the epithet given to *Aladdin, or the Wonderful Scamp* by Henry Byron, or another recurring favourite of these years, *Black-eyed Susan*, first performed by Oratory boys in 1895. Having fun on stage seemed to come naturally to Oratory schoolboys, but much credit is also given to the producer of these entertainments, Mr J Wybert Toms, ably assisted by Miss Jennings, who trained the dancers and helped the boys to win praise: in *Chiselling* 'J Fraser and J Church performed the pretty dance in the sculptor's dream very beautifully.' These annual productions formed part of a round of entertainments put on at Christmas time by the different schools associated with the Parish, and sometimes included a performance by the Oratory Cadet Corps. As well as playing to parents and parishioners it was also usual for the different schools to stage a performance for each other.

The performances by the Central School boys were attracting considerable renown and consequently productions were well anticipated and the demand for tickets could not be met. In 1935 the decision was taken to transfer the production to the London Academy of Music's Harrington Hall in order to accommodate the large sell-out audience. That year's production was *Charley's Aunt* by Brandon Thomas, and the 'sight of a young man pretending to be an old woman', with the added amusement of 'the fact that all the female parts were taken by boys', contributed to the enjoyment of the evening. Anyone who saw the 2012 London Oratory School Junior Drama production of *Sherlock Holmes* or the senior school production of *A Comedy of Errors* in 2011 will appreciate that little has changed in this regard.

The London Oratory School – *Part III: An Oratory Education*

On a more poignant note, one of the cast mentioned in the parish magazine review of *Charley's Aunt* was Wilfred Shirley, who played his part 'with old fashioned sweetness, somewhat dispelled when he began to "make eyes" in a prodigious and apparently detached fashion'. These were halcyon days for Wilfred and his schoolmates. When he left school in March 1939 Wilfred took up a position with Thomas Cook and Company in Berkeley Street, but shortly afterwards when war broke out he joined the RAF Volunteer Reserve serving as a bomber. Sergeant Shirley was killed on 5 May 1943, just 20 years old. Fellow actor Desmond Downer, who had played the part of Sprules in the 1934 performance of *Tons of Money* was another casualty of the war.

School plays ceased over the war years and it would be some time before performances would once again reach the heights of acclaim they had attracted before the war.

By the time Simon Callow attended the school in the 1960s drama was yet to recover its strength within and beyond the curriculum, and it seems there would be few opportunities for young Mr Callow to take to the school stage. That is not to say, however, that the talents which were in time to bring him to a position of prominence in cultural life were not in evidence in these formative years. Mr Callow's pen bears witness to his eloquence. In an essay of 1965 published in *The Oratorian* S Philip Callow of form VL speculates on *The World in 2050*, presented in the form of a debate between four men: 'Sir Andrew Lovatt, scientist and doctor; Peter M Marshall, celebrated historian; Lord Turnbull, philosopher; Samuel Profitt, shop-steward … seated in low Scandinavian chairs, drinking coffee.' There follows a very assured piece of writing. Simon Callow has not always looked back fondly on his schooldays, having described the school as he saw it in his time as 'utterly undistinguished', and apparently to him something of a cultural desert. He was, however, keen to pursue what opportunities there were, and along with fellow sixth formers, including Sheila O'Higgins, became a founder member of the Literary and Debating Society under the guidance of Mr Dent. This gave a platform for reading from plays and poems – no doubt an early sign of an inclination towards performing on a more public platform on stage.

Not all of Simon Callow's contemporaries share his view of the school of the 1960s. Many have fonder memories, and even Mr Callow acknowledges that there were individual teachers who 'threw open windows onto possibilities of life of which we had not been aware' (*Evening Standard*, 3 March 2011). That coming together of an inspiring and dedicated teacher with a young pupil hungry for knowledge and possessed of talent can account for the path taken by that pupil in later life.

It would be an individual teacher who would for many provide the spark that inspired them in school productions. David Wilson was first appointed to the English department in 1966; Simon Callow left the school in July 1967, so would not have had more than a brief acquaintance with Mr Wilson, and would not witness the revival in drama which the new master brought to the school. Despite the limitations of the old building and the scarcity of resources he staged a number of plays in the Stewart's Grove School, the last being Molière's *Le Bourgeois Gentilhomme* (*The Would-Be Gentleman*). Mr Wilson helped see the school hall in the new building established as the venue for many more productions, and although he left the school in 1971 he returned in 1974 as Head of English and Drama, a post he held until 1983.

In 1975 a House Drama Festival was announced to broaden participation, and to expand the scope of House competition. The winners in this inaugural year were More House, with their presentation of *Three Gentlemen of China,* directed by Mr Brunwin with the aid of Mr R Murphy. Thomas Smyth was deemed to have given 'the best performance, probably of the whole evening' (Orat. 1976). *The Oratorian* 1976 shows that in addition to the House Competition there were three other plays performed that year, all indicating that the pupils of The London Oratory School were now enjoying and benefiting from a fresh emphasis on drama and theatre. The main school play of that year was J B Priestly's *An Inspector Calls,* reviewed for the school magazine by Jeremy Trafford, another

Left: Simon Callow attended the school (1961–7) and is now a Patron of The London Oratory School Schola.

Right: Former pupil Hayley Atwell in the acclaimed 1999 sixth-form production of *The Duchess of Malfi*.

memorable name in the history and progress of drama at The London Oratory School. As well as teaching English he directed many school productions and also took to the stage himself when in 1989 at short notice he stepped in to play the part of Marco in Arthur Miller's *A View from the Bridge*. This performance was reviewed by Mr Trafford's colleague Mrs Walton, who commented on 'the subtlety and intelligence' which Sofia Mozoro brought to the role of Beatrice, and on Scott Clancy's 'professional and sensitive' portrayal of Rodolpho, as well as the excellent performances of Grace Campos and Agostino Orsini. Regarding Mr Trafford's performance she observed that the age difference between himself and his young cast 'created a rather difficult visual hurdle', but he performed with 'commendable conviction'. She conceded that 'to expect the director to shave off his distinguished beard in the cause of art for a mere three nights would be asking too much' (Orat. 1990). This review was just one of many enjoyable critiques of school productions written by Maureen Walton, who first joined the English department in 1972. Her untimely death in 2005 was a great sadness to so many to whom she had been an inspirational teacher. As Father Paul Keane, one of her former pupils, put it most succinctly: 'she loved English literature and because of her we loved it'.

Another and very perceptive review by Mrs Walton appeared in the 1999 school magazine when the senior school production was *The Duchess of Malfi*, directed by Evan Artro-Morris and Roy Peachey, with a stylish set designed by David Gifford. The performance of the evening was that of the eponymous Duchess. 'She has a wonderful voice and an impressive sensitivity and maturity… She filled the stage with supreme confidence and her performance grew in stature as the play developed. Her death scene aroused all the pity, terror and admiration needed for the scene.' This talented young lady was Hayley Atwell. Hayley joined The London Oratory sixth form in 1998 and went on to study at the Guildhall School of Music and Drama.

> I absolutely loved my time at LOS: choir practice every lunchtime, performing with the choir and orchestra, playing Lady Jane in Gilbert and Sullivan's *Patience*, and playing the piano in accompaniment to the play in my final year. All of this performance experience gave me the skills and confidence to pursue a career in the theatre. As an actress, being able to sing is invaluable; in my ten years in the theatre, only two of my shows have not required this skill, one being *The Mousetrap*, in which I am currently performing as Mollie Ralston. Other recent shows include *Half a Sixpence*, in which I played Helen Walsingham alongside Gary Wilmot, and at the Unicorn Theatre in London I had to use my piano and vocal skills as Beatrix Potter in *Jemima Puddleduck and Her Friends*, which was challenging and delightful. The London Oratory School provides a structured and disciplined environment which enables pupils to constantly achieve and explore various types of performance, thereby instilling the confidence and determination which is required for a life in the arts.
>
> Zara Plessard (Tomkinson) 1991–3

The London Oratory School – Part III: An Oratory Education

> *During my time at the school I was a regular fixture at Drama Club. I must acknowledge the great deal of inspiration, insight and guidance I received from Evan Artro-Morris, Robert Tilbury and the much-loved Maureen Walton in my development as a young performer. Their commitment and passion carried me into new heights of enthusiasm. The Arts Centre blew me away when as an 11-year-old I first entered the theatre, purpose-built to professional standard; I knew this was where I wanted to be educated. My artistic education was formed on stage after school, every summer and every winter, much as in a professional company. Our abilities were honed on that stage, developing the practical experience of how to adapt and communicate with an audience which was formative in my decision to become a professional actor.*
>
> *Amongst my memories I remember we played A Midsummer Night's Dream in the Chapel courtyard; and there was the time we ran through the audience screaming in Lord of the Flies; and the pride when a young man approached me and recalled a play he'd seen me in when he was small. The memories are precious because of the crucial encouragement I received as a young boy in developing confidence and maturity as well as tentative interpretations of text and character in a public forum where I could pursue what fulfils me. This is why I am so grateful to have had the opportunity to learn at a fine institution with facilities and teachers that prepared us for professional life.*
>
> Matthew Houlihan, 1994–2001

Now she is a highly acclaimed actress of stage and screen with such film credits to her name as *The Duchess* (2008), *Brideshead Revisited* (2008) and *Captain America, The First Avenger* (2011).

Another successful actress who for two years, 1991–3, graced the sixth form at The London Oratory School is Zara Plessard, formerly Zara Tomkinson. Zara went on to study music at university and later moved into acting. In 2012 she took the part of Mollie Ralston in the longest-running West End play, *The Mousetrap*. Zara recalls the profound influence of her teachers, Mr Breen and Mr Flanagan, in nurturing her talent and how she was able to bring her musical gifts to the school stage, something she is still doing on the professional stage.

As Zara was leaving The London Oratory School a new actor in the making was starting on his Oratory career. This was Matthew Houlihan, who over seven years gave some outstanding and memorable performances on the school stage. Matthew now earns his living performing on the London stage.

Making his debut on the London stage alongside Matthew and his fellow cast members in the 1999 production of *Lord of the Flies* was Old Oratorian Mr Randall, at that time teacher of economics and rugby coach, and soon to be Fisher Housemaster. Playing a royal navy officer, his was judged to be 'an impressive debut'. There are, however, no reports of a second stage appearance.

Others whose acting talent were nurtured at The London Oratory School include Obi Ugoala. In 2006 he gave a memorable performance as Caliban in *The Tempest*, speaking his lines in 'mellifluous vocal tones' (J McKenna, Head of English, Orat. 2007) with a natural intelligence. Maybe Shakespeare is in the blood; older brother Chi had played Theseus in the excellent 2000 production of *A Midsummer Night's Dream*. For Obi, however, the Oratory stage was but the prelude to drama school and

Matthew Houlihan in *A Midsummer Night's Dream.*

Right: The sixth form 2012 production, Dry Rot.

the professional stage. His first West End role was at the Donmar Warehouse, and in 2012 he took up a position with the Royal Shakespeare Company in Stratford.

Old Oratorians do not just appear on the stage, though. There are many former pupils working in different branches of theatre, with lighting, design and choreography all represented. Jack (Sean) Murphy, who attended the school in the 1970s, works as a choreographer and movement director, with many film credits to his name. In 2009 when working on the film *Young Victoria* he found himself devising the ballroom scene with actors Emily Blunt and Rupert Friend in Fulham's Dance Attic Studios on North End Road. Jack remembers the building as the old Fulham swimming baths. He never imagined he would be waltzing with the stars where once he had swum with his Oratory pals. With Old Oratorians Patrick Walshe McBride (1999–2006) and James Mack (2003–10) both currently at drama school, who knows whether Jack Murphy might one day find himself directing a fellow Old Oratorian?

James and Patrick, like many of the stars of senior school drama performances, belonged in their early years at the school to the Lower School Drama Club, which was established in 1985 and continues to nurture acting talent from first and second form. Mr Ashenden, whose credits for senior school performances include the highly acclaimed productions of *The Tempest* in 2006 and *A Midsummer Night's Dream* in 2008, along with the very amusing *Dry Rot* of 2012, has also brought out some wonderful, sparkling performances from younger casts in delightful productions such as the 2009 version of the Marx Brothers' *Duck Soup*.

With such enthusiasm in the lower years the future of London Oratory drama looks secure. In the Junior House Maurice Cole has already made his mark in film and television. Maurice, who joined Junior House in 2010, may

> *From my first school play in J1 when I was a villager in Paradise Island through to playing the Princess in The Princess Bride to Caliban in The Tempest in the sixth form, the John McIntosh Arts Centre was always a special place for me. Be it Lee Ward directing an opera or musical, James Trapmore and Steven Sumner taking Lower School Drama every Wednesday or being directed by the legendary Simon Ashenden, the effort and extra dedication by each of the members of staff helped bring out the best in budding thespians throughout the years, in a theatre space which rivals many theatres in London for technical support and acoustic. After 12 years at the Oratory, one of which was spent assisting Mr Ashenden teaching on the AS drama course, and three years at Drama Centre London, I have in the past six months made my West End debut at the Donmar Warehouse and am currently in Stratford-upon-Avon performing with the Royal Shakespeare Company. I don't know where the journey ends, but I know that it started at the Oratory under the tutelage of drama teachers who went beyond the call of duty in facilities that matched up to their dedication.*
>
> Obioma Ugoala, 1997–2008

The London Oratory School – *Part III: An Oratory Education*

The cast of the senior school 2012 production of Molière's *The Hypochondriac*.

be familiar to fans of *Doctor Who*, as he appeared in the 2011 Christmas Special. His first feature film, *Foster*, was released in 2011.

For pupils with an interest in drama and the theatre but perhaps not necessarily with the talent or inclination to take to the stage themselves, the opportunity to revel in the theatre has long been encouraged through visits to performances on the London stage. In the 1930s the Dramatic Club organised visits to a number of Shakespearean dramas, including in 1933 an outing to Sadler's Wells Theatre to see Charles Laughton as Henry VIII, a role he played in the classic film of the same year.

Decades later the opportunity to see the great plays of Shakespeare performed by the outstanding actors of the day, though not always to positive critical acclaim, was not lost on the members of the Arts Society, which flourished in the 1980s. For Catherine Haughton (1979–82), Peter O'Toole as Macbeth in 1981 'spoilt the evil plot of possibly Shakespeare's best known play, turning tragedy to comedy by his inappropriate and exaggerated actions'. Catherine had a more enjoyable evening watching Timothy West in the title role in *The Merchant of Venice* alongside Maureen O'Brien as Portia, when they gave 'a romantic, comic but intensely realistic' performance. Ian McKellan as Coriolanus in 1985 was 'brilliant and compelling', whereas Anthony Hopkins as Lear in 1987 was 'too young and too vigorous' as judged by English teacher Mrs Walton, 'but always highly intelligent and frequently very moving'.

In 1982 the Shakespeare enthusiasts were satisfied with seeing Terry Hands' outstanding production of *Richard III* with Alan Howard playing the title role. That year's dramatic excursions included the added bonus of seeing a former pupil on stage in Molière's *The Hypochondriac*. Peter Lovstrom, who was playing the role of Punchinello, had attended the school from 1971 to 1978. In his final year he had taken the role of Argan in the very same play that the Oratorian Arts Society members were watching four years later. His career since his Oratory days has taken him from performances on stage to screen and includes those stalwarts of many an actor's CV, television roles in *The Bill* and *Casualty*. Another former pupil, Mairead Carty (1982–4), has also appeared in *The Bill*, and in other popular television dramas, as well as being an accomplished stage actress.

The Arts Society was briefly renamed the Theatre Society in 1985, but 'a copious store of unused posters' prompted a reversion to the original title in 1986. The most

112

9 / *The Creative Arts*

The 2011 production of The Comedy of Errors *featured real-life twins Daniel and Martin Freely as the Dromio twins.*

popular excursion that year was to see Martin Shaw in *Are you Lonesome Tonight,* despite facing competition from a new play by Stephen Poliakoff and from classics of English and Russian theatre at the National Theatre. The London Oratory sixth form is a broad church when it comes to the arts! Musicals, comedies, tragedies and avant-garde productions all featured in the Arts Society calendar each year. Of course not all members appreciated all genres. In 1984, when presented with the opportunity to see Noel Coward's *Hayfever* starring Penelope Keith, 'some of our more intellectually fastidious members refused to attend' (Orat. 1984).

Today London Oratory pupils continue to enjoy theatre visits. The opportunity and privilege of relatively easy access to the West End and South Bank is not lost on staff or pupils and with both established and up-and-coming talent there continues to be the possibility of seeing a former pupil on the stage there in front of them.

The Princess Bride was the lower school drama production in 2011, as it had been in 2002.

113

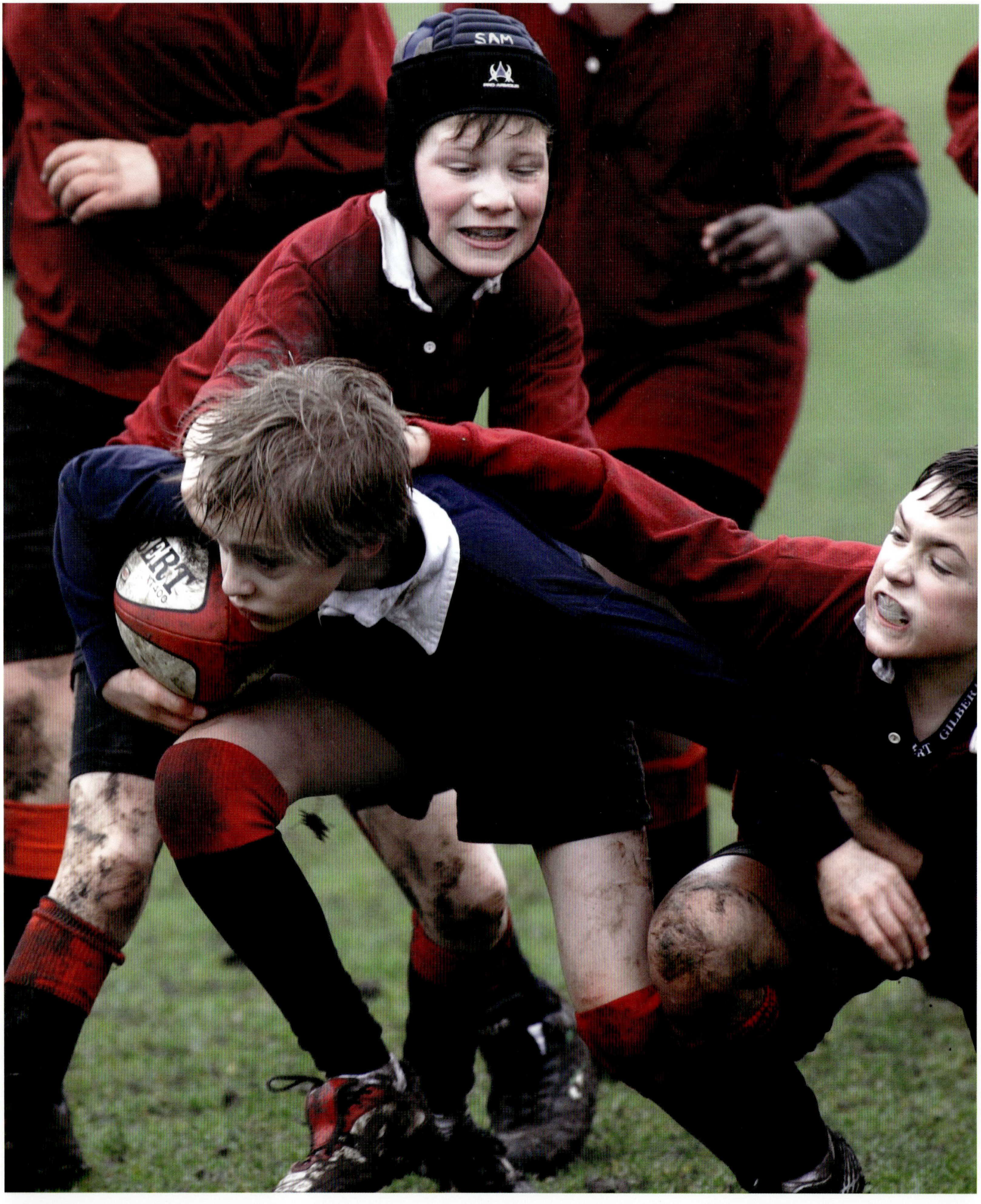
SAM

10

Sport

Opposite: Howard and Owen House competing in the House Rugby Competition.

Below: J C Burns, Old Oratorian, Brentford footballer and England international.

'Rugby, rugby, then some more rugby' is how Gerry Power (1973–80) summed up school sport in his day. This will ring true for many of his contemporaries and for anyone who attended the school from the 1960s onwards, but it might come as a surprise to know that it was not always so. For many years football was the main competitive sport of the school.

In the very early years it was a case of weekly drill with a drill sergeant to keep the boys fit. School records make no reference to participation in any particular sports or games, but once competitive games started, football was the main sport for the boys of the Oratory long before any one of them held a rugby ball. From the 19th century young Oratorians played football. At first it was the game of the playground. The school log book in 1891 records the purchase of footballs for play at recreation time. Once the Oratory Central School was established in the 1920s the school was eligible to take part in the Chelsea Schools' League and the Central Schools' League. The young players could look for inspiration to one of their teachers who was himself playing football at the highest level, representing his country.

James Charles Burns, born 1906, had been a pupil at the Oratory Middle School and trained as a teacher at St Mary's College, Twickenham, before taking a post at his old school. At this time he was playing left half for Queen's Park Rangers, who were struggling at the tail end of the third division. He signed for Brentford in 1930. J C Burns played 145 games as an amateur with the club while he continued to teach the boys of the Oratory. He was with Brentford at an exciting time in the club's history, as from 1926, with the appointment of Harry Curtis as manager, the team began to work their way through the divisions, eventually making it to the first division in 1935 to compete with the top clubs (this was of course long before the Premier League was in existence). On 23 November of that year Brentford lost to Chelsea 2–1 at Stamford Bridge before a crowd of over 56,000. At this time The London Oratory School was not on its present site, but it is an interesting thought for today's pupils as they look across to Stamford Bridge from school to think that an Oratory teacher played a top-class game there, and indeed on other famous pitches, as J C Burns not only made over 260 league appearance in his career but also represented his country. He won his first international cap playing for England against Wales. He was to win 16 England Amateur Caps in total and captained the team on nine occasions. He was also selected for the Corinthians and captained Middlesex Wanderers, a touring team with the aim of bringing football to a continental audience. Although Mr Burns was playing as an amateur the school records show that when matches fell on schooldays he was released from teaching duties on unpaid leave. This was standard practice at the time and does not diminish the respect and admiration for his achievement, with regular congratulations appearing in the school and parish magazines. When Ted O'Sullivan, who was at the school in 1930, looked back with mixed feelings on his Oratory schooldays, he had nothing but admiration for his old form teacher, recalling him as 'a kind and generous man, and an excellent teacher of mathematics… He was a popular hero throughout the school and we considered being in his class an honour' (Edmund O'Sullivan, *All My Brothers*, 2007, pp82–4).

J C Burns is not the only Old Oratorian to have played a football 'international'. Kevin John McLoughlin, from Clapham, was at the school from 1937 to 1943, and was evacuated to south Wales with the school during the Second World War. While in Tonypandy the Oratory boys began to play rugby rather than the football they were used to, but during Spitfire Week, when the children were asked to take part in activities to help raise the money to buy a Spitfire, young Kevin took part in a fundraiser football game. He was seen by scouts from Cardiff City Football Club and at the age of 14 was signed as their goalkeeper. Even after leaving school, when he was enrolled at St Mary's College to train as a teacher, he continued to turn out for Cardiff, staying with the team for seven seasons. In one memorable match he was in goal for Cardiff City when they welcomed Moscow Dynamo to Wales for an international game at Ninian Park. The Moscow Dynamo tour of 1945 is of historic interest, not just for the football. This was November 1945, the Second World War was over and Russia and her former allies in the west were no longer bound by a common cause against Germany; this was the coming of the Cold War. The football tour was conceived 'in the name of peace' to try to show good relations still existed between the USSR and Great Britain. The tour drew plenty of interest and the first game, against Chelsea, resulted in a 3–3 draw. The Russians then travelled to Wales, where a 40,000-strong crowd saw 'Dynamo shock Cardiff' as the Welsh team were outclassed, succumbing to a 10–1 defeat; and in goal for Cardiff, picking the ball out of the net, was Old Oratorian Kevin McLoughlin. Before the match the Welsh side had presented their guests with miniature mining lamps as a memento of their visit to the Valleys. David Downing in his book about the tour reports that one sharp reporter noted of the mining lamps, 'it would have been a fine idea if the Russians had worn them. Cardiff would have at least seen which way the Russians were going.' Downing goes on to give an account of the game and the goals, noting that the Russians' eighth goal was the result of a dropped corner from the Cardiff goalkeeper but adding 'this was unfortunate – despite the score the keeper had been one of Cardiff's best players' (D Downing, *Passovotchka*, 1999, p139). Although he continued to play football and cricket at a serious level Kevin McLoughlin was to follow the footsteps of former Oratorian J C Burns by training as a teacher at St Mary's College. He taught in a number of schools, including a period as Headmaster of Bishop Marshall School in Manchester, until his retirement in 1991. He died in 2010, a sportsman to the end.

For J C Burns and Kevin McLoughlin a football career had to be combined with a 'real job'. It was to be a while before an Oratory pupil or teacher could consider football alone as a means to a living. Alan Hawley, who was engaged by the school as a games coach in 1974, followed in the footsteps of J C Burns, playing for Brentford – although not in such successful times. In 1994 one young pupil, Wayne Andrews, decided to make a living in football, and to the great disappointment of the school rugby coaches he signed for Watford FC. John Quigley played Under 16 football for Ireland, winning his international shirt while in the fifth form in 2004.

Football continued as the principal Oratory sport on into the 1960s, and the school teams met with considerable success. In the 1930s the teams – of which there were five at one point – were often in good positions in the local leagues, and Oratory boys were selected to represent the West London Central Schools. The selections followed trials which took place on Eelbrook Common, a pitch familiar to many of today's Oratory boys. On 16 May 1936 Oratory player F Brown was selected to represent London in the match against Glasgow played at Hampden Park. The London boys won 2–0. This was the first time a Catholic Central School boy had been selected to play for London. The importance of football for the whole school was evident when in 1933 the Headmaster announced a whole-day holiday on St Patrick's Day in celebration of the year's examination successes, explaining that this would enable all the boys to go along to Battersea Park to support the school team in the hotly contested Lipton Cup Match. Such was the Headmaster's enthusiasm that he encouraged the boys to support their team 'with the old Maori war cry which goes like this:

K-O-RA, K-O-RA
COO-MA-GHEE, COO-MA-GHEE
AKEE-AKEE
OR-A-TO-RY'.

The image conjured up by the thought of the usually stern-looking Dr Summerbell leading the Oratory crowd along the touchline in the 'war cry' is an interesting one.

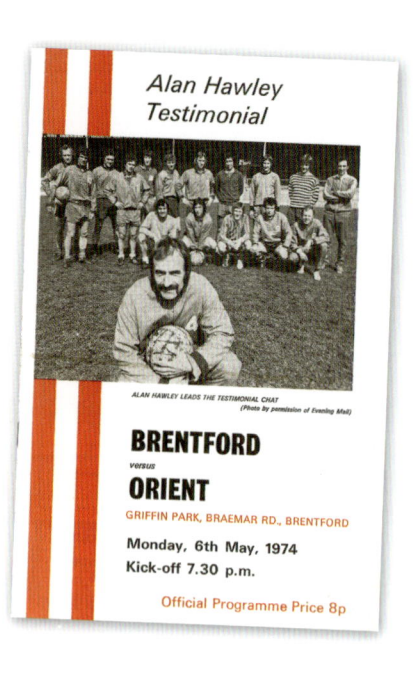

Alan Hawley was a games coach at the school in the 1970s.

John Quigley presenting his Ireland shirt to Mr Moran.

Right: The London Oratory Senior XI, 1963 from the days when football was the main sport at the school.

As with all school activities, musical, dramatic and sporting, the reports of the 1930s bring forward names which are now engraved on the school War Memorial. A J Fuge and R C Whiffen are two of those who were regularly commended in football reports and who played for their House in the inter-House football league, which gave many of the boys a chance to compete against each other on the football pitch. Today the boys get a once-a-year opportunity to do the same in the annual House Competition, but no longer do boys represent the school at football. Eamonn Malone (1966–73) was Head of School and First XI Captain in 1973, but he was also representing the school at rugby. For so long the mainstay of Oratory sporting life football was by this time making way for rugby; this was one of the changes as the school moved into the new era at Seagrave Road.

The arrival of Mr Gaffney as Headmaster was also very significant in moving the school towards the adoption of rugby as the main sport. Football lingered in a one-off entry into the West London Soccer Cup for a third-form team in 1979, and had a very brief renaissance in 1987 when a group of sixth-form pupils approached the PE department and asked if they might organise a sixth-form team. In the words of one of the delegation, Stephen Nolan, 'the reception was not enthusiastic and for a time it seemed the idea would have to be shelved. We were persistent, however, and to our great surprise and delight we found Mr Pearce, who was willing to help organise the team.' After discovering a long lost pile of 11 soccer tops in a gym cupboard the team was just about sorted and the fixture list was drawn up. A successful round of games followed against opposition which included Latymer Upper, Salesians and Westminster City. This was, however, to be the last gasp of Oratory football, and apart from the annual House competition no sign of a return is imminent.

So it is rugby on which the modern Oratorian is reared. There had been two brief encounters with the game in earlier years for the school. When the young boys of the Oratory School were evacuated to south Wales during the war they soon realised that in the Valleys they play rugby, so the London boys acquainted themselves with the rules of the game and soon proved very adept. By 1941 in matches against local Welsh schools the Oratory Junior XV had played ten games and won ten, with 117 points for the school and only 17 against. The Senior XV had won five out of six matches played, with a total of 56 points against 18.

The only other excursion into the world of rugby before the Gaffney era was an attempt by Dr Summerbell to introduce the game one year, but as Bernard Liengme (1949–52) summed it up simply, 'unfortunately this was not successful'. It would be down to the determined Scotsman and rugby enthusiast Mr Gaffney to get the game well established. He believed competitive rugby would bring the boys of the Oratory into the sphere of some of the smarter

The London Oratory School – *Part III: An Oratory Education*

Above: The early days of Oratory rugby at Barn Elms, 1963.

Right: Paul Stapleton, the school's first rugby international and his 1978 England shirt.

schools. He had the support of some keen staff, such as Tom Hartigan. The annual School versus Old Oratorians fixture played at the London Irish ground was established before rugby was secure as the main sport in the school, and victory tended to go the way of the Old Oratorians until the 1965–6 season, when school won for the first time, defeating the old boys by 12 points to nine. Under the captaincy of Richard Ellis they repeated this success the following year. The first full fixture card against other schools was established in 1967, and it was not long before The London Oratory was making a name for itself on the rugby pitch. Tom Hartigan recalls how he suggested to Mr Gaffney that the boys should have school jerseys to play in. Not keen to spend too liberally, Mr Gaffney instructed Mr Hartigan to source shirts at five shillings per boy. The PE department were not impressed. They went to Harrods and bought good-quality rugby jerseys, instructing that the bill be sent to Mr Gaffney, who apparently nearly fainted at receiving it, but it was paid and the boys turned out to represent the school in quality kit. At this time both rugby and soccer were being played in competitive fixtures, but by 1972 rugby was taking the lead, evident in the comparative length of the articles in *The Oratorian* that year.

In 1973 a new member of staff who shared the Headmaster's interest in rugby was appointed to the PE department. This was Kevin Moran, who would do much to influence sport and in particular rugby over the next 40 years. It seems the Oratory PE department has a tradition of recruiting and retaining some long-standing highly driven teachers. From J C Burns, the football hero of the 1930s, to Johnny Jenkinson – 'he worked you to death', recalls Roger Knight (1956–62), but was 'a great source of encouragement', adds his contemporary Michael Sheehan – to Kevin Moran, who became Head of Department in 1975.

The 'Moran years' have seen further expansion in sport at the school; the number of pupils participating in school teams across a wide range of sports is higher than ever. It is rugby, however, that dominates, and the records and trophies bear witness to great success. There have been many highlights, for teams and for individuals. In 1978 Paul Stapleton became the first London Oratory pupil to win international honours in rugby when he was selected for the England Under 19 side to play against France at Chateauroux. He is one of seven boys who have to date played international rugby. Jose Seijido played for the England Under 18s in 1984, as did Tom Malaney in 1992 and Michael Swift in 1996. At Under 16 level Alex Philiotis played in 1992, Michael Swift in 1994, Thomas Smallbone in 2010 and Lorcan Dow in 2011. Alex Philiotis now plays international rugby for Cyprus. Michael Swift is playing professional rugby for Connaught. Tom Malaney, with Patrick Crossley, was in the Cambridge University team for the Varsity match in 2007. To have two players from the same school playing together in the Varsity match is quite something, so this was a great occasion for the young rugby players of the school who went along to Twickenham to watch these former pupils play, and for added value to see Tom score the winning try for Cambridge.

By the time these players represent their country and university they have been playing rugby for years, and their potential will have showed in their earlier years at school. With up to six first-form teams training and competing every week the fresh intake each year brings new prospects. There are of course some year groups that bring forth more talent than others and some seasons that yield more silverware than others. The year 1992 was one to remember, with the Under 15 team making it to the final of the Daily Mail National Competition, picking up the Middlesex Cup on the way, and team manager Mr Barney Nisbet of the mathematics department gaining enduring status in the annals of Oratory rugby. The semi-final game against Loughborough was hard fought in wet and windy conditions, but with excellent work from the defence the team held out, and when the final whistle blew there was delight at making it to Twickenham for the final. Final day was a big day for the school and although the team was defeated by a very strong side from Skinner's School, the Oratory boys knew they were making Oratory rugby history. It would be 2004 before another team came even close to matching the 1992 boys, and then it was as far as the semi-finals of the Plate Competition.

Another great season for a team was that of the Under 14s in 1997–8. They won all 18 of the games they played in the XVs season and then went on to win all three of the Sevens tournaments they entered. This included a final against Wellington College in the Reigate Grammar School Sevens competition, the score being The London Oratory School 30, Wellington College 0. Captain of the Under 14s was Tom Malaney who, as we have seen, went on to play for Cambridge at Twickenham.

Records are made to be broken, however, and the outstanding achievement of the Under 14s in 1998 was surpassed in 2011 by the Under 13s, who won all 21 of their fixtures in XVs and three Sevens tournaments, including the prestigious Rosslyn Park Sevens, which they secured with a 19–0 victory over Whitgift School in the final.

The Sevens competitions have given players the opportunity to compete against the top rugby schools which might not normally feature on the Oratory's fixture card. Looking back over the years Mr Moran highlights four Sevens sides who demonstrated the best of Sevens rugby.

Above right: Oratory sports master John Jenkinson presenting a trophy on Sports Day.

Below: The Cambridge Varsity Squad 2007 – The London Oratory School is the only school to have more than one player in the picture, with Patrick Crossley, third from right, and Tom Malaney, in the centre on the back row.

Left: The Under 16s in the 1992 Daily Mail Cup Final.

Below left: The Under 13 winners at the Rosslyn Park Sevens, 2011.

These are the 1979 side, which included Paul Stapleton and Stef Marty, who both went on to play for London Irish RFC (and in Mr Marty's case returned to teach at his old school); the 1984 side with its amazing pace; the 1989 Seven captained by Kevin Moran junior; and the 2002 side with a tremendous Sevens record over their school career of ten tournament wins, five semi-final stage and three quarter-final stage. In selecting what he described as 'The Magnificent Seven', Kevin Moran compiled a team of the best of the best (see table right).

The aforementioned Middlesex Cup win by the 1992 Under 15s is one of a record number of wins for London Oratory sides in this competition. With 57 and counting, the school has more victories than any other school in the county. There have been many great performances and some tense moments on the way to glory. On one memorable occasion in 1984 a closely fought game brought a 16–15 victory against Bishop Douglas School, with Michael Carr scoring two important tries and Martin Saunders kicking an injury-time penalty. To add to the honour of victory the trophy was presented to Oratory Captain Jonathan Bowes by Cardinal Hume.

In 1988, when the school was celebrating the 125th anniversary, the First XV added to the cause for celebration with the Cup, theirs after defeating St Ignatius 18–0 in the final. From 2005 to 2007 The London Oratory First XV secured a hat trick in the Middlesex Cup, winning three years in a row.

'The Tour' is an important part of a rugby career and the boys – and indeed girls – of the school have travelled

THE MAGNIFICENT SEVEN

Prop	Stef Marty	1979
Hooker	Anthony Isturis	2002
Prop	Tom Malaney	1989
Scrum Half	Jose Seijido	1984
Fly Half	Edward Mole	2002
Centre	Paul Stapleton	1979
Wing	Nigel Murray	1984

Right: Mr Gaffney presenting a rugby cup, with Mr Moran who had recently joined the staff, on far left of the picture.

Bottom right: Jonathan Bowes, Captain of the 1984 Middlesex Cup-winning team, with Cardinal Hume and Mr McIntosh.

far and wide to play the game, to represent the school, to bond with team mates, to explore different cultures and to make memories.

From the annual tour to south Wales for the Under 13s, to journeys to Sevens tournaments around the country, to the girls' tour to Hinckley and the long established tour to Galway, hundreds of pupils have travelled and represented The London Oratory School at rugby over the years. In addition major overseas tours have taken players to the US and Australia.

The first Galway tour was in 1971 and the pattern of touring every second year and hosting the visitors from Ireland in the alternate year was established. The main fixture of the Oratory tour is always against St Joseph's College, Galway, known locally as 'the Bish'. Encounters with 'the Bish' over 40 years have cemented an association that extends beyond the rugby field.

On the first large-scale overseas tour to New York in 1979 Messrs Moran, Hartigan and Kuczynski accompanied the party of 19 sixth formers. On arriving at the airport they were welcomed by a New York cousin of First XV player John McEllin who greeted the tour party with a selection of ham and cheese sandwiches. Over 30 years later some of the tourists still recall the disappointment on finding there was also a dollop of sweet mustard between the slices of bread which did not meet with approval. Then there was the matter of getting out of the airport and off to Philadelphia, the first destination of the tour. The party were travelling in two minibuses; the lead vehicle was driven by Mr Moran, with Mr Hartigan as co-pilot, while Mr Kuczynski followed in the second bus. With Mr Moran at the wheel the first navigational question arose as the road ahead split. A dispute between driver and navigator ensued, 'go left', 'no it's right', and then, 'it's too late', as the vehicle was stranded in the no man's land of the chevrons between the two roads. Thereafter Mr Moran and Mr Hartigan did not travel in the same bus. This tense start was not, however, a sign of things to come, and the tour was a great success. The boys enjoyed excellent hospitality and four games of rugby played in great spirit against schools from Philadelphia, Washington and New York. The New York game was against St Francis School and was played on a pitch situated under the freeway. Conditions were not good; there were so many stones on the rough ground that Mr Hartigan refereed the game in his hush puppies.

In 1983 a tour group went once again to the US, though this time they were based in San Francisco and the party comprised 26 pupils, accompanied by Mr Moran, Mr Tierney, Mr Coyle, Mr Matthews and Mr Guinness, the latter two geographers being particularly informative on the long flight, noting the spectacular scenery in Greenland, pack ice of Baffin Island and the grid iron field patterns of the Great Plains over which the plane was flying. This was another successful tour, with the team playing and winning four games, but not doing so well in an inaugural California Sevens competition.

North America was the destination once again in 1988, but this time as well as returning to California the Oratorians took the game to British Columbia in Canada. Mr Moran, Mr Tierney, Mr Matthews, Mr Williams and Mr Bamford accompanied the tour.

By 1990 Oratory Rugby Tour USA was a well rehearsed formula, so Mr Williams decided it was time to break

Rugby tour brochures and action from the Australia tour 2011.

new ground and head for a new continent; it was time to tour Australia. This was a brave venture. Not only would there need to be an incredible amount of planning and fundraising but the Oratory boys would need to be prepared for tough opposition. Australians would present a more challenging prospect on the field than the Americans. Accompanying Mr Williams on tour were Mr Guinness, more of a basketball player, and Mr Rose, a talented footballer. How would the 26 players and this coaching team fare down under? Played seven, won two, lost five, tells only part of the story. The tour was an overall resounding success. The Oratory boys had been to Perth, Sydney, Cairns and Brisbane. They had played some excellent rugby in some closely contested matches and had a wealth of experience to look back on. In Perth the party had been hosted by Aquinas College, where former London Oratory pupil, First XV player, and teacher David McFadden was then working. Twenty-five years after hosting his old school while they were in Australia he would return to London as their Headmaster. *The Oratorian* magazines provide a sequence of photographs featuring David McFadden which chart this interesting journey: 1976 First XV player, 1984 Under 15 coach, 2008 Under 13C coach.

The Australia tour was a great success but such an ambitious venture was unlikely to happen too often. It would be 21 years before another Oratory touring side would travel to the southern hemisphere, when in 2011 the First and Second XV went on their great Australian tour. A Singapore stopover gave a game against St Andrew's School and then it was on to Australia with fixtures in Brisbane and Sydney. Amongst the staff accompanying the boys this time was Brian Maguire, another Old Oratorian with a

Right: Mr McFadden as a First XV player (third from left on back row) in 1978.

Below: Mr McFadden as Under 13 coach in 2008.

distinguished rugby career, having played for London Irish between 1978 and 1998, with over 100 games played for the First XV, and taking the captain's role.

Girls have also had their turn with the rugby ball, with somewhat mixed fortunes but plenty of fun and team spirit. The best season has been 1999, when they were losing semi-finalists in the Rosslyn Park Sevens and winners in The London Oratory Sevens.

While rugby has been well established since first introduced, cricket has had mixed fortunes in school history. The school competed in the Central Schools' leagues with varying success. For example, on the same day in May 1931 that the senior school were securing an impressive win by eight wickets over Richmond Central School the Juniors were losing to Mortlake Central School, put down in part to a 'common fault which must be remedied, and which resulted in many missed catches, that of moving from the position in the field given by the captain or the bowler', and noted by the Headmaster in the school newsletter (Orat. vol. 1, no. 7). The frustration of the Headmaster with the lack of success in the 1930s can be detected in this biting report after losing the game against Acton Central School in summer 1933: 'our batsmen seem imbued with the idea that they will be given out if they hit a boundary … our fielding was bad and lacking in vim'. Although the school might not have been producing great teams there were some memorable individual achievements in these years. In the same season that drew the above comments G Hammond was awarded 'the Star', a two-guinea Oval bat autographed by Jack Hobbs, in recognition of young Hammond's performance against Wembley Central School, when he took eight wickets for nine runs.

Cricket's fortunes fluctuated in the post-war era, and there is little on record to suggest there was much distinguished play in the 1950s, 1960s and 1970s. The 1980s and 1990s, however, saw some strong performances as Mike Matthews, Senior Master, ably assisted by keen members of staff such as Paul Johnston, Head of History, brought a new lease of life to the game. The opportunity for developing the school's cricketers to the full was, however, limited by the poor wickets at Barn Elms and the lack of nets at school. The school was able to field three or four serious teams each season though, and with some boys playing for clubs outside school and representing London in the London Schools' Cricket Association county sides there was a good deal of talent in evidence. In 1987 two new first formers, Kervin Marc and Eugene Cariaga, came to the fore in the Under 12s XI, Kervin as an impressive fast bowler and Eugene as wicket keeper. As these two moved to Under 13 level the incoming Under 12s, coached by Mr Johnston, had an extremely successful season, winning the London Cup final, owing much to their Captain, Sean Byrne. With an average run tally of 93.25 and a top score of 114 in the game against Latymer Upper, he certainly led by example. That century was the first in a London Oratory school game for about 20 years. In 1990 Sean was selected for the English Schools Cricket Association Under 14s and Kervin Marc was playing for the Under 15s in the South of England XI. These were the best years for Oratory cricket, with more boys from The London Oratory School playing in the London county sides than from any other school. Sean was not the only impressive Byrne on the cricket pitch. He and his older brother Michael both represented Surrey and were presented with awards in 1992. Sean received the Barclays Bank Most Improved Cricketer Award from Doug Insole, and older brother Michael (also of LOS rugby fame) was presented by Denis Compton with the LCCA Young Cricketer of the Year. Kervin Marc went on to a first-class cricket career between 1994 and 2000, including two seasons playing for Middlesex.

Left: Kervin Marc (back row centre) went on to play for Middlesex.

Far left: Cricket under a lowering sky at Barn Elms.

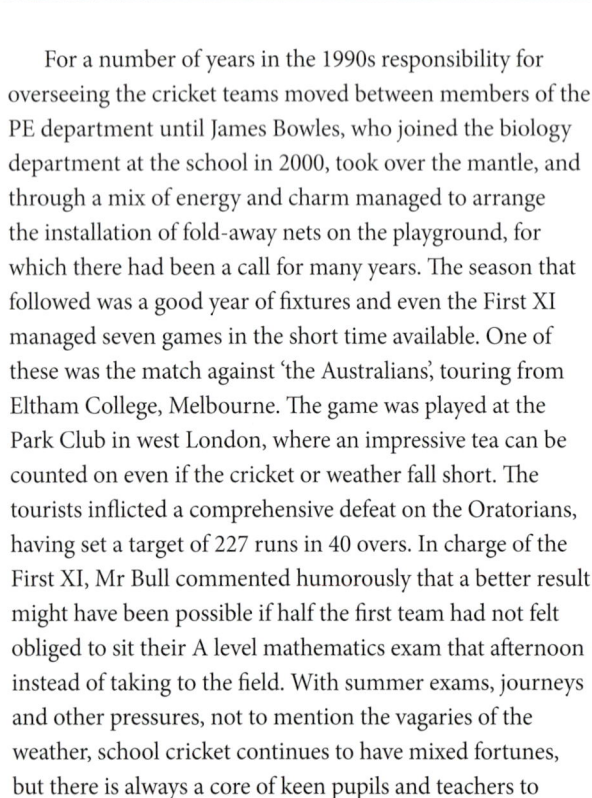

For a number of years in the 1990s responsibility for overseeing the cricket teams moved between members of the PE department until James Bowles, who joined the biology department at the school in 2000, took over the mantle, and through a mix of energy and charm managed to arrange the installation of fold-away nets on the playground, for which there had been a call for many years. The season that followed was a good year of fixtures and even the First XI managed seven games in the short time available. One of these was the match against 'the Australians', touring from Eltham College, Melbourne. The game was played at the Park Club in west London, where an impressive tea can be counted on even if the cricket or weather fall short. The tourists inflicted a comprehensive defeat on the Oratorians, having set a target of 227 runs in 40 overs. In charge of the First XI, Mr Bull commented humorously that a better result might have been possible if half the first team had not felt obliged to sit their A level mathematics exam that afternoon instead of taking to the field. With summer exams, journeys and other pressures, not to mention the vagaries of the weather, school cricket continues to have mixed fortunes, but there is always a core of keen pupils and teachers to ensure what can be played is played.

Rowing was expanding in the mid 1960s as Mr Dent and Mr Bamford, under the auspices of Mr Hooper, assisted with teams at different levels. In the 1964–5 season the school First Eight secured a good win over Westminster City School. Rowing was offered to boys as one of their games options in the 1980s, using the facilities at the Barn Elms Rowing Centre. Competitions were organised amongst the different schools training at the Centre. The appointment in September 1980 of a new member of staff brought a fresh impetus to rowing; Alan Whitwell had rowed in the British Eight which won the Silver Medal in the Moscow Olympic Games. While Olympic standard was probably too ambitious a target, he aimed to bring Oratory rowers on to compete with top-class school rowers in the Schools' Head of the River Race and other challenging events. A number of boys were already rowing with clubs outside school and this boosted the school squad. One of these rowers was Nicholas Kapica, who coxed with Kingston Rowing Club in National and International regattas.

After disappearing from the curriculum for a while rowing was reinstated in 1998 under former pupil David Harte. He laid the ground for a revival which really took off when Ali Boileau assumed command of the school rowers and school registrar Jackie Darling, a very experienced and competitive rower, assisted with the organisation. Talent now began to emerge, and in 2003 the school acquired its first boat. Readers of *The Oratorian* might have noticed that this was the year when the rowing report was elevated to the sports section, having previously occupied a place somewhere between junior drama and pottery in the Clubs and Societies section. One of the rowers for the school that year was Michael Dolan. Two years later he won his Oxford blue rowing against Cambridge at Henley. Oratory rowing was now a serious sport and in 2006 the J16 coxed four of

Above: London Oratory rowers on the river at Putney.

Right: The J14B winners of the gold medal in the National Schools Regatta 2012.

James Flahive, Billy Jerry, Feargal Mostyn Williams and Johnny Cullinan, with Alistair Adams as cox, secured the first National Schools' Head win for The London Oratory School, setting a new event record at the same time. In 2009 Albert Gora was the first Oratory pupil to be selected for the Great Britain Junior rowing team trials. London Oratory rowing has not looked back since. That same year Mr Gerald Elphicke, with a strong background in rowing and coaching, was appointed Head of Rowing, and with no end of interested young rowers and talented and enthusiastic coaches the Oratory oarsmen continued to go from strength to strength. The London Oratory School Boat Club is now a serious challenger in major competitions against first-rate opposition. In June 2012 the J14B Octuple made school history as they took the Gold Medal in the National Schools' Regatta, the biggest event in the rowing calendar for schools.

Current pupils might have a chance to emulate or exceed their forerunners in the sports reviewed so far but there is one sport at which the school once excelled which is no longer on offer, and that is the noble art of boxing. Boxing flourished at the school between the 1920s and 1950s and only disappeared in the 1960s. It was regarded as a good sport for boys, encouraging fitness, teaching discipline and demanding respect for the rules and for one's opponent.

In the 1920s and 1930s the school competed in the Chelsea Schools' Sports Association Boxing Tournament and often recorded winning performances. J C Burns, footballer and mathematics teacher, helped to coach the young Oratory boxers. In 1932, encouraging talented pupils to attend training sessions to keep up their practice, the Headmaster assured the aspiring boxers that 'there are always plenty of sparring partners to act as "chopping blocks" for the prospective champions'. One 'prospective champion' was John Wright. His ambitions to succeed at boxing were to be realised when on Saturday 30 November 1936 at the Holborn Stadium he won the six-and-a-half-

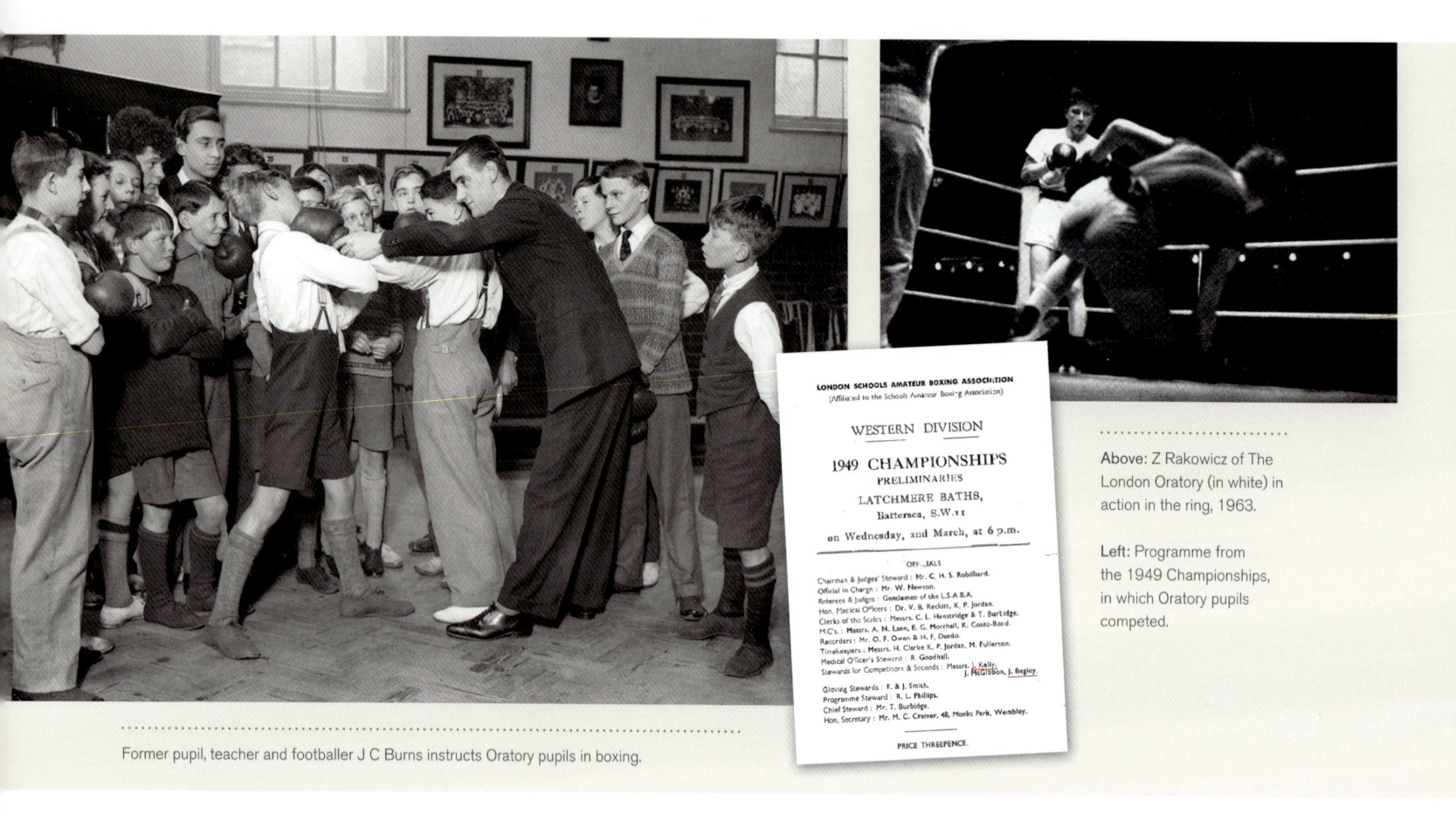

The London Oratory School – *Part III: An Oratory Education*

Former pupil, teacher and footballer J C Burns instructs Oratory pupils in boxing.

Above: Z Rakowicz of The London Oratory (in white) in action in the ring, 1963.

Left: Programme from the 1949 Championships, in which Oratory pupils competed.

stone Championship of London. He went on to win the Great Britain Schoolboy Boxing Championship, in the eight-stone intermediate division in 1937. Colin Burran was runner up in the six-and-a-half-stone junior division in the same championships. It is sad to note that John Wright and Colin Burran, two successful and dedicated Oratory sportsmen, were both killed on active service just three years later.

Boxing was still a school sport in the post-war years and continued into the 1960s. Roger Knight (1956–62), not himself a practitioner of the art, tells how, by way of punishment after he thumped another pupil, he was put in the ring with the school boxing champion. Faced with such a formidable opponent young Roger decided 'the best course of action was to keep hitting him so he didn't have a chance to punch me'. As Roger recalls the school champ was apparently not impressed. 'He got fed up and left the ring saying I was a waste of time.' This young champion obviously took his art seriously, and in this he followed a line of committed Oratory boxers. By the 1970s boxing was no longer on the curriculum but there were still boys who boxed outside of school. Patrick (P J A) Murphy was a member of the Brunswick Club who became a London Federation Champion, and as a fifth former in 1976 reached the semi-final of the Great Britain Boxing Championships.

One of the longest-surviving Oratory sports is swimming. The first Annual Swimming Gala seems to have been held in 1882. Swimming has always been encouraged and popular with young Oratorians and it seems it served them well as more than a leisure pursuit on many occasions. In 1931 Norman Turner, a 14-year-old pupil at the school, showed great bravery, diving fully clothed into the River Thames near Putney Bridge in an attempt to save the life of a boy who had fallen into the river. Although the rescue was in vain the Battersea coroner complimented Norman on his heroic action. As Norman's Headmaster said, 'well done Turner, school is proud of you'. School was proud again in 1933 as the holiday jottings in the September newsletter reported that 'Terence Cane rescued a little girl from drowning off Canvey Island and was rewarded by the grateful mother.' The following summer it was

Below: The boxing medal won by Eamon Malone as an Oratory schoolboy in 1966, the last year boxing was permitted in ILEA schools.

126

Above: Water polo in the school swimming pool.

Above right: Father Tighe presents a winner's cup to a delighted pupil at the Annual Swimming Gala at Chelsea Baths.

the turn of Frank Flynn to 'save a boy from drowning at Shanklin'. It seems that the hours spent learning to swim in the Chelsea Baths were not wasted on Oratory boys.

The Chelsea Baths was the location for the annual swimming competition. As well as the familiar races in the established strokes there were diving competitions and the novelty races. The costume race was always 'amusing' and the finale to the evening was generally either the nightshirt and candle race or the apple scramble. In 1938 the 50th gala was recorded as a special day in school history. The swimming gala was revived in the post-war years, and from Chelsea to Fulham and from Kensington to Richmond pools The London Oratory School Annual Swimming Gala, after well over 100 competitions, is still a keenly contested annual event. The gala is now one of the House Competitions, which has brought additional excitement as the points are accumulated and the totals are calculated. Each year the champion swimmer is named Victor Ludorum, and there have over the years been a number of exceptionally strong swimmers who have carried off the award more than once. Between 1998 and 2007 Harry Dunne, Peter Kowalski, Lori Peri and Alex Wahnon all won the title on two occasions. Before them Peter McGinty had carried the accolade for three years in a row, 1989–91. This record was beaten in 2012 when Rory McMonagle took his fourth title. Any good swimmer who joined the school in 2006 was going to have a tough time in swimming competitions as they would always be up against Rory, who swims for Ireland and holds two national records. Another pupil who made his mark in the water is Matthew Fox (1997–2004); a keen water polo player, he represented Wales in the Commonwealth Games in 2006.

As the venue for the swimming gala has changed over the years there have been different grounds for outdoor sports. Today Barn Elms is the school's home ground and the venue for most of the annual House competitions, but earlier Oratorians trained and competed on a variety of other sports fields. In an Inspection report of 1914 the Inspector noted that 'the playground is small but the boys have a private playing field at Ealing'. In 1932 the school travelled from South Kensington to Hampstead Heath for the first School Sports Day. It was organised on an inter-House basis with the Champion House Shield at stake, and special medals were struck to be presented to the Victor Ludorum of the upper and lower school. The first House Champions were Francis House. The following year the Fathers of the Oratory donated a cup, the Oratory Cup, to be awarded each year to the Sports Day winners. For Sports Day 1933 the school found a venue a little closer to home, the Duke of York's Headquarters in Chelsea. A great deal of preparation went into the event; the Fathers provided the refreshments, and 200 chairs were made available for parents and pupils. The boys were given clear instructions for the day: no one was allowed to leave until the Championship Cup had been presented and, the venue being a military barracks, it was necessary to warn the boys that no one was allowed in the gun park. The Headmaster took a dim view of those boys, albeit only seven in number, who did not attend this Sports Day, and an even dimmer view of their parents, who had 'aided and abetted in their absence'. It was generally agreed, however, that Sports Day was a resounding success.

The events of these early Sports Days were a blend of the serious athletic disciplines and the more amusing school sports day events, with the egg-and-spoon race, the three-legged race and the slow-bicycle race all providing the opportunity for House points. The fourth Sports Day in school history was extra special, coinciding with the Chelsea Silver Jubilee Celebrations, on which account Chelsea Council provided a bumper tea for the pupils.

In 1937 at the Sixth London Oratory School Sports Day, St Edward's House were House Champions, and they would have the interesting honour of holding the title for 12 years, as it was not until 1950 that the Seventh Sports Day was held. In that year St Wilfred's House took the title and House Captain Brian Cheesman was declared Victor Ludorum.

Sports Day and other athletic events continued at the Duke of York's Headquarters up until the move to Seagrave Road. Bernard Liengme (1949–57) recalls a memorable day in 1954. He and some friends were practising on the track at the barracks when they were politely asked to clear the area for a while. Then they watched as three or four young men had a race, at the end of which the timekeeper shouted 'Roger, you did it.' The next day, 6 May 1954, Roger Bannister ran the first official sub-four-minute mile.

Over the years there have been some very talented athletes at the school, who have not only competed for their House but who have also represented school, borough and nation. In 1935 F O'Sullivan of form IVC was the All London half-mile Champion and came third in the All England competition. Just over 20 years later another half-mile champion was Rod Hamilton (1952–8), who at the age of 17 set a new record in the Under 19s half-mile in the London Schools' Championships and was selected for London in the English Schools' Championship. He also came fourth in the 800m final in the European Catholic Schools' Games. Another English Schools' Champion was Kevin Murray, an excellent all-round athlete and Champion in the 110 hurdles. He went on to success in the European Championships in Germany. In the following decade the school had another champion hurdler, Jan Kijowski, who won the 110 hurdles in the London Championships 1965 and in 1967 was Champion in the 200yd low hurdles.

The desire to beat the record works at all levels, and The London Oratory School Sports Day has always been a hotly contested affair, as pupils seek to write their name in the school record book. Since moving to Seagrave Road Sports Day has been held at the Hurlingham Park track or at Barn Elms, and records have been made and broken on many an occasion.

Seeing a record fall, particularly one that has stood for years, is of course part of the thrill for the spectators at Sports Day, though maybe not if it is your record being smashed, as former pupil and Deputy Headmaster Mr Rooney can testify. In 1999 he watched his 800m record, which had been set 21 years earlier, being taken by Denis Murphy, knocking nine seconds off the Rooney record of 2 minutes 8 seconds. At least niece Natasha was able to uphold the family honour that day by setting a new record in the girls' 100m race. The following year Christian Morris broke the 20-year 1,500m record. In 2003 a 30-year record went when the first-form 100m record held by Paul Stapleton was broken by Ian Odiwe. This was quite an achievement for young Ian; the record had stood for so long because Paul Stapleton wasn't just a fast runner, he was so fast that he even earned the admiration of Linford Christie, who put it on record in his autobiography that the only person who could challenge him in training at the White City track was one young London Irish rugby player by the name of Paul Stapleton.

It is not just on the track, however, that records are set and broken, but in the field too. Liam Clancy, who won the third-form shot-put in 2006, was ranked in the top ten in the country in the event. A similar national ranking

An old photograph taken with a box Brownie of Brian Cheesman with the Victor Ludorum and House Champion Cups after Sports Day 1950, and the commemorative programme.

Above: Steve Collins jumps the hurdles at Sports Day at the Duke of York's Barracks. The picture was taken in 1963 by fellow pupil Mike Moran, who went on to become a professional photographer.

Below: The girls' javelin event at Sports Day at Hurlingham Park.

was earned by Adrian Assinor in the triple jump. Many Oratorians have represented borough and county in the whole range of athletic and cross-country events, and many have continued to excel at university and at an amateur level. Teachers keen to show that they still run a good race after schooldays are done had for many years the chance to take on the senior boys in the Paul Quinn 300m Challenge Trophy. Mr Moran and former pupil Matthew Sullivan share the record of three wins a piece in this challenge.

That word 'challenge' is music to Mr Moran's ears, and in 1986 he introduced a new challenge to young Oratorians. This is the annual fitness challenge which still takes place each year. Over 500 pupils from third form to sixth form test their fitness in a series of challenges assessing speed, strength and endurance. Not only do pupils aim to improve on their own score year on year, but as the years have passed there is now the opportunity for some pupils to beat a score set by their own parents.

There have been many different sports on offer to young Oratorians over the years. First offered in the 1930s, badminton has always had a following, but opportunity for competition has fluctuated. In July 1932 the school purchased a complete badminton set and announced the establishment of a School Badminton Club, with those wishing to join contributing subs of 6d a term. It took a little while for the Oratory teams to really make their mark in competitive fixtures, but they were soon holding their own against teams from St Joseph's Club, Roehampton and St Mary's College. Once a certain Roche was established as the Oratory's 'brilliant captain' (Orat. vol. 1, no. 51) the school began to secure more victories. Membership of the club was steady, with around 20 regular players. Badminton was still enjoyed, with considerable success, in the 1940s and 1950s. Bernard Liengme still has proud memories of the Oratory sixth-form badminton team beating the London University Champions – he gives the credit for the win to Chris Byrne. In the 1980s the school was running a

Badminton League for the senior boys, but with only one court available participation was limited. Friday after school was for many years the badminton slot, with staff and senior pupils occupying the gym for that purpose.

The Friday after-school gym session transferred to volleyball shortly after Dr Virgili took command of a revival of the sport in 1993, and there have been some successful teams competing on both a city-wide and a national level. Attracting strong talent from the Polish pupils in the school, these boys – and occasionally girls – form a dedicated group. Another sport that flourished under the auspices of a talented coach is fencing, in which English teacher Paul O'Dwyer formerly represented Great Britain. Under Mr O'Dwyer's tuition and with the Sixth Form Common Room as a modified fencing salle, The London Oratory fencers have brought forth some serious talent. Fabio and Gianfranco Artesi, members of Camden Fencing Club, were already proficient before starting at the school in 2005, and both boys went on to achieve excellent national rankings in their age group and many competition successes. Christopher Mollard (2003–8), who was introduced to the sport at school, has gone on to fence for Brunel University, winning a sports scholarship. He got his GB vest in 2011 and started 2013 ranked 39th in Great Britain. He was recently invited onto the Scottish team and is ranked fourth in Scotland. Sights are now set on the Commonwealth Games in Glasgow 2014.

A more unusual activity for games afternoons was introduced by Mr Gaffney when he made arrangements for small groups of sixth formers to take up horse riding, first at Coombe Stables, and later at the stables in Wimbledon Village. Initially it was to offer the girls of the sixth form an alternative to the games which dominated the curriculum of a boys' school. The first group of girls to mount the saddle did so with relish, with 12 passing their 'green standard test', denoting a basic knowledge of the horse's tack and competency at the walk and trot. Mr Gaffney had a love of horses going back to his time in the army, so it was perhaps also for this reason that he agreed to the Metropolitan Police using the school for the mounted officers to gather before Chelsea matches, an arrangement that continued into the 1980s, when there was still the occasional sight of horses

Long jump at Barn Elms.

memory that will always stay with me is winning the rugby House Cup with the rest of my class'; Matthew Thoumine will not forget being part of the Octo that came fifth at the National Schools Rowing race; Lorenzo Vilona looks back on the rugby Sevens tour to the Wirral; George Kearney's best memory is being unbeaten in over 40 rugby games; and for Joe Stapleton the highlight is winning the Middlesex Cup in second form. David Bull believes that playing rugby for the A team 'has been great fun, with huge success and a great sense of achievement, and the chance for new friendships with other boys in the year. We will always be a team.'

As these memories and comments show, so much of the success in sports at The London Oratory School can be attributed to the enthusiasm and commitment from pupils. This combined with the dedication of staff, who in many cases have played and competed at a high level in the sport they are coaching, points to the prospect of many more great sporting moments to add to the Oratory record book.

Above: Former pupil Christopher Mollard represents Great Britain at fencing.

Right: Pupils learned sub-aqua skills in the school swimming pool in the 1970s.

tied to posts in front of the main entrance while police officers tucked into a pre-match meal in the houseroom.

Another activity that for a short time was on offer to pupils on account of a personal interest of a Headmaster was sub-aqua diving. Mr McIntosh was a member of a sub-aqua club in Chelsea, and from there he recruited an instructor, Mr Lionel Blandford, founder and Director of the National Snorkellers Club, who offered training to boys who were attending the youth centre at the school. He thereafter found so much interest, no doubt inspired by *The Undersea World of Jacques Cousteau*, that an after-school snorkelling and scuba diving club was established. This is certainly one of the more unusual sports experienced by schoolboys. The list of sports offered at some time or other in school history is indeed extensive. In addition to all those mentioned there will be pupils past and present who remember participating and representing the school in netball, basketball, tennis, hockey, trampolining, water polo, golf and even lacrosse.

When asked to consider what they think will be amongst their most abiding memories of their schooldays, many current pupils cite a sporting moment. Dara Spring says 'a

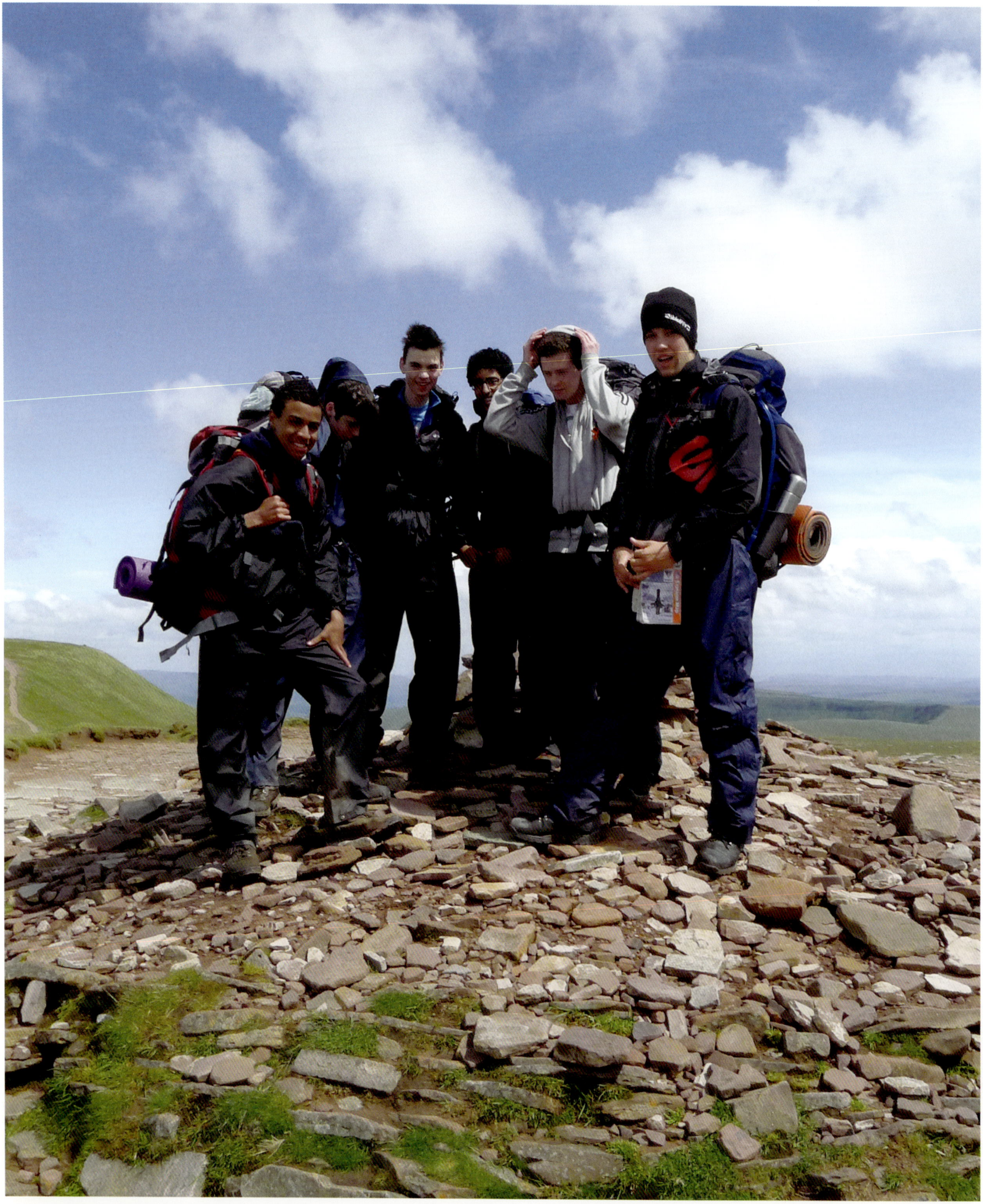

School Journeys

The benefits of travel and the educational experience of a school journey have long been recognised at The London Oratory School. From days out at Sydenham to Baltic cruises, from the museums of South Kensington to the Battlefields of the American Civil War, from Hampton Court Palace to the Tokpaki Palace, from the mountains of North Wales to Kilimanjaro, the Oratorian travel gazetteer is a comprehensive volume.

The first recorded 'school journey' was to Sydenham, where the parkland surrounding the Oratory Fathers' House, St Mary's, became the regular destination for the 'annual summer treat' for the Oratory boys, although in July 1887, by way of a change, the whole school went on the annual treat to Hampton Court. This then became the preferred destination for the whole school outing for many years to come. As the name implies, the idea of the school outing was to give the boys a treat, taking them to the open spaces of Sydenham, Hampton Court and Bushy Park. This gave these London boys a day in the fresh air and an opportunity for cricket, races and an outdoor tea – a novelty for many of the Oratory schoolboys in the early 20th century. The 'annual treat' became an important tradition in Oratory school life and was looked forward to with happy anticipation each summer, although it seems a day of rain also became part of the expectation. So much so that the fact that it had not rained was deemed worthy of record in 1926, with the parish magazine noting that the boys had enjoyed 'a day without rain' and observing that 'it is a tradition that it always rains on the day the school goes to Hampton Court'. The better weather was thus explained: 'this year they took the extreme step before they set out of saying some prayers for a fine day, and a fine day St Philip obtained for them'. The Hampton Court treat continued into the 1930s, by which time the residential journey had entered Oratory life.

The first school journey of this sort was in the summer of 1931, when a party of 70 boys and three teachers, Mr Braun, Mr Crawley and Mr Blight, set out for a two-week camp at Dymchurch in Kent. Over the two weeks they were to enjoy specially devised lessons and outdoor pursuits. Each day there was a timetable, with classes in mathematics ('becomes quite enjoyable when it takes the form of survey work'), literature, history, geography, botany, agriculture, science ('why have the pebbles on the beach no sharp corners?') and French. In addition there were to be 'games,

Opposite: The Duke of Edinburgh's Award mountain expedition.

Below: St Mary's Sydenham, destination for the 'annual summer treat'.

The first residential school journey was to Dymchurch in Kent.

bathing parades, and interesting rambles, inland and along the shore' (PM, xi, p111). The camp food was deemed 'amazing', with second helpings on demand. The tours and activities included excursions by charabanc and by the Romney, Hythe and District Railway, the smallest railway in the world. The party visited Canterbury for a guided tour of the Cathedral, and on all their visits Mr Braun enthralled his pupils with his architectural and botanical knowledge. The boys entered fully into the spirit of camp life and on departure received 'three hearty cheers of "speed well" from the camp Commandant and his staff'. Early the following term parents were invited to an exhibition at school to inspect the photographs, guide books and botanical specimens accrued from the trip and to listen to speeches from some of the participants.

The Dymchurch expedition was deemed a great success, and the tradition of the 'School Journey' was begun. As soon as the plans for the 1932 camp were announced boys were enrolled and saving began towards the £3 cost to secure a place for camp at East Cowes on the Isle of Wight. This camp was another great success, and concluded with the distribution of accolades to boys of the four Houses. St Philip's House deserved special mention for neat beds, St Francis' for smartness and neatness, St Wilfred's for concert work and St Edward's for good, orderly work. It seems all were winners on a London Oratory School Camp. Perhaps this is no surprise if all abided by the rules of Camp as laid out in 1933: 1) be obedient, 2) be cheerful, 3) be gentlemanly.

While Dymchurch and the Isle of Wight gave a good dose of fresh air and a taste of the great outdoors to city children, there were plans afoot for more ambitious travel, and late in 1933 the Summer Cruise to Northern Ports was announced. The following summer a party of 32 senior boys accompanied by three masters travelled on the SS *Neuralia* from Tilbury Docks on a fortnight's cruise, visiting Norway and Denmark. The holiday cost £5 5s 6d and all on board had a very enjoyable time, with excursions to the castle at Elsinore and to the top of the Fløien Mountain by 'wire-rope' railway. This was one of the inaugural cruises for schoolchildren run by the Secondary Schools Cruise Association under the title British Cruises for British Boys. The first of these had been organised in 1932 for schoolchildren from Scotland and was then expanded to a wider range of schools. The voyages were operated along the lines of a camp, with strict timings, rules and orders. As well as helping with duties on board the schoolchildren were expected to participate in all the entertainments. The Oratory boys were once again on board the *Neuralia* in 1935, this time cruising the Baltic, visiting Oslo, Stockholm, Copenhagen and the Kiel Canal. The arrival in Norway after an eerie journey through a foggy North Sea brought relief, and all fears were soon forgotten as the party were welcomed by what seemed like the entire population of 'blue eyed and fair haired maidens and men' (Orat. vol. 2, no. 25). In 'hospitable, jolly Copenhagen' they were welcomed by the Mayor himself. On their visit to Kiel the Londoners observed 'Krupp's Yards with torpedo boats and submarines on the stocks and battleships in the harbour with Hitler's beautiful armed yacht'. Four years later these very vessels were in action in the seas in which the Oratory boys were passing their summer, as Norway became the target of Nazi expansion. The very ship on which the boys were enjoying their holiday would become a casualty of war in 1945 on service in Italy.

In 1936 the London Oratory boys were once again one of the schools on the Secondary Schools Cruise, this time to the Mediterranean, taking in Lisbon, Madeira, Gibraltar and Casablanca. The ship was the HMT *Dilwara*, a brand new trooper, fitted with 'swimming pool, sun decks, sports decks, twin-screw diesel engines, thermostatic ventilation and convenient hammock storage'. Which of these selling points had most influence in attracting customers it is impossible to know, but there was no shortage of interested parties, and it was a happy crew of young Oratorians who set sail on the two-week voyage in August 1936. They had a wonderful time, visiting sights which included the Jeronimos Monastery and Vasco da Gama's tomb in Lisbon, as well as the Sultan's Palace in Rabat. They enjoyed leisure time also, bathing in Madeira and watching the action at the bull ring in Lisbon. Souvenirs picked up on the trip included fezzes from the market in Casablanca and picadors' darts as a memento of the bull fight. It was also recorded that the Oratory boys were specially commended by the cruise organisers for 'rolling and stowing hammocks'. No sooner were the travellers of 1936 back on home shores than plans were underway for the following year's cruise to the Baltic. Upon arrival in Helsinki on 15 August 1937, the Feast of the Assumption, the Oratory party hurried to church. To their astonishment they there encountered a former pupil, probably the only Old Oratorian in Finland. He had seen the visitors in the familiar school blazer and came to speak with them, saying that the sight of the old school uniform made him feel homesick. The Baltic journey also took the boys to Denmark and Sweden. 'The cruise' had become a regular feature in London Oratory School life, until the outbreak of war and all the change that wrought.

As well as participating in these school journeys the pupils were encouraged to show enterprise in their own holiday plans, and a feature in *The Oratorian* newsletter of the 1930s records some of the exploits of pupils under the heading 'where the Oratory cap was seen'. Each September pupils would share their adventures, and these make for interesting (and amusing) reading. While Bruges, Liege and Ypres sound like understandable holiday destinations, figuring out what was done on the visits to Stoke Poges or Widnes undertaken in 1931 requires greater imagination. By 1932 boys were adding competitive detail to their jottings: now J Bushell and P Fleury did not just visit Yarmouth, they saw 'a great fire at Yarmouth'; H Gesdurian 'witnessed a mad bull chase at Ashford'; J McElroy 'saw the legless American Channel swimmer aspirant, Charles Zibelman, at Dover'; and Gasser saw 'three ships in collision off Dover'. It seems the gauntlet (or cap) had been thrown down. The following summer adventures were had beyond English shores, with France, Belgium and Italy mentioned in dispatches. Energy and enterprise were encouraged and by 1936 visits all over Europe were recorded alongside added information such as the assurance that wherever Malone of 2A was when 'he chased a run-away elephant' he did so 'from a safe distance'.

Above: Oratorians took part in British Cruises for British Boys aboard the SS *Neuralia*.

Left: The house in which the Oratorians stayed on the journey to East Cowes on the Isle of Wight in the 1930s.

The London Oratory School – Part III: An Oratory Education

With such pioneering travellers before them it is little wonder that Oratorians continued to relish the prospect of school journeys. David Wailen (1949–56) recalls a trip to Paris after which he 'got a life-long appetite for overseas travel'. His contemporary at school, Bernard Liengme has wonderful memories of the school trip to Rome, which involved 24 hours of travel by train and ferry. Then there was the theft of the boys' clothes from the hostel in which they were staying, which was resolved courtesy of the Italian Ministry of Education and resulted in the boys seeing the Pope on Easter Day, dressed in their 'smart Italian clothes'. Did the Pope notice the winkle-picker shoes and the bright green tie in which young Bernard was attired?

Italy remains a favoured Oratory destination to this day. In 1960 a party went to Chiavari on the Italian Riveira. Roger Knight and Michael Sheehan, pupils on the journey, both recall the long train ride across Europe and the impression of seeing the Alps from the window. Neither boy had been abroad before; both found the whole experience amazing, and both are still able to recall visits to Milan, Genoa, Portofino and Pisa, as well as 'bullet' soup on the hotel menu.

Retracing the steps of some of their forebears on the Baltic cruise, a party of Oratorians visited Denmark and Sweden in 1965, and in 1966–7 two journeys were organised to Yugoslavia. The parties travelled by coach through Belgium, Germany, Austria and Italy to their final destination of Dubrovnik. They visited the main tourist sights along the route and all were treated to spectacular scenery as they drove through the mountains of Central Europe, apart from 'the young man who read Superman comics until an irate Mrs Edwards snatched them off him and ordered him to look out of the window' (Orat. 1967). They experienced local cuisine (spaghetti for the first time, in Venice). For the writer of the report of the 1966 journey, however, all the magnificent architecture, the wonderful sights and the cultural delights were reduced when measured against 'the most single exciting moment, when we witnessed on television England's final victory in the World Cup'.

The advent of the skiing trip brought new Oratory adventures. Mr Rooney, then a pupil at the school, recalls the phone call he received on Boxing Day 1979: 'Mr Tierney calling, a space has come up on the skiing trip but you have to be ready in ten minutes!' 'But I haven't got any skiing gear' replied the pupil. 'Never mind we'll sort that when we get there, just have your passport ready and I'll collect you.' And so it was that a young Mr Rooney found himself heading to the Dolomites for a week on the slopes.

By this time the skiing trip was a well-established event going back to 1970, when Mr Bamford and Mr Wilson had organised a skiing holiday to Le Mont-Dore in France, the success of which would ensure more to follow. In 1972 the Oratorian skiing party went to Italy, once again under the charge of expert skier Mr Bamford. Mr McIntosh was the second teacher on the trip; however an unfortunate accident on the first day left him *hors de combat*, and Mr Matthews arrived to join the party while Mr McIntosh

Left: Ian Davidson (1959–66) on the 1961 school journey to Norway. He recalls 'the horrendous crossing on the SS *Leda* from Newcastle' during which 'most of us were sick'. While in Norway the party took a cruise through the fjords, visited Bergen and had the opportunity to try skiing in the mountains.

Below: By the 1990s the London Oratory skiing trip was well established.

Above: Tynecot Cemetery is visited each year on the Battlefields Tour.

Right: Mr McCarthy of the history department in the trenches.

rested. The ski journey became a regular fixture, with destinations moving between France, Austria and Italy, and new generations of skiers were emerging from amongst the young Oratorians, no doubt destined to spend holidays on the slopes in years to come. Such was the enthusiasm for skiing amongst pupils and staff that in the Christmas holidays of 1977 two separate groups set off to Italy. The progress of Oratory skiers was rewarded, with a Gold Star Award in the tests arranged by the Italian Ski School going to one pupil in each of the school parties: Paul Carr and Santiago de Barry. Unfortunately for Peter Lovstrom, now an established actor, then a sixth former, 'break a leg' was not a reference to his future career but rather the consequence of a fall on the slopes which resulted in him spending Christmas Eve in an Italian hospital. He was not the only young Oratorian to have the Italian hospital experience as part of the skiing expedition. Abraham Arthur of third form and second former Stephen Tynan both broke a leg in accidents in Italy in 1978, and Mr Brunwin found himself on an extended Christmas holiday in Italy looking after 'the legs' until they were able to fly home nine days after the rest of the party.

The occasional injury has also been experienced on the annual tour to the battlefields of the First World War, usually on account of tripping on a duckboard or inadvertently touching a piece of barbed wire in the trenches. The experience of a visit to the scenes of conflict and memorial in France and Belgium has left a lasting impression on many pupils. The vast Tynecot Cemetery near the site of the Battle of Passchendaele is the largest Commonwealth War Cemetery in the world, the last resting place and memorial to 11,954 Commonwealth servicemen and the scene of many speeches, studies, prayers and quiet reflection on school tours. For nearly 30 years Oratorians have retraced the first day of the Somme at Beaumont Hamel or Serre, have walked through the tunnels at Vimy Ridge and fallen in the mud at Sanctuary Wood. They have gasped at the massive Lochnagar Crater – and in less health and safety conscious times, scrambled into said crater – looked out for silent pickets and unexploded shells, attended the Last Post Ceremony at the Menin Gate, heard Mass in Flemish and eaten lots of chips and chocolate! Battlefields further afield were added to the history department travel brochure when Mr Johnston led the first visit to the US Civil War sites in 1995.

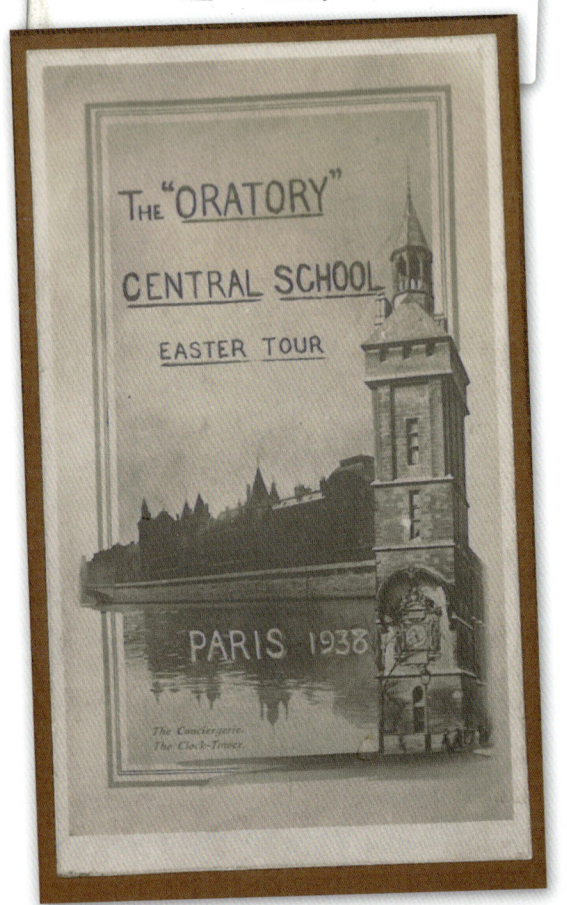

The second-form journey to France organised for many years by Madame Ressort is always popular with young Oratorians who are billeted *en famille*. For many years these groups were based in Fontainebleau and in more recent times in Reims. The modern languages department continues to organise regular journeys to France and Germany, with many pupils taking the opportunity to test their skills in the native language and to experience local culture. Today's young Oratory travellers, however, are unlikely to show such relish for local pastimes as the Oratory girls on a visit to Spain in 1964, where Susan Carragher and Kathleen Allan enjoyed the excitement of a bull fight, writing of the event: 'marvellous, one Matador nearly got gored by the bull and two of the Matadors cut off bulls' ears'.

Oratory boys and girls have always been ready to engage in outdoor pursuits from mountain climbing to waterskiing, along with more gentle pursuits such as fishing or golf. For many years from 1981 the annual journey to Galway was the occasion for such activities, as well as a chance for the city boys from London to meet the country girls of Galway in the disco at Ballinasloe. Adventure holidays such as those enjoyed in France at Port Grimand, with sailing, snorkelling, walking and horse riding on offer,

Left: In 1938 pupils on the tour to Paris were issued with an informative guide.

Below: Tyn y Berth was a regular destination for Oratorians in the 1970s and 1980s.

At the top of Mount Kilimanjaro on the World Challenge Expedition to Tanzania.

bring back memories for pupils of the 1970s and 1980s, as do the third-form expeditions to Tyn y Berth in mid Wales, where the challenge of climbing Cadair Idris was always part of the experience, as it may still be for boys and girls on expedition for The Duke of Edinburgh's Award. Also in more recent years the rain-soaked Lake District or sunny Isle of Wight have been the adventure destinations for second formers. Each year Junior House pupils in J4 look forward with great anticipation to the Kingswood adventure, with the opportunity for exciting exploits such as caving, with underground tunnels and tyres to pass through, or, as has been known in the case of teachers, to risk getting stuck in. These adventures are but the beginning for some of these boys, who have progressed by the time they are in sixth form from the thrill of the zip wire to the thrill of climbing Mount Kilimanjaro or swimming in Lake Titicaca on a Team Challenge expedition. Through the latter organisation pupils in the past ten years have been on expeditions to countries in Africa (Namibia, Kenya, Rwanda, Uganda and Tanzania), Europe (Romania), Central and South America (Belize, Argentina, Bolivia) and Asia (India, Thailand, Cambodia). They have trekked and climbed; travelled by mountain train, in canoes, on elephants; encountered spiders and snakes, and may have eaten some; built a village square, constructed a monkey cage; painted a school; taught English; and have had the experience of a lifetime. Oratorians have certainly travelled many miles in the past 150 years, over many countries and continents with, it seems, only Antartica left on which the metaphorical 'Oratory cap' has yet to be seen.

The London Oratory School – *Part III: An Oratory Education*

Left: Pupils on an activity camp at Marchant's Hill, Hindhead, Surrey.

Above: The Duke of Edinburgh's Award participants on expedition in the Brecon Beacons.

Expeditions also feature in The Duke of Edinburgh's Award, which hundreds of pupils are involved in from bronze to gold level, involving journeys from the overnight camp on the South Downs to mountain climbing in south Wales to a trek through the Fish River Canyon in Namibia. Alongside the expedition, regular voluntary service, skill and physical activity are requirements of the Award.

Music and sports have also given many boys and girls the chance to travel and tour. From Australia to the US and all around Europe, rugby teams, choirs and orchestras have flown the Oratory flag. Perhaps the most luxurious school tour ever was that to Japan, where the choir performed in *Carmen* in Tokyo and were provided with accommodation in a five-star hotel.

The Tokyo experience may have been the rare height of luxury, but nonetheless many of the modern-day Oratory travellers expect a level of comfort in their travel that their counterparts of the 1960s, 1970s and 1980s would have only dreamt of. The boys on 'the Riviera Run' in 1979 endured a nine-hour minibus drive in a vehicle that was ultimately written off by French mechanics before the end of the tour, requiring 'Messrs Guinness and Brunwin to empty

11 / *School Journeys*

These were also the days before coaches were subject to rigorous mechanical checks and compulsory seatbelts. On the classics and history departments' Italian tour in 1992, the 'Amalfi Run' lost some of its romantic appeal when experienced in a battered old coach, at speed, clinging precariously to the road with a sheer drop straight into the sea alongside.

This is just one of a multitude of memories which all the pupils and staff who have participated in journeys over the years have amassed, a collection of memories and experiences which stay with them long after they leave school, and in some cases open eyes to new horizons and a lifetime of travel. If it is true that travel broadens the mind then the pupils and staff of The London Oratory School should have broad minds indeed.

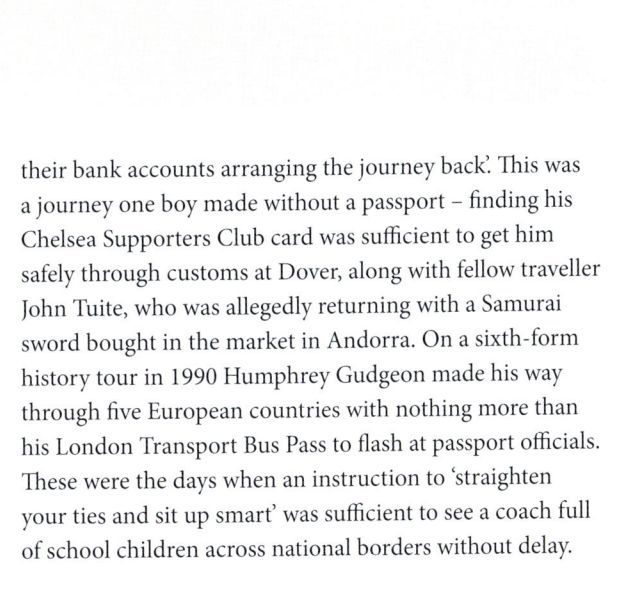

their bank accounts arranging the journey back'. This was a journey one boy made without a passport – finding his Chelsea Supporters Club card was sufficient to get him safely through customs at Dover, along with fellow traveller John Tuite, who was allegedly returning with a Samurai sword bought in the market in Andorra. On a sixth-form history tour in 1990 Humphrey Gudgeon made his way through five European countries with nothing more than his London Transport Bus Pass to flash at passport officials. These were the days when an instruction to 'straighten your ties and sit up smart' was sufficient to see a coach full of school children across national borders without delay.

'The most luxurious school journey', Tokyo 1989.

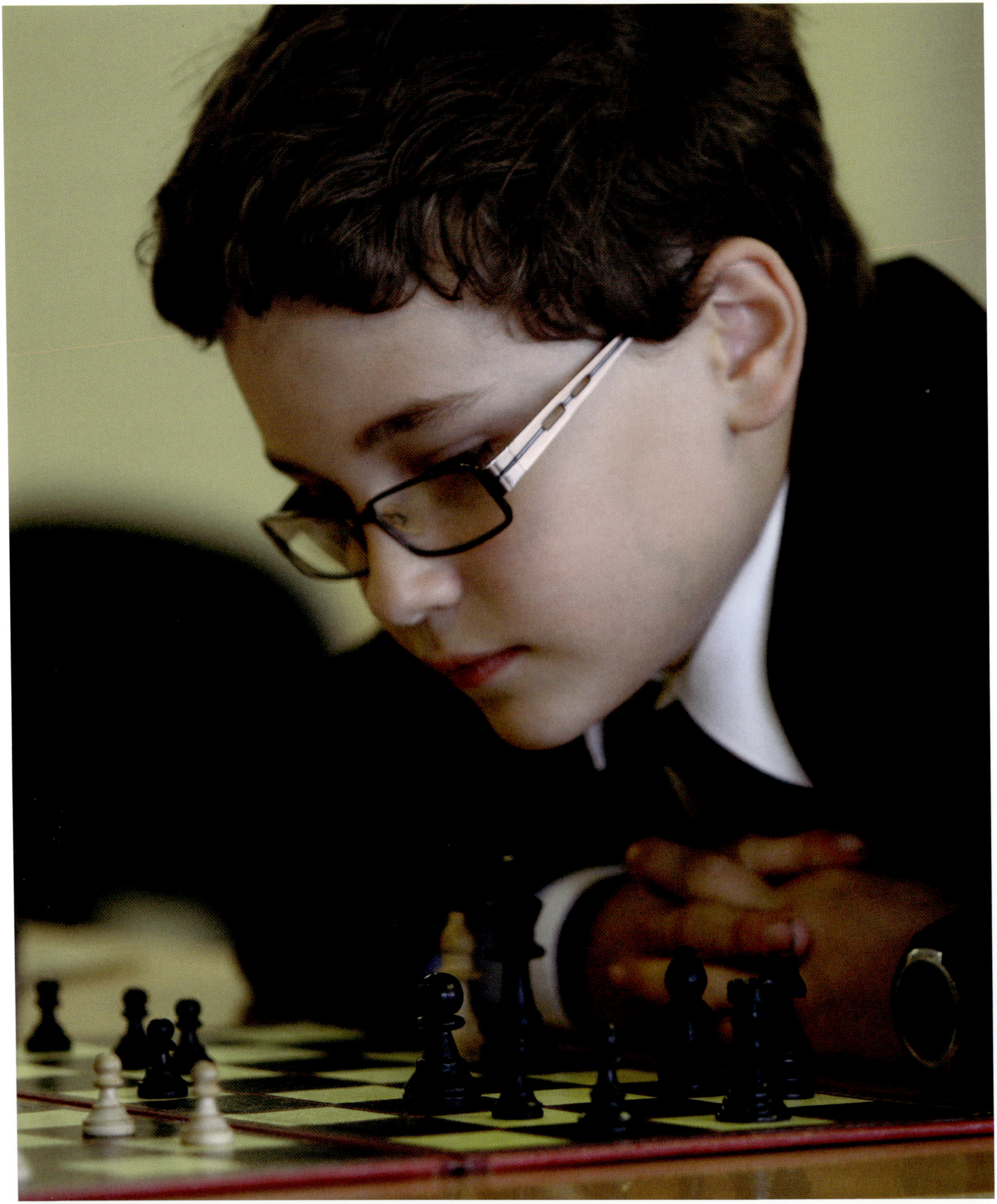

12

Clubs and Societies

The list of clubs and societies offered over the years at The London Oratory School runs literally from A to Z, with activities ranging from angling to zumba. The former enjoyed its heyday in the 1970s, while the latter would be a mystery to boys and girls of earlier generations, and possibly to many of the current era. These two clubs illustrate the scope and changing tastes of the offerings on the Oratory 'extra-curricular menu'.

One of the longest-running clubs is the Chess Club, which has varied in size and strength over the years but has always attracted followers. In the 1930s boys competed against other Central Schools, such as the neighbouring West Kensington Central School, who threw down a challenge in 1931. After an 'excellent tea' the two schools engaged in a tourney, the final result going 10–6 in favour of the Oratory boys. Success was also theirs in a competition a few months later against the Oratory Girls Central School. Much of the enthusiasm for the game came at this time from the inspiration of Mr Locock, the teacher in charge, and under his direction membership grew to 46 boys. The club had formal rules and the benefits of 'this excellent game' were promoted by the Headmaster, Dr Summerbell, as he pointed out that chess, 'besides being a very enjoyable pastime is an excellent training for the mind, and will help in ordinary school work'. An increase in popularity and numbers did not necessarily mean competitive success was maintained in the years ahead, however, and when in June 1936 the boys suffered 'an overwhelming defeat', losing four games to 12 against the girls, Dr Summerbell issued the stern warning 'that the moral to be drawn from such an unfavourable result was the necessity of more regular and intensive practice'. Practice and competition continued until the war brought an interruption to the regular round of tournaments.

The fortunes of the Chess Club continued to rise and fall over the years, often reflecting the enthusiasm for the game amongst teaching staff and pressure from pupils. Michael Barry (fourth form, 1965), in an article in the school magazine, echoed in some respects the sentiments of the Headmaster quoted above, urging fellow pupils to take an interest in chess problems, and remarking that 'chess problems are not only amusing, but help you pass your time in a way that is creative and rewarding'. He assured fellow pupils that 'not only intellectuals solve problems, people of all kinds and classes play chess'. In the 1960s and

Opposite: Chess Club.

Right: The boys and girls of the Oratory Central Schools competed against each other in chess competitions. Here Rosemary Spraggon, representing the girls, ponders her next move, 1939.

PART III : An Oratory Education

1970s the school was again entering chess leagues, and in the 1970s Peter Khan emerged as something of a school champion, being selected to play for Middlesex Schools. After a quiet period the club was strong again in the 1990s with Mr Brandt in charge, and once again players were entered into competitions such as the Times National Schools' Competition. Today's Oratory chess players engage in friendly 'in-house' tournaments. The game of bridge, since its introduction by Mr Spencer in 1967 and its revival by Mr Fitzpatrick in the early 1980s, has found a place alongside the chess players and still attracts a small group of enthusiasts today.

There was a period of time when the Chess Club lost its independent status and was subsumed into the Games Club in the 1980s and early 1990s until rescued by Mr Brandt, with support from Mr Banwell and Mr Dyson. The Indoor Board Games Club – to give it its full formal title – had introduced a wider, and to many a more tempting range of pursuits, for an after-school hour or two. Chess was being challenged by games with names such as Diplomacy, Kingmaker and Colditz, all presented to an eager audience by Mr Isaaks. He did permit members of the Indoor Board Games Club to bring their own games, but 'to be aware that the teacher in charge rarely loses'. Mr Isaaks, former pupil, teacher, Housemaster and current Assistant Head, still enjoys a competition or a wager, and challengers might still do well to remember that 'he rarely loses'. By 1984 the top-choice pursuit at the Games Club was most definitely Subbuteo, the definitive football game. A challenger came on the scene the following year, however, and sparked a Club within the Club as Mr Stableford launched the Dungeons and Dragons section. Generations may be defined by the games they play and to the pupil of today Dungeons and Dragons will seem an archaic pursuit, but a visit to War Hammer Club might lead older and wiser heads to conclude that in essence nothing much changes, and it was probably the case that the Oratory schoolboys of 1863 devised and played their own strategy games, and no doubt future Oratorians will do the same.

Members of the different computer and programming clubs look to the future and seek to stay in command of the latest developments in computer technology and the application of the latest programs. In a history of the school which surveys the past 150 years the Computer Club is but a recent feature. Launched in 1981 under the auspices of Mr Cheal, this was taking school clubs and societies into ground-breaking territory. Commenting on the first year of the club, Mr Cheal was able to report that 'in February a Research Machines 3807 arrived at the school and is now the centre of attraction'. In 1984 the advance of technology was announced with a 'second RM 3802 with mini disks' and 'we also have an RML 4802, a stand-alone system with cassette backing store'. By 1985 the advance of technology seemed unstoppable, as the members of the Computer Club were now meeting in a new room on the third floor with 12 machines. The past 25 years have seen many changes in this area, but there has always been a committed group of enthusiasts keeping abreast of change and using the new technology at their disposal for various ends. The early members of Computer Club were fascinated by Adventure, a game of hidden treasure requiring 'a keen sense of direction and a clear mind to unravel the clues.' Today boys might look at Adventure with derision: in the changing world of computer and digital technology, however, will the next generation of Oratorians look back at today's latest game and scoff, or will we find, as we do in other areas of extra-curricular life, that the medium might change but the games and the boys who play them are actually not that different?

That young people like to make things is a long established fact, and for boys who wish to turn their hand to something practical there is the chance to make things in extra-curricular activities. At the old school in Stewart's Grove the art rooms were the hub of creativity and production. Art, pottery, metalwork, woodwork, technology: these have all been offered as after-school pursuits. In 1947 the school even boasted a Puppet Club.

The early days of Computer Club.

Right: The 'mad scientist', Dr Andrew Szydlo, visits the Science Club.

Below: In 1931 the Science Society visited the HMV Gramophone Works.

Radio Club in the 1960s gave boys the chance to work on a 'push-pull transistor amplifier'. In the Airfix and Model Making Club boys today recreate the battleships and aircraft of past eras, but with scope for the construction of spacecraft and more futuristic models. Those who prefer their model-making on a larger scale work in Technology Club on projects such as constructing a hovercraft and a mechanised buggy.

Camera Club was the forerunner to Photography Club which has now been subsumed into Digital Media. Members of Camera Club in 1931 received instruction in how to avoid particles on their photographs by ensuring no dust was present in the camera. Any dust should be removed with 'a damp cloth or vigorous blowing with a bicycle pump'. Unfortunately the school archive holds no examples of the work of these early camera enthusiasts. By the time the Photography Club was active in the 1980s members were given assignments to carry out-taking photographs at school events. The negatives were developed in the darkroom in the technical department. When the Arts Centre was built in 1991 a dark room was created in the basement, but with rapid changes in camera technology it never really came into use. Photography Club also faded for a time until revived by Mr Flanagan and Mr Kelly in recent times, now with an emphasis on digital processes as well as encouraging pupils to view photography as an art form. Those who prefer moving images can take themselves along to Film Club and enjoy watching and discussing classic films, with occasional popcorn.

There is a long tradition of lectures by distinguished and informed guest speakers at The London Oratory School. At Stewart's Grove boys were treated to lectures, sometimes with accompanying slides, on subjects as varied as 'Light Music by French Composers' and 'The Internal Combustion Engine'. The former was under the auspices of the French Society and the latter under the Science Society. Science Society was a very active organisation in the 1930s, arranging visits to places of scientific interest, usually with an industrial emphasis, in and around London. In 1931 alone visits were made to Price's Candle Works in Battersea, the Gas Light and Coke Company in Fulham, Ironclad Mantles in Earlsfield, the Osram Works in Hammersmith, United Dairies in Willesden, HMV Gramophone Works in Hayes, the Hovis Flour Mill in Vauxhall, the Bryant and May Factory in Bow, Western Electric Talking Films at Bush House and the LGOC Depot at Chiswick. The members of today's Science Society incline to more theoretical and academic subjects, with speakers from universities and research institutes heading the bill. There is also room for spectacle though, and St Philip's Hall is always packed when the 'mad scientist' Dr Andrew Szydlo visits to set off a few explosions after school. Mathematicians have paid homage to Euclid in their own society, the Euclideans, with lecture visits including the Royal Institute lectures on the history of mathematics, featuring academics in costume, enabling sixth formers, and Mr Morgan, former Assistant Head at the school and a mathematician, to avail of a photo opportunity with Isaac Newton.

The Model United Nations organisation is a flourishing activity, with pupils enjoying conferences and debates along the lines of the United Nations.

The History Society and the Newman Society also have a focus on lectures to broaden the mind and to encourage debate. The latter began in 1998 with the aim of encouraging sixth formers to consider issues of a moral and ethical nature, with the occasional tinge of politics. The first speaker to address the Society was the journalist Melanie Phillips. There was also a History Club running in the 1950s which encouraged boys to sign up for events such as 'a visit to places of Catholic interest in the City of London' (Orat. 1955). In more recent times the History Society was established, with Lady Antonia Fraser as the first guest speaker in 2002. It has flourished ever since, with a regular programme of talks on subjects from all periods of history.

Debate generally follows any Society talk, but for those who prefer not to wait until after the event to discuss issues there are the Debating Societies for more immediate and direct debate. In 1965 Mr Dent founded a Literary and Debating Society to encourage sixth formers to engage in debates, play readings and discussions. In one debate the male members of the Society announced that they fully expected their future wives to go out to work (while the men remained at home). When after a lapse in existence the Debating Society was re-founded in 1987, with Mr Johnston, Mr Griffiths and Mrs Franks directing sixth-form debaters in the art of oratory, it is perhaps not surprising to hear that 'the liveliest debate of the year was centred on the motion 'this House believes A Woman's Place is in the Home', with the motion opposed by Bridget Murphy and Emma Heald. Bridget was to go on to a successful legal career (and in a nice turn of events, also went on to marry Dr Howells, who would himself some years later end up as an Assistant Head directing the sixth formers of his wife's old school). The Debating Society continued to thrive and the school entered teams into competitions such as the prestigious Observer Mace Competition. Now the keenest debates take place in the Model United Nations (MUN). This is a format introduced by school Chaplain Father George and involves pupils in formal discussions on real issues that might be placed before the United Nations. Meetings mirror the structure of the UN with its Committees and protocols, as pupils represent different nations. This is truly an international affair, with pupils having taken part in MUN conferences in Qatar, the US and Scotland, as well as many on home soil. There is every possibility that the Oratory MUN will be nurturing a future diplomat or two.

Sport and music, art and drama always feature in extra-curricular life, from the strict training and competitive rugby sessions to the various choirs, from the playing of the School Orchestra to the tentative notes of the junior ensembles, on stage or backstage, there is scope for all.

And what of the Angling Club with which this section opened? The club started in 1975 with 'twenty members and a waiting list' and at first instruction was confined to theory, with practical craft sessions on float making and rod building. It was hoped that opportunity would be found for some weekend fishing. Mr Rooney, now Deputy Headmaster, then aspiring angler, recalls a fishing expedition to Wales under the direction of Mr Raw. The party stayed at Tyn y Berth, scene of many memorable London Oratory journeys, and fished at the top of Cadair Idris, where the young angler 'caught a trout'. Angling Club was but a relatively brief chapter in the 150 years of the school, but recently a revival was investigated. Fulham is not, however, the most convenient starting point for the pursuit and only time will tell whether the Oratory fishermen will ever cast again.

Table tennis attracts a strong following in after-school sessions.

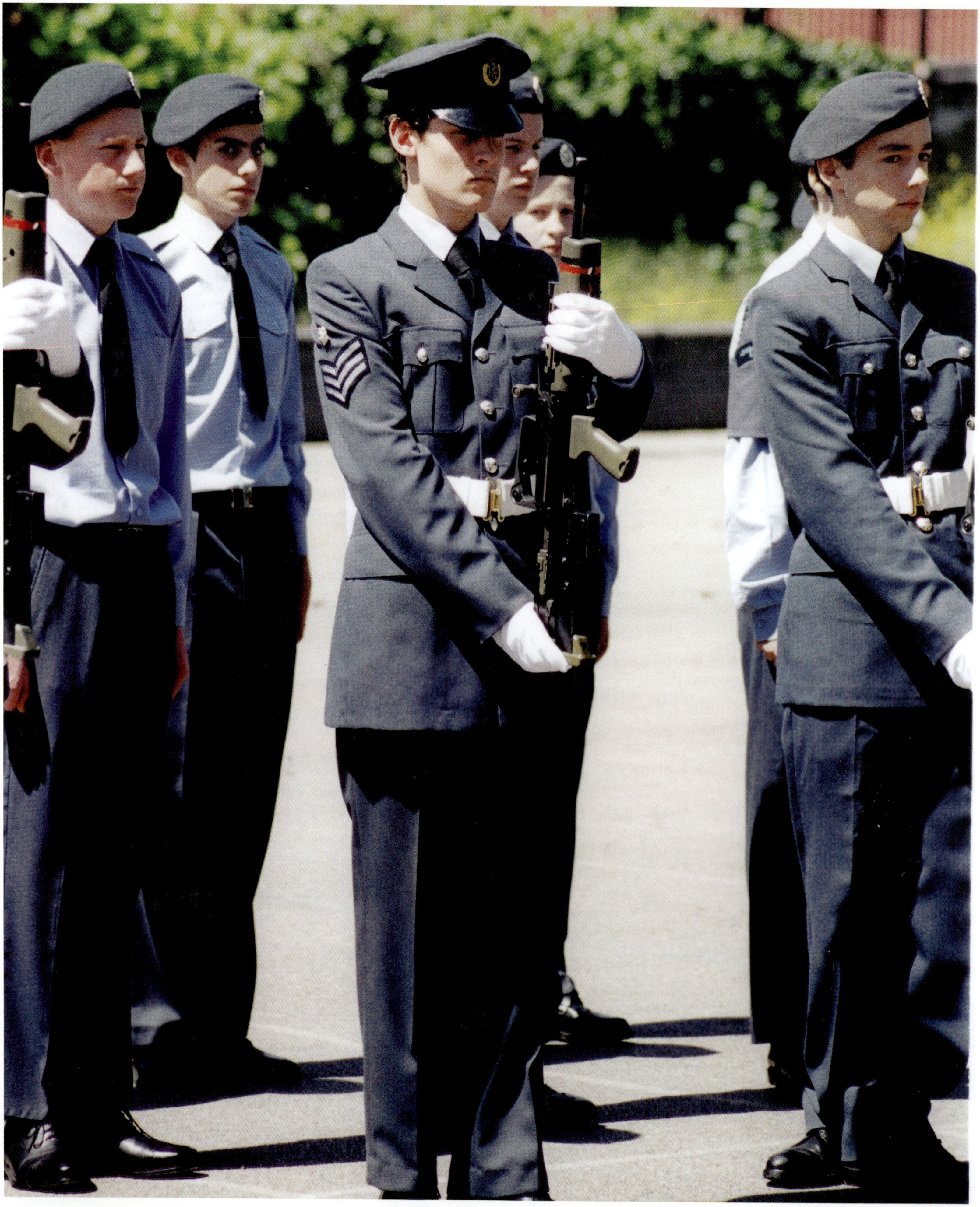

The Cadet Force

The first Oratory Cadet Force with which boys of the school were associated was linked to the Oratory Church and had its origins in the Confraternity of St Joseph and St Philip, an association for boys which was formed in the Oratory Parish in 1866. In 1875 it became the Confraternity of St Joseph and shortly afterwards Father McCall established a marching band for the members of the Confraternity. The Confraternity became the Oratory Boys Brigade in 1903 and in 1911 the Brigade became the Oratory Cadet Corps (OCC). Many boys from the schools joined and participated in Cadet activities.

When the call came for volunteers in the First World War many from the Oratory contingent responded. The company returned to regular routines after the war, and in 1921 Sergeant Major W Hill retired after over 30 years in command. He was succeeded by Sergeant Major A P Manzi, who had himself been a Cadet in the Corps. He had been awarded the Military Medal for his actions in the war and would command great respect from his young charges. The Cadets continued as a Parish organisation throughout the 1920s and 1930s, with weekly drill and sporting activities as well as the Annual Camp.

The Annual Camps were always a highlight in the Cadet Calendar. On a number of occasions in the 1930s the contingent camped near Bognor Regis, and the week would include a route march on Bank Holiday weekend, taking in the streets of the town and attracting the interest of many holidaymakers. The Cadets made a great impression 'with their smart appearance and their splendid steadiness in marching' (PM, x, p146). As well as drills, competitions and sport the Camp of 1939 included a 'Gas Mask Parade' – a sign of things to come, as this would be the last Camp for some time, as by December 1939 the meetings of the

Opposite: The RAF on parade.

Right: Oratory Cadets on camp on the Isle of Man, 1960.

The London Oratory CCF in 2004.

Cadet Corps were suspended; not only did the black-out regulations make it impossible to use the drill hall in the evenings, but most of the boys had been evacuated and the older Cadets had joined up or were being enlisted. Present and former members of the Oratory Cadet Corps did their duty during the war, with boys from the school amongst those whose names would be recorded on the parish War Memorial.

From the start the Cadet Band was an important element of the unit, and this continued in the post-war years. In June 1950 the Band was selected to perform alongside other military bands at the Royal Tournament at Earls Court. As well as marching with the band, Cadets were learning many more skills. Once a week the young soldiers had shooting practice above the Drill Hall at the Duke of York's Barracks in Chelsea. Camps were also a part of Cadet life. Richard Bond recalls the Isle of Man camp of 1960:

The camp on the Isle of Man was an ordeal! We had already had a summer camp the year before in Lydd in Kent and then the Manx adventure and also at some stage a camp in Rainham. We left London by train with several hundred other boys from all over London and spent most of the day and part of the night travelling to Liverpool, where we went by dedicated ferry to the Isle. It was a really great place for us as I don't think many of us had seen so much open country.

In terms of organisation the Oratory Cadet Corps were a Company of the County of London Army Cadet Force, and training came from officers assigned from different regiments. Membership was open to Catholic boys over the age of 13 and the Company met every Friday for weekly parade in the school hall of the Cale Street school, now the Oratory Primary School. The school CCF of today has been part of the Irish Guards since 2010, but maybe current Cadets do not realise that there was an association with the Guards before that time through their connection with the Oratory Cadet Corps. The different Guards' Regiments based in London provided support and training at different points in the Company's history. The Irish Guards and Scots

Left: Oratory cadet, Richard Bond on camp in 1960.

Right: Lieutenant Colonel Thorn at his farewell parade in 1996. Captain Paul Belcourt, Head of School 1983, is on the left and Mr Peter Harvey is on the right.

Guards, along with the Grenadier Guards and Coldstream Guards, all gave instruction in drill and physical training, as well as providing training for the Band and assisting at camps. Although not a regimental corps there were times when the Oratory Cadets might have been mistaken for such, as for many years they were unofficially known as the Munster Fusiliers (when Father Munster was the priest responsible for the Cadets) and then as the Leicester Regiment (when they were Father Leicester's charge). When Father Tighe took over in 1960, however, no apposite epithet was coined.

Staff from the school assisted with the running of the Cadets, with Mr Kelly, Mr Carr, Mr Crowley and Mr Burns all participating in camps in the 1930s. Leading by example, however, was Mr Monaghan as Commanding Officer. Mr Monaghan had taught for ten years in the Parish Junior School before the Second World War and was with the school during the evacuation to Cambridge. After the war he moved across to teach in the Boys Central School, becoming Deputy Headmaster from 1950 until his retirement in 1958. He had a great interest in sport and encouraged the pupils in a range of activities. He promoted boxing and was a judge for the London Schools Boxing Association. He first became associated with the Oratory Cadets in 1926, succeeding Captain Angel as Commanding Officer in 1927. He continued in that capacity until 1952, when he became Area Commander of the North West Division. As the Oratory Cadet Company fell within his division he maintained links with the contingent for some years afterwards. When he died in 1968 a report in *The Chelsea News* paid tribute to his work with the Oratory Cadet Corps.

Throughout the Stewart's Grove years there were a steady number of boys in the Oratory Cadet Force who went on to a career in the Forces. For those who did not pursue a military career, however, there was still much to look back on and benefit from as a consequence of their years in the OCC.

When the school moved to Seagrave Road the connection with Oratory Parish organisations would inevitably not be quite so closely intertwined, and while there might still have been some boys in the Oratory Cadet Corps there were nothing like as many as there had once been.

Meanwhile it was not too long before The London Oratory School in Seagrave Road had its own Cadet force. It was something of a chance encounter that gave rise to the school Cadets. John McIntosh was, in the early 1970s, responsible for the Youth Centre based in the school. One evening Roy Thorn, Officer Commanding of a Cadet Unit based at the Territorial Army Centre near Putney Bridge, called into the school when the Youth Centre was in session as he hoped to make use of the welding equipment in the workshop to carry out a mechanical repair to his Cadets' vehicle. This became the beginning of an association between the Youth Centre and the Cadets, with some combined activities and sharing of facilities. When a little time later the Cadets were facing eviction from their headquarters it was not surprising that Roy Thorn should approach John McIntosh about the possibility of using the school premises. Arrangements were made and The London Oratory Cadet Force was born. What had been a TAVRA-operated unit was in due course transferred to the Royal Green Jackets. In 1989 the LOS Army Cadet Force gained their own separate headquarters at school, Peninsula Lodge, or more colloquially 'the Cadet Hut', at the far end of the playground. The benefits of having their own building were considerable; the LOS Cadets were always large in number with at times over 100 members, the largest CCF in a state school, and now their identity and organisation within the school were bolstered with their own HQ.

In 1994 the ACF became a CCF; now the airforce blue would line up with the army green on parade on the playground every Friday. Mr Sullivan, Head of Classics, assumed command of the new section. Flying became a regular part of Cadet life, and wider training opportunities and greater resources for both sections were on offer.

Over the years a steady number of pupils have gone on to careers in the Army or RAF or have continued

The London Oratory School – *Part III: An Oratory Education*

their training with the TA. Paul Belcourt (Head of School 1983) served with the regular forces in the first Iraq War, Ollie Sanandres (1992–4) with the TA. George Cowdry (1994–2001), Tom Cowdry (1996–2005), Max Railing (1998–2005) and Daniel Hickey (1994–2001) are amongst those who have served in Afghanistan. Fergus Atkinson O'Sullivan (Head of School 2005) is with the RAF, as is Jamie Meighan (1989–96), who is working in Intelligence. Tom Wood (1990–7) is an army doctor, as is Tom DeBurgh (2001–5), and Chris Keri Nagy (1986–94) was with the Parachute Regiment. Martin Woytyna (1999–2006) got his introduction to flying in the CCF, has since qualified as a commercial pilot, and now runs his own ACF Cadet Unit. These former pupils provide examples of the opportunities opened up by the experience of life in the Oratory CCF; these and many others were first introduced to service life in the school Cadet force. The roll continues and year on year boys from the school are awarded Army or RAF scholarships when they leave school. There are at present nearly 100 members of The London Oratory Cadet Force, and of these 40 are with the RAF.

In 1996, on the retirement of Lieutenant Colonel Thorn, command of the CCF passed to Lieutenant Colonel Western and then in 1998 to Squadron Leader Sullivan, who remained in command of an excellent unit until 2010. Squadron Leader Chandler (aka Mrs Chandler, School Estate Manager, or Ma'am) assumed command and continues to lead a fine body of men. Throughout all this time the unit has benefited enormously from the services of Major Bill Coombes MBE as Officer Commanding of the Army section of the CCF. The Major (and his dogs) have had a great influence on the organisation and training of the Cadets, and in his other role as workshop technician Major Coombes is busy dispensing resources and no-nonsense advice to staff and pupils in the design technology department.

Over the years the range of activity and opportunity brought by the CCF has been considerable. It is summed up in the opening paragraph of the 1993 *Oratorian* report: 'rock climbing, canoeing, mountain biking, pony trekking, hill walking, skiing, night exercises, military training, assault courses and rifle shooting, just some of our many activities'. The boys in today's CCF enjoy a wide range of experience and receive some valuable training. They learn 'Skill-at-Arms' using a Cadet version of the SA80, fieldcraft such as camouflage and concealment; cooking; patrolling; map-and-compass skills; drill; leadership; self-reliance and teamwork. Cadets must keep their kit clean and tidy, with emphasis on shiny boots. In theory this routine should transfer to civilian life, though whether the boys' teachers and mothers are always convinced that this is so is open to question.

Left: Major Coombes, Officer Commanding of the Army section.

Below: Flight Lieutenant Chandler and RAF cadets, 2005.

152

Longmoor in Surrey is the regular base for Oratory Cadet camps.

The CCF camps at Longmoor in Surrey became, and still are, a regular feature in Oratory Cadet life, with a camp usually occurring each half term. A coach full of Cadets leaves school on Friday evening for a weekend of camp life: military training, outdoor activities and ration packs. Under Lieutenant Colonel Thorn an element of fine dining also featured, at least on the officers' and staff tables, with a sit-down dinner served for all on the Saturday evening. Mr Sullivan remembers one weekend when returning from camp on the Sunday afternoon the coach broke down on the outside lane at the junction of Fulham Palace Road and Lillie Road. This was in the days when for security reasons military uniform was not worn in public and the Cadets, with 44 rifles in hand, were certainly not able to walk the relatively short journey back to school. A replacement coach was called and the coach company sent the only available vehicle: an open-top double-decker bus. The rifles had to be transferred from one vehicle to another as discreetly as possible, to avoid panic and invasion fear on the streets of London! The weapons were stored on the lower deck of the bus, and Cadets sat on the open top deck in pouring rain, singing 'we're all going on a summer holiday' as they made the short journey back to school.

Christmas Camp, with full Christmas dinner served in the mess followed by presentations and promotions, has always been a highlight of the CCF year. Once Mr Dyson volunteered to relieve Mr Sullivan of chef duties and to cook the Christmas dinner. This was in exchange for Mr Sullivan agreeing to take Mr Dyson's Under 16 rugby team to Trinity School for a fixture. Mr Dyson arrived at camp only to find that all the ovens in the cookhouse but one were broken. Undaunted he still managed to rustle up full Christmas Dinner with all the trimmings, and only two hours late.

As well as weekend camps for the Cadets, each summer there is the week-long annual camp. Mr Sullivan recalls the impression made on camp by the Oratory contingent the year sixth former Joseph Cooney was in charge of drill; the soldiers in the guardroom came out in amazement to watch the Oratorians being marched out of camp on their way to Sunday Mass.

Memories of skills learned, of night exercises, of survival and challenge abound. For Pierce Ferris there is the recollection of disaster averted when in 1996 he backed a forklift truck into a £16 million Jaguar fighter aircraft; fortunately he just missed clipping a wing. It seems Oratory pupils ought to have been kept away from Jaguars, as on another occasion at the same base Dean Williams

The London Oratory School – Part III: An Oratory Education

managed to press a red button which set off the emergency fire extinguisher and filled the plane with foam. The fact that RAF Coltishall is now closed and Jaguars have been withdrawn from service is, of course, in no way connected to these events.

In 2010, after the Royal Green Jackets were assimilated into the Rifles, The London Oratory School CCF was attached to the Irish Guards. The official adoption was a memorable day in the unit's history and brought the unusual sight of Conmael, Irish wolfhound and mascot of the Irish Guards, in attendance at the service in the school Chapel that formed part of the day's ceremonies.

The CCF also takes part in competitions against contingents from other schools. The London Oratory unit have acquitted themselves very well over the years. The Celer et Audax (Swift and Bold) competition to find the best Royal Green Jacket Cadet company was, from 2003, a chance for Oratory boys to demonstrate their prowess in a range of military skills, which they did with considerable success. In just the second year of entering the competition the eight LOS Cadets who represented the contingent won six individual awards and came first overall in the contest, which was held at Stowe School. It is perhaps not surprising to note that three of these Cadets, Matthew Hickey, George Cowdrey and Max Railing, later went on to careers in the regular Army. The victory was repeated the following year – quite an achievement, and as the only state school in the competition the Oratory boys showed that they could more than hold their own against what some might have regarded as more elite contingents.

In 2012 eight members of the unit took part in the Irish Guards Military Skills Competition, at Magilligan, Northern Ireland. Cadet Colour Sergeant Jack Wells of LOS CCF was voted Best Cadet and the contingent also completed the march 20 seconds faster than any other team. Despite having never entered before the Oratory Cadets had two trophies. The runners-up in the entire competition were The London Oratory School CCF, just 23 points behind the winners, Ballygowan ACF.

Impressive individual endeavour has over the years earned for some Cadets the opportunity to take part in activities beyond the unit itself. In 1991 members of the Cadets spent a week in Gibraltar with the Royal Green Jackets. Cadets were recruited for a six-week Leadership and Survival Course in the Rockies, Daniel Parish (1991) and Thomas Ward (1994) both being awarded the opportunity. In 1992 Nick Hayes joined Operation Raleigh on a trip to Borneo.

The CCF is regularly inspected, with biennial inspections providing an opportunity for the school to see the Cadets on Parade and for the members to receive a distinguished guest. In 2010 it was Major General Sir William Cubitt, Regimental Lieutenant Colonel of the Irish Guards, and in 2012 it was Group Captain Stuart Jack. Another proud occasion each year is Patronal Festival, when the CCF forms the Guard of Honour for the Principal Guest at the Oratory Church; these have included a Cardinal and a Prime Minister, as well as other distinguished public figures. As yet the school contingent cannot quite match the old Oratory parish company, who could boast having been reviewed by Monsignor Pacelli (later Pope Pius XII), and by Lord French (Commander in Chief of the British

Left: Conmael, Mascot of the Irish Guards, at the school in 2010.

13 / *The Cadet Force*

Special days for the CCF (clockwise from top) – Biennial Inspection 2012; meeting Guards' Patron, The Duchess of Cambridge on St Patrick's Day 2012; and at Buckingham Palace for a Garden Party to mark 150 years since Cadets were first established.

Expeditionary Force in 1914). In 1960 it was an eminent Oratory parishioner, Field Marshall Sir Francis Festing, Chief of the Imperial General Staff, who conducted the review. He declared himself honoured to be inspecting the same unit that the late Pope Pius XII had inspected when he was Papal Legate to England.

The history of the school CCF is indeed an interesting one, having its origins in two different units and establishing itself as a distinct, strong and successful contingent. As the school enters its 150th year the CCF has much to look back on and much to look forward to as the unit continues to prosper in its association with the Irish Guards.

155

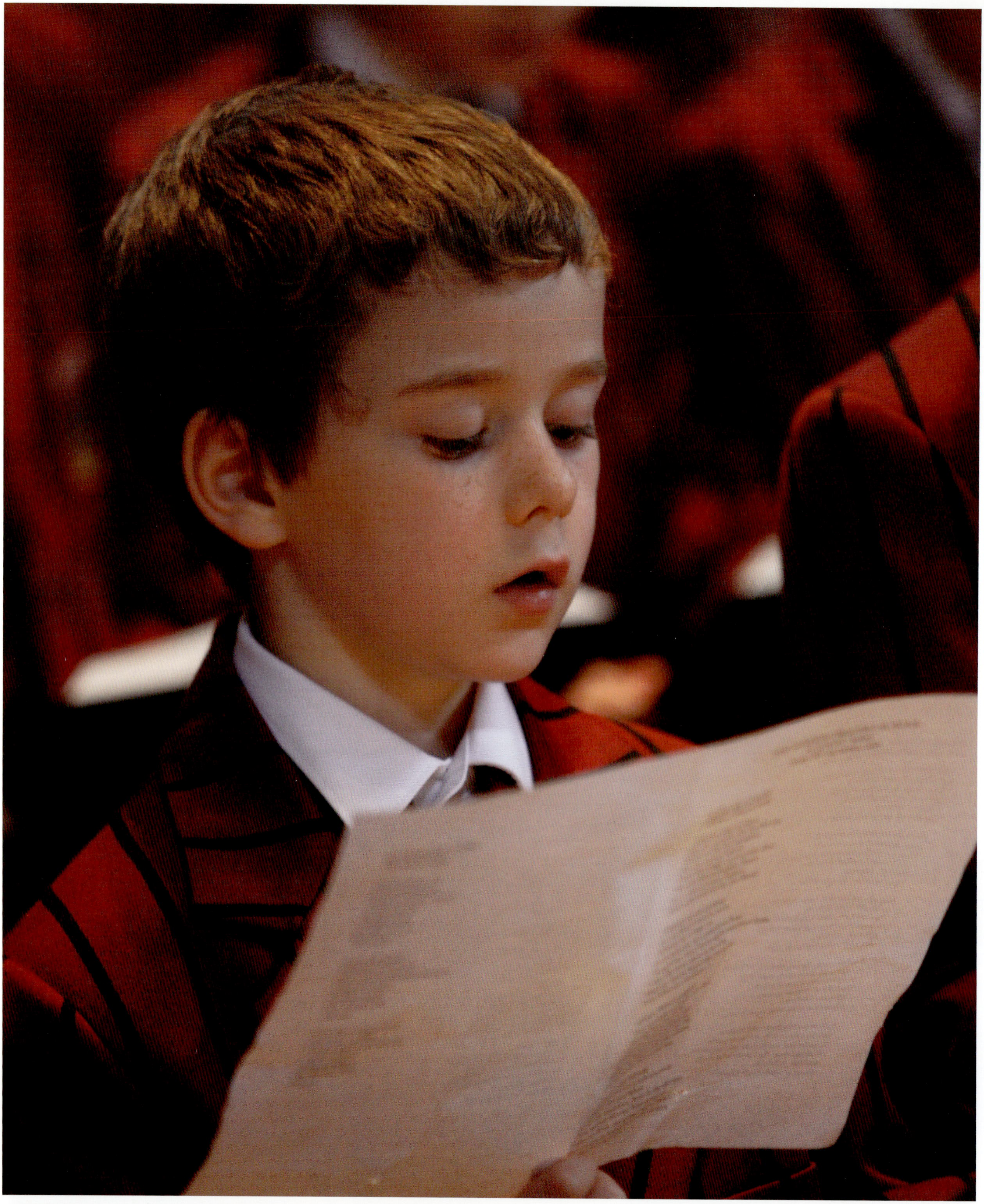

14

Respice Finem:
Look to the End

Opposite: The beginning of an Oratory school career.

Below: The heading from the school newsletter announcing the adoption of the new school motto.

By 1932 the school showed many of the distinctive features which characterise The London Oratory School of today: the religious and educational philosophy, the strong link between home and school, the House system, the uniform and *The Oratorian* were there in some form, but as yet there was no school motto. A competition was announced with a prize of 2s 6d offered to whoever, 'in the opinion of the Headmaster, composes the most suitable' school motto. Over 50 entries were received and after much deliberation the Headmaster settled upon *Respice Finem*.

When the winning motto was announced the rough translation was given as 'remember the end', with the comment that this was 'a principle well worth putting into practice both in work and in life generally'. Often translated as 'look to the end', the motto has many applications: in the practical sense it drives ambition and reinforces the school's philosophy of asking pupils to be the best they can be in all that they do; in the spiritual it is an exhortation to pupils to always remember the importance of their faith in this life and in looking to the next. The 2/6 prize was never claimed, as the entrant 'unfortunately omitted to add his or her name and address' to the entry, so we do not know to whom we owe the credit for the motto which Oratorians for over 80 years have made their own. We would not dare suspect the Headmaster of a 'fix', so it seems we remain forever in ignorance as to the identity of the 'winner' of the school motto competition.

LOOKING FORWARD

As the school celebrates 150 years the work of the Oratory Fathers, the governors, teachers, support staff and pupils of the school goes on and the mission for which the school was first established – to educate Catholic boys from across London – is still the purpose of the school. In the words of current pupils, 'At The London Oratory School you are taught a wide range of subjects with excellent teachers, providing an all round Catholic education,' in a 'fun and friendly place'. All in all this sounds like a good mix for a happy and successful future.

PART III · An Oratory Education

The London Oratory School – Part III: An Oratory Education

Choristers in the organ loft of the Oratory Church.

> "Reflecting on my time at the school really made me realise just how much has happened in seven years; as clichéd as it sounds, the school has the job of overseeing the transformation of boys into men, and if I can say anything at all about my experience, it is that I have matured not only in age, but also in mind and spirit. The school is much more than just a place for lessons, and the experience I have had has given me life-long friends, a solid academic grounding, and seven years to look back on and miss when life becomes much more complicated!
>
> Kim Slim, Head of School 2012–13

THE SCHOOL SONG

The school song was first sung in the 1950s. Although no official record remains regarding its composition, it seems that the words were written by Latin master Mr Hooper, and Mr Myerscough and Mr Handyside of the music department had the task of setting the words to music.

Today the school song is sung at the Oratory Church on the occasion of the annual Academic Mass to mark the new school year each September and at the Patronal Festival in May.

Quam bonum est	*How good it is to lead a life*
In hac fraternitate	*Of joy in this fraternity*
Vitam jucundam agere!	*O Philip Father in our strife*
Te duce nostro	*For victory we look to thee*
Philippe Pater	
In vitae proelio	
Vincemus.	
Vivat academia!	*Long live the school and masters all*
Sint tibi professores	*Who lead us in our youthful days*
Qui nos in juventute dirigant.	*O Philip Master help us all*
Magister noster	*To work forever to thy praise*
Philippe Bone	
Nos in operibus	
Adjuva!	
Vivat Rex! Vivat Grex!	*Long live the King, long flourish the flock*
Potens in caritate	
Vivat et floreat in saecula!	*Whose strength doth lie in charity*
Legifer noster	*O Philip Ruler make thy stock*
Philippe Iuste	*In heaven always to dwell with thee*
Fac nos in patria	
Vivere!	

> For me, like so many other Old Oratorians, The London Oratory School holds many stories and has become a special place. Our shared stories create a picture of rich traditions in work and play, of tremendous vibrancy and dynamism, a strong sense of community centred on the extraordinary vision of life that faith in Jesus Christ offers to us all. Along with the many changes since our establishment in 1863, the common threads of our Christian, Catholic, Oratorian ethos run through the years.
>
> The London Oratory School will celebrate its 150th anniversary in 2013. The school is busy making plans for what will be a year of celebration, one that not only looks back on a tremendous heritage, but one that looks forward towards an exciting future as it builds a new legacy for the years ahead.
>
> As with our predecessors there are numerous challenges ahead that have to be met and overcome, especially those that challenge the school in creating an authentic Catholic ethos in an increasingly secular society. The signs however are exciting: the school is thriving, and admission applications, academic results in public examinations and performance in sport, arts, drama and music have reached new heights for the school. The Old Oratorian Association is gaining momentum and our community has a wonderful vision for our future. A School Strategic Plan emphasising new growth has been established and we have commenced a major capital redevelopment and refurbishment of the school.
>
> If the founders of our school could reflect on us today, I am sure they would be pleased that we are continuing to meet our challenge of *Respice Finem*.
>
> David McFadden, Headmaster, 2013

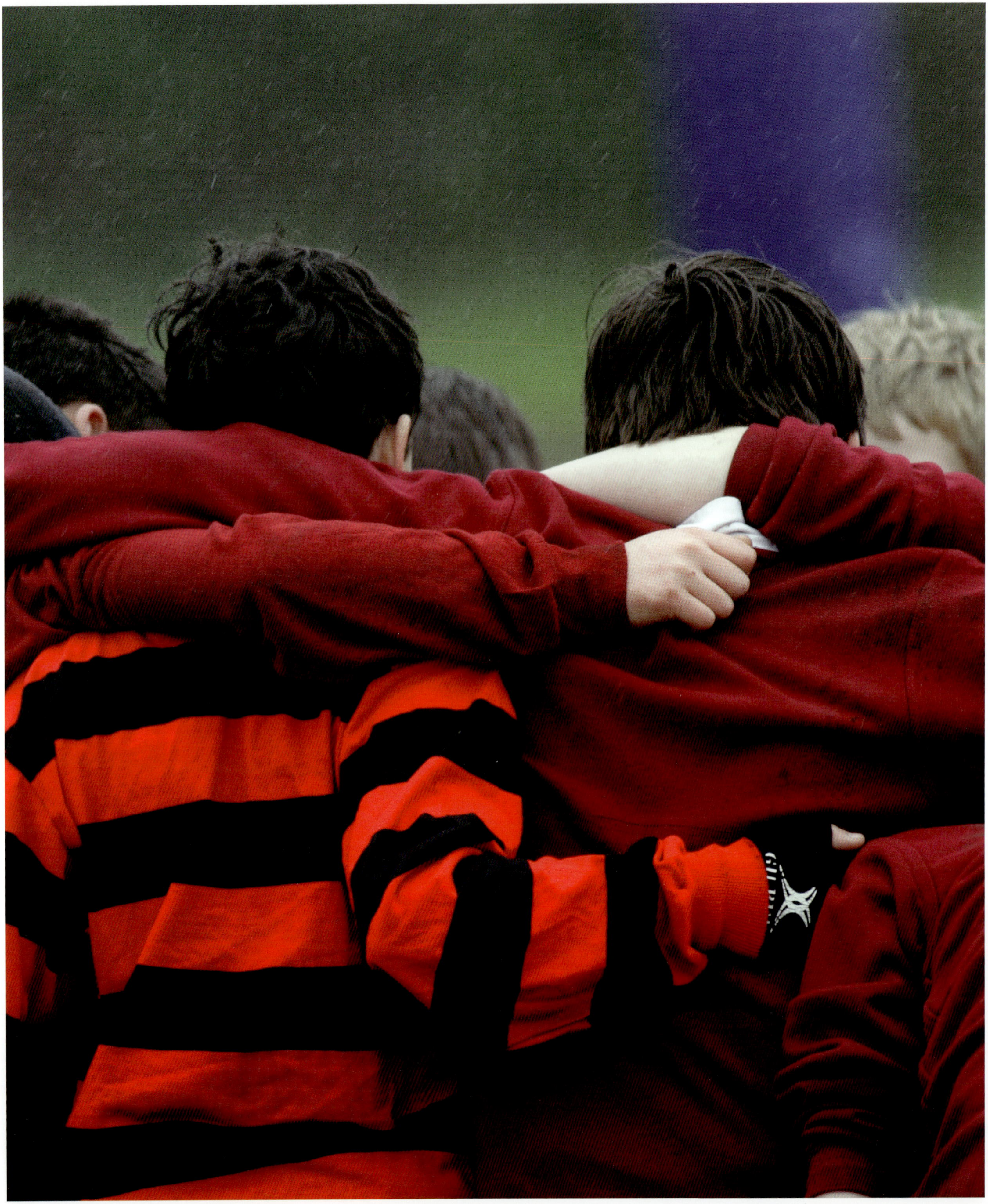

Heads of School
since moving from Stewart's Grove to Seagrave Road

1970–1	Bob Kibble	1985–6	Marc Dodd	2000–1	Harry Dromey
1971–2	Christopher Burton	1986–7	Shane McCabe	2001–2	Christopher Marcel
1972–3	Eamonn Malone	1987–8	Mark Lucas	2002–3	Neill Cahill
1973–4	Johnson Ogiste	1988–9	Peter Marden	2003–4	Jonathan Casey
1974–5	Sean O'Donovan	1989–90	Luigi Chu	2004–5	David Howell
1975–6	Vincent O'Brien	1990–1	James Hanley	2005–6	Fergus Atkinson O'Sullivan
1976–7	Michael McDonald	1991–2	Mark Thomas	2006–7	Alistair Adams
1977–8	Anthony Hammond	1992–3	Sanu de Lima	2007–8	William Jerry
1978–9	John Wade	1993–4	Christopher Keri-Nagy	2008–9	Joseph Steptoe
1979–80	Carlo Ferrario	1994–5	Steven Kalynuk	2009–10	Joseph Gibbs
1980–1	John Reilly	1995–6	Anthony O'Connell	2010–11	Nicholas Votier
1981–2	Franco Porcella	1996–7	Alex Obreja	2011–12	Conor Godsall
1982–3	Paul Belcourt	1997–8	Mihalis Walsh	2012–13	Kim Slim
1983–4	Martin Saunders	1998–9	Louis Cadier	2013–14	Peter Morris
1984–5	John Botia	1999–2000	Cliff Andrade		

A reunion of Heads of School and staff in 2007.

List of Subscribers

This book was supported by the generosity of the subscribers listed below.

Maksymilian Adach	2004–11	Eleanor Bocarro	2005–07	Stephen Carter	2010–	Jonathan Crisp	1998–2005
Peter Adams	2007–	Elliot-Geoffrey Bocarro	2003–10	Thomas Carter	2012–	Mary Crompton	1982–2002
Simon Adams	2010–	George Bodakh	2000–07	Carlo Caruso	2010–	Daniel Steven Cruise	2010–
Fernando Aguilera Rodriguez	2008–	Edward Boden	1996–2007	Giorgio Caruso	2007–	Jerome Curran	1968–75
Gonzalo Aguilera Rodriguez	2009–	James Boden	1996–2005	Kirsty Carvalho	2012–	Toby Curran	2010–
Caitano and Beryl Albuquerque		Richard Boden	1998–	Joe Carvill	1969–82	Christopher Curtin	1967–73
Kirsty Alderton	2007–	Stephen Harold James Bond	1991–7	Stewart Casey	2005–12	David Cuss	1979–84
Edward Allaker	2011–	Patrick Bone	2006–13	Caolan J Cassidy	2006–13	Helen D'Amico (née McGrath)	1986–9
Sebastian Allon	2010–	Niall Bones	2011–	Eligia Cattini		Mario D'Amico	1986–9
Christopher Allsden	1989–97	Margaret Bourke (née Jennings)	1986–8	Victor Cattini		Juan Dagorret-Martínez	2011–
Duchess Kerrol Williams Alonga		Finn Bowcott	2008–	Michael Caulfield	1977–83	Alan Daly	1959–66
Michael Abure Alonga	2011–	Redmond Bowcott	2008–	Filipe A Cerqueira	1993–2000	Matthew Daly	2008–
Olivia Anderson-Davies	2013–	Conor Elliott Boyle	2005–12	Paula Chandler	2002–	Stephen Daly	
Joshua W R Andrews	2011–	Kieran Breen	1979–86	Daniel Chapman	2006–13	Benjamin Daly-Jones	
Jeremy Ansbro	2009–	Thomas Breen	1979–86	In Memory of John Chater	1874–1900	Noah Daly-Jones	
Simon J Ashenden	1988–	Julen Brennan-Garmendia	2013–	In Memory of Robert Wilfrid Chater		J E Darling	
Liam Aslin	2012–	Colm Brito	2013–		1882–92	Arminas Daujotas	2006–13
Maclyn Augustine	2008–	Gonzague Brochard	2012–	Brian Cheesman	1944–50	Ben Davidson	2012–
Marcellus Augustine	2010–	Anthony Brophy	1968–75	Adrian Edward Siu Kei Cheung	2013–	Mr and Mrs M Davies	
Michelle Austin-Peden	1982–4	Evan Bryant	2007–10	Massimo Chiocca	2012–	Adam de Almeida	2008–
Cormac Auty	2009–	George Bryant	2007–10	Minu Choi		Daniel de Almeida	2002–
Callum Ayres	2012–	Mark Buchinger	1997–2004	Hungta Chu		Santiago de Barry	1973–9
Daniel Ayres	2012–	Paul Buchinger	2008–	Lucia Chu		Alessandro de Besi	2002–08
Melanie Bacchi	2000–02	Felicity Burling	2001–03	Luigi Chu	1983–90	Luca de Besi	2000–07
Charlotte Marie Bailey	1997–9	Magnus Burling	2006–	Michele Chu	1980–7	Matteo de Besi	2000–07
The Balacky Family	2004–	Daniel Burnand	1995–2002	Konrad Chudzik	2008–	Pietro de Besi	2004–11
The Balfour Family	2000–12	Joshua Burnand-Witter	2012–	Oliver Bradley Clark	2005–	Adrien de Germiny	2006–11
Gianluca Ballarini	2011–	Michael Burrows	2009–	Tiernan James Eoin Clarke	2011–	Alban de Germiny	2008–13
Brian Bamford	1965–95	Joseph John Bushell	2012–	Tomás Joseph Clarke	2009–	Felix de Meeûs d'Argenteuil	2008–
Roman Bannock	2007–	Peter Augustine Bushell	2008–	Antonio Clegg	2013–	George R F de Voil	2000–11
Zygmunt Bannock	2009–	Anthony B Byrne	2010–	Wendy Coakley	1985–2012	Charles Dean	2011–
Daniel R Bariente	1984–91	Ciaran J Byrne	2008–	Maximilian Cogan	2007–	Tobias Thomas Quezado Deckker	2004–
Maximiliano Barria Rodriguez	2009–	Oisin Eugene Patrick Debarra Byrne		Tamsin Cogan	2010–12	Ray Delaney	1947–
Henry Barrington	2010–		2010–	Edward Collier	2007–	Jules P Deruelle	2012–
Jonathan Barrington	2006–13	Camilla Cadier	2000–02	Declan Collins	1985–92	Eilis Devaney	2001–
Will Barrington	2008–	Louis Cadier	1992–9	Fergus Collins	1983–90	Benjamin Dickens	2011–
David Barry	2013–	A S Campbell	2012–	Patrick Collins	1964–70	Samuel Dickens	2009–
Patrick W M K Barton	2011–	E G Campbell	2012–	Liam Connery	2007–	Milo R H Dickins	2003–
Finn Bengtsson	2008–	Christopher Capon	1983–90	Dylan Connolly	2012–	William Diffey	2012–
Lukas Bengtsson	2010–	Pat Carberry	1974–81	Linus Cooper	2013–	Luca Digrandi	2012–
Max Bengtsson	2010–	Euan Carr	2012–	Milo Cooper	2013–	Matteo Digrandi	2009–
Simon Bennett	1982–9	Finuala Carr	1982–4	Anne Couch	1971–3, 1987–2004	Daniel James Docherty	2011–
Luca Bentivoglio	2012–	Michael Carr	1977–84	The Coulter Family		Marc Dodd	1979–86
Rachelle Bernardino	2012–	Denise Carrere	2011–13	Finlay Coward	2010–	Christopher Doig	2007–
Hunde Berri	2013–	Martin Carrere	2011–13	Ben Cowdry	1995–2002	Michael Doig	2010–
Zoe Bickell	2004–	Andrea Carroll	2004–	George Cowdry	1996–2003	Robert Doig	2005–
Jose A Blanco	1992–9	Denis Carroll	1970–8	Tom Cowdry	1994–2001	Geoffrey Doran	1981–7
Alexander J A Blaney	2009–	Laurence Carroll	2001–12	Joseph Cracknell	2007–	Alex Doyle	2007–
Benedict T O Blaney	2013–	Cliona Carson		Matthew Cracknell	2004–	Thomas Doyle	2007–
Linus C P Blaney	2012–	Joshua Xavier Carson	2010–	William Cracknell	2002–13	Philip Duffy	
Simon Blyth	1995–	Anthony Carter	2007–	Tom Craven	2006–13	Lorenzo Dufour	2012–13

Oisín Duggan-Dennehy	2010–	Luke Gompertz	2003–	Abbie Hopkins-Flanagan	2011–13	William Kramer	2006–
Laurence Dynes	2010–	Oliver Gompertz	2001–08	Tom Hopkins-Flanagan	2004–11	Tomasz J Krzyzewski	1986–93
Tim Edge		The Gonzalez Metello de Napoles Family		Benjamin Hovey	2012–	Alexander Kummelstedt	2005–12
Olivia Edwards	2011–13	Jessica Gooch		Gary Howells	2008–	Eric Kummelstedt	2007–
Sarah Jane Ellis (née Cahill)	1996–8	Dominic Goodall	2006–13	Fabian Hubner-Clarke		Roberto Kummelstedt	2012–
James Philip Emery	2011–	H K Goodlife		Miles Hubner-Clarke	2013–	Santina La Porta	1987–9
Thomas More Emery	2008–	Jamie Gosnell	2008–	Tobias Hubner-Clarke	2011–	Adrian Laing	1990–2001
Lola Epiphaniou Louca	1950–6	Benedict Grady	2003–09	Ann Hughes (née Walsh)	1983–5	Alastair Lane	2009–
Jessica Evan-Hughes	2009–11	Dylan Philip Grant	2012–	Edward Hughes	2009–	Fionnuala Lane	2012–
Thomas Evan-Hughes	2007–	Les Gray	1937–9	Jack Daniel Hughes	2012–	Jonathan Lau	2010–
Felix Faillace	2008–	Vincent Gray	2011–	Simon Hunt	2008–	Kieran Laurie	2011–13
Mateus Fairbank	2008–	Adam Green	2000–11	Philip Hurtado	2009–	Ben Lavin	2009–
Matthew Falcone	2004–	James Green	2003–	Daniel Jan Hutton	2012–	Tobiloba Lawson	2012–
Nicholas Falcone	2001–12	Roy Griffiths	1972–2000	Elizabeth Hyams	2010–12	Jack Lawton	2008–
Olamide Fayankinnu	2008–	Joseph Anthony Griso Dryer	2011–	Sebastian Hyams	2003–	Tom Lawton	2005–12
Martin Fedenczak Garcia	2010–	James Gross	2006–13	M Isbell	2007–	Jordan Le Blanc-Burrows	2009–
Jeffrey Roque Fernandes	2007–	Katy Gross	2009–11	Nicholas James	2009–13	Jack Lee	2008–
Beltrán Field	2007–	Harley Hachem	2006–13	Oliver Jarvis	2000–07	James Lees	2007–
Liam Fitchett	1997–2004	Zack Hachem	2008–	Andrzej Jastrzebski		M-A Lees	
Cormac Flahive	2006–13	Gregory Mario Hadeed	2011–	Renata Jastrzebski		Grazyna Lewinska	1961–7
Declan Flahive	2008–	Fintan Hall	2012–	Filip Nykiel-Jastrzebski	2011–	Bernard (Bill) Liengme	1949–57
Lorcan Flahive	2012–	Ciáran Hallbery	2013–	Piotr Nykiel-Jastrzebski	2011–	Raymond Little	1985–2001
Paul Flanagan	1986–	Christopher Mark Halsey	2007–	Martyn Jenkins	2005–12	Gabrielle Loader	2011–13
Richard Flanagan	1999–2006	James Michael Halsey	2009–	Angus Johnston	2010–	Anita Lobo	
Peter Flannery	2000–05	Rod Hamilton	1952–8	Kathleen Johnston	2007–09	Edward Lobo	
Emma Flynn	2010–12	Thomas Hankin	1999–2006	Patrick Johnston	2006–13	Russell Lobo	2011–
Matthew Flynn	2005–12	Dylan Hanley	2009–	Paul Johnston	1980–2001	Tom Longfellow	2005–
James Foley	2008–	Max Harcombe	2006–13	Edouard Joiris de Caussin	2012–	Daniel Lord	2008–
Joseph Ford	2005–	Charlie Hardman	2006–	David Jones	1986–93	Eliot Lord	2008–13
Jackie Forde	1977–9	Freddie Hardman	2006–	Glyn Jones		Sebastian Lord	2007–
Jon Forss	2009–	Peter Hardman	2006–	Lucas Jones	2011–	William Lord	2009–
Mark Forss	2011–	Thomas Hargy	2009–	Robert Jones	1989–96	The Lury Family	2001–
David Forster		Sam Harney	2006–13	Alexander Joseph	2003–10	Aengus Lynch	2006–
Annette Foy	1983–5	Tim Harrington	1977–84	Rianna Julian	2012–	Hugo Lynch	2004–11
Daniele Franz and Family	2002–	Kevin Harrington Arango	1995–7	Pierre Kacary	1975–82	Kevin Lynch	1952–8
Cecilia Freely	2009–11	Roberto F Harrington Arango	1995–7	Stanislaw Kaleta	2013–	Kieran Lyons	2011–
Daniel Freely	2006–13	Ned Harris	2010–	Mr and Mrs A Kazanji		Victoria Macdonald Hill	
Martin Freely	2006–13	Kevin Hart		Zuhair Kazanji	2013–	Alistair J Mackay	2000–12
Monica Freely	2006–08	Rory Hart	2012–	Paul J Keane	1986–93	Fiona Mackay	2000–
Patricia M Frith (née Hogan)		Stephen Hart	2000–	George Kearney	2009–	Paul Mackay	
Ashley Gabriel	2007–	Kevin Patrick Haughton	1951–5	Patrick Kearney	2007–	Edward Makin	2011–
In Memory of Ian Gaffney		Annette Hayes		William Kearney	2012–	Alexander Maljkovic Mena	2013–
Isobel Gaffney		Luca Hayes Lorente	2012–	George Kearse	1962–9	Milan Maljkovic Mena	2011–
John Gallagher	2004–11	Nicholas Hayes	2001–08	Gerry Keegal	1971–6	Eamonn Malone	1966–73
Nicholas Gallagher Maury	2010–	Benjamin Haynes	2012–	Samuel J A Keeler	2001–12	Kenneth D Malone	1973–80
Charlie Gallant	2013–	Elizabeth Healy Bottriell	1974–6	Angela Kelly (née Evans)	1995–7	Matthew Malone	2007–
Daniel Gallant	2012–	Claire Heffernan		Patrick J Kelly		Conor Maloney	2009–
Tomas Bautista Garau		Peter Heslop Smith	2005–12	Therese Kennedy-Laing	1994–2001	Finnian Maloney	2007–
Julie Gardner		Daniel Hickey	1994–2001	Aedan Kerrigan	2011–	Rónán Maloney	2011–
Nicholas Gardner		Mark Hickey	1997–2004	Ruairi Kerrigan	2008–	Benedict Manfield	2013–
Andrea Garzolini	2011–	Matthew Hickey	2000–07	Christopher Khan	2009–	Hugo Manfield	2011–
Luca Garzolini	2008–	Patrick Hickey		Michael King	2011–	Francesco Manzi	2004–
Adam Gibbs	2006–13	Jack Hicks-Flynn	2005–12	Robert King	2013–	Giuseppe Marasco	1996–8
Joseph Gibbs	2003–10	Liam Joseph Higgins	1971–8	Scott King	2007–	Denise Marchant	
John Gilmartin	1973–8	Oliver Higgins	2012–	Maximilian Kinsky	2013–	Jeffrey Mariampillai	2004–11
In Memory of Simon Gipps-Kent		Timothy Higgins	2005–12	Wenzel Kinsky	2009–	Roland Maryniak	2012–
	1970–4	In Memory of John Dennis Patrick Hogan		Felix Kirby	2012–	Antonio Masella	2008–
Francesco Gnudi	2006–13		1929–34	Henry Kirby	2007–	Rosa Maria Masoero Webster	
Conor Godsall	2005–12	Cathal Holloway	2008–	Archibald Knox	2009–	Mr and Mrs P Mattar	
Benjamin Gompertz	2012–	Neil Holloway	2006–13	Thomas Knox	2009–	Oliver Mattar	2012–
Joseph Gompertz	2002–09	Shea Holloway	2010–	Peter Kordeczka	1965–72	Marcus Mazuri	2012–

John McAleer	2000–07	John-Joe O'Connor	2009–	Benedict Rangasamy	2007–	Marek Skibinski	2006–
Liam McAlinden	2005–11	Rory O'Connor	2004–11	Christopher Rea	2002–	Luca Felipe Slade	2012–
Terry McCarthy	1942–7	David O'Donnell	1992–8	Dominic Rea	2000–	Dr and Mrs Andrew and Dominique Smith	
Margaret McCondach	2012–	Joe O'Dwyer	2013–	Jamie Rea	2008–		
Patrick McConnon	1982–9	James O'Keeffe	2010–	Oliver Rea	2006–	Joe Soares	
Riordan McCready	2010–	Nicholas O'Keeffe	2009–	Mary and Jim Redmond		Michael André Soares	2007–
Joseph McDowell	2009–	G A O'Neill		Odhran Redmond	2011–13	Stefanos Stathis	2011–
Matthew McDowell	2012–	William O'Neill	1968–74	Armand W T Rego	2009–	Cameron Maclean James Steel	2008–
Declan McGarry	2008–	Mr and Mrs J O'Regan		James Reilly	2009–	Dr and Mrs Jeffrey H Steel	
Paul McGee-Renedo	2004–11	Louis O'Regan	2012–	Sean Reilly	2009–	Lawrence Ashley Steel	2006–
Elliot McHugh	2012–	Liam O'Riordan	2011–13	Charles Rennie	2006–11	John and Frances Stobbs	
Fenton McHugh	2010–	Alexander O'Sullivan	2008–	James Rhodes	2003–10	Davide Strappelli	2003–10
Gill McIlvenna	1997–13	Harry O'Sullivan	2010–	Francis Richards		Gian Marco Strappelli	2005–12
Justin B McKenna	1987–2012	The Ochei-Okpara Family	2012–	Thomas F A Richardson	2010–	Lorenzo Strappelli	2001–08
Eric McKenzie	1971–8	Robert Ojeda-Sierra Garcia	2013–	Matt Richbell	2001–10	Stefan Suchcitz	2011–
Oliver McLaughlin	2008–	Michael Omisore	2012–	Daniel G Rooney		Matt Sullivan	2001–08
Jackie McRoberts	2004–	Connor Osborne	1999–2006	Danny Rooney		Aidan E Swietochowski	2005–12
James A G McWalter	2006–	Hubert Ostoja-Petkowski	2007–	Aaron Rose	2009–	Andrzej Szadkowski	1951–8
Ludovic Meaby	2006–13	Sebastian Ostoja-Petkowski	2011–	Hayden Rose	2013–	Alexander Szerezla	2006–11
Valleran Meaby	2004–11	Lukasz Ostrowski	2005–12	Rhys Rose	2004–10	Nathaniel Szerezla	2010–
Elliot M Mead	2009–	Michal Ostrowski	2009–	Alexander Ross	2010–	Tom Szychowski	1995–2002
James Mead	2007–	Judy Owen	1981–96	William Ross	2012–	Renata Szymaniak	1973–5
Krystyna Medwicz-Starba		Sarah Owen		David Rotchelle	1965–70	Gianluca Tartaro	2010–
Catherine Meinertzhagen (née Gudgeon)	1990–2	Jessica Peacock	2010–12	Bernard Russell	1984–91	Ben Taylor	2006–
		Joseph Peacock	2008–	Lisa Russell		F E Taylor	
Hazel Mendoza	1996–8	Thomas Peacock	2003–10	Thomas Russell	2010–	Jacob Taylor	2008–
Moses Mendoza	2001–09	Bevan Anthony Gordon Pereira	2010–	Joseph Russell-Bishop	2010–	Luke Taylor	2012–
Paul-Eric Mendoza	1989–6	Alexander Pereira Barker	2012–	John Ryan	1974–81	Timothy Frank Christopher Taylor	2010–
Cornelius Mitchell	1973–8	Jespy and Michael Pereira Barker		Tom Ryan	2008–		
Sam Modi and Olga Celda Real		Chantelle Perriman	2004–06	Mr and Mrs Saade		David Terry	
Oliver Modi-Celda	2013–	Curtis Perriman	2001–08	Julian Saade	2009–	Lisa Tham	1995–7
Kieran Moggan	2008–	Peter Perry	1942–6	Vincent Saade	2004–	Mark Thomas	1985–92
Laurence Mohan	2011–	Conrad Pollock Spadavecchia	2009–	Mostafa Sadeghi	1994–5	Les Thompson	2005–12
Christopher Mollard	2003–10	Joseph Finnian Pongracz	2012–	Andrew Saffrey	1993–2000	Mr and Mrs C J Thoumine	
Sebastien Mollard	2004–11	Thomas Anthony Pongracz	2010–	James Saldanha	2008–13	Eilish Thoumine	2012–
Euan Moore	2012–	Gregory Potter	2008–	Luke Saldanha	2006–11	Matthew Thoumine	2009–
Lorcan Moore	2009–	Michael Potter	2006–13	Matthew Saldanha	2010–	Mr and Mrs Tishler	
Marianne Morris		Aidan J Preston	2013–	Sergio Salveti	2009–	Eric Tishler	2011–
Reece Peter Moss	2011–	Conall Preston	2011–	Amadi J L Sanderson	2001–12	Grzegorz Todryk	2013–
Mr and Mrs D Mugwanya		Mark Pryjma	1972–8	Dan Saul	2005–11	Bernadette Tracey (née Wells)	1973–5
Liam Mugwanya	2012–	Ilario Pucino	1991–8	Tom Saul	2001–08	David Tracey	1968–75
Douglas Murch	2000–07	Hubert Puzio	2007–	James Scantlebury	1993–2010	Mr and Mrs Charles Trustram Eve	
Robert Murch	2001–12	Natalie R Queffurus	2007–09	Myles Scantlebury	2006–	The Ryan Tucker Family	2006–
Bridget Murphy	1986–8	Nicholas J Queffurus	2006–13	William Scantlebury	2010–	Joe Tulasiewicz	2004–11
Jack Murphy	2012–	John Quigley-Nicholson	1989–96	James Schiele	2006–13	Joseph Louis Tullett	2010–
Norah P Murphy	1994–2005	James Quin	2010–	Archie Scott	2008–13	Paul Tuszynski	1971–6
Patrick Joseph Murphy	1971–8	Thomas Quin	2008–	Luca Seemungal	2007–	Charles Tyldesley	1996–2007
The Mylchreest Family	2013–	Lorenzo Quirke	2003–	M A Shanahan		George Tyldesley	1996–2001
Samuel Hannibal Nabli López	2012–	Matteo Quirke	2005–	Karolina Shaw	1994–6	Harry Tyldesley	1993–2000
Freddie Nicholls	2006–	Milo Quirke	2007–	Mr and Mrs Guy Shelley		John-Joseph Tyldesley	2000–11
Harry Nicholls	2008–	Owen Raccani	2012–	Deborah Sheppard-Keenleyside		Alaeze Ugoala	1996–2006
James Nicholls	2005–12	Patrick Raccani	2009–	Conor Sheridan	2012–	Chijioke Ugoala	1996–2003
Helen Nolan	1977–9	Petronella Raccani		Alexander Shickell	2007–	Obioma Ugoala	1997–2008
Josephine Nolan	1977–9	I Raess		Daniel A Siemaszkiewicz	2004–11	Fabiola Unazoi	1995–7
Adam John Nowak	2008–	Navin Raess	2010–	Szymon Siembida	2008–	Peter Utley	2007–
Vincent O'Brien	1969–76	Nyan Raess	2012–	Donald and Jenny Sinclair		Zane Utley	2006–
Aidan O'Byrne	1981–9	Oliver Raess		Eileen Sinclair (née Gaffney)		Hazlitt van Goethem	2008–
Alex O'Carroll	2013–	Paul Rainsford	2009–	Ian Sinclair	2000–07	Oliver van Goethem	2010–
Dominic O'Carroll	2004–11	Johann Rajakarunanayake	2009–11	Martin Sinclair	1993–2000	Pier Francesco V Verdese	1970–3
Jack O'Carroll	2013–	Hiroko Raleigh		Roy Sinclair		Roberto Vernazza	1978–82
Sean O'Carroll	1999–2006	Patrick Raleigh		Michael A Siravo	2009–	Pedro Virgili	1990–

List of Subscribers

Alexandra Votier	2011–13	Charlie Warren	2005–12	Daniel Williams	2008–13	Leo Wyard	2002–09
Nicholas Votier	2004–13	Luke Weaser-Seychell	2004–	Deborah Williams		Nicolas Garrido Ybanez	2011–13
David A Wailen	1949–56	Annelies Webber	2004–06	Dylan Williams	2013–	Callum Douglas Young	2002–09
Benedict Wain-Blissett	2004–	Charlie Webber	2001–08	Jonathan (Jo) Williams	1999–2001	Peter Zaki	2009–
Alexander Wakefield	2010–	George Webber	2006–13	Jordan Williams	2009–	Edward Zakrzewski	2005–12
Daniel Wakefield	2013–	Marcus Weedon	1978–85	Rhianna Williams	2010–12	Roman Zakrzewski	2003–10
Aodhan Walsh	2010–	Abib J Wellington	2012–	James Willis	2006–13	Jack Zammit	2006–
Cormac Joseph Walsh	2011–	Zac West	2011–	Rhiannon Willis	2008–10	Matthew Zammit	2008–
Matthew Walsh	2010–	Sam White		Ethan Wolfe	2009–	David Zimmerer	2007–
Michael Walsh	2012–	Bruno Wieringa-Diaz	2011–	Fabian Worthington	2012–	Philipp Zimmerer	2002–09
Niall Walsh	2008–	Alexander Wild	2002–09	Phoebe Worthington	2012–	Thierry Zoghbi	1999–2005
Clare Wareing	2004–	Mark Wild		Alexander Wright	2007–12	Richard Zuk	1969–74
Nathan Wareing	2004–	Oliver Wild	2005–10	Oliver Wright	2010–		

School Coat of Arms.

Governors, Staff and Pupils

THE GOVERNING BODY

Chairman of Governors
The Very Revd Ignatius Harrison
Vice Chairman
R Boden
Foundation Trust Governors
R Adams
T Edge
The Revd John Fordham
M Ginn
R Jones
Mrs R Kummelstedt
The Revd Michael Lang
The Revd Rupert McHardy
M Morgan
P Thimont
P Ward
Parent Governor
G Jones
Staff Governors
D McFadden
Miss P Devereux
D Rooney
Clerk to the Governing Body
S Hart

TEACHING STAFF

Senior Staff
DA McFadden MA, Headmaster
Miss P Devereux MA, Deputy Headmaster
D J Rooney BA, Deputy Headmaster
P M Flanagan BMus, Assistant Headmaster
G K Howells PhD, Assistant Headmaster
P C Isaaks BSc, Assistant Headmaster
R A Jones MA, Procurator
S W Marty BEd, Assistant Headmaster

P Adey BSc, Physics
Miss S F Adkins BSc, Mathematics
Mrs K Alderton BSc, Director of ICT
P Alexander MA, English
Miss S M Allen BA, French
S Allon BSc, Mathematics
S J Ashenden MA, English
Miss E J Bennett MPhil, English
Miss Z M Bickell BA, French
A Blackmore BSc, Biology
S Blyth BA, Head of Design and Technology
E A Boileau MA, Geography, Physical Education
Mrs S Burden Griffiths MA, Junior House
Miss A Celentano BSc, Head of Physics
G Clottey, PhD, Biology
C Cole BA, ARCO, Director of Schola
Miss L J Costello BA, Geography
M Couch MSc, Chemistry
Miss M-P D'Aversa, French, Fisher Housemaster
Miss P Damsell BSc, Mathematics
M I Daniels BSc, Head of Geography
Miss C Dawson BA, Assistant Director of Music
Miss L Davenport MA, History
Miss S Deane BSc, Mathematics
D Deegan BA, Head of Art
Miss C de Lotbinière BA, French, German
Miss E C Devaney BA, Head of History
Miss C N Dove MSc, Acting Head of Religious Education
S D Edwards BA, History
G Elphicke BSc, Rowing
Mrs M Farmery MA, French
D Fox BA, Religious Education, English
Mrs J Fox BA, Geography
Miss E Gomersall BSc, Biology
N Hazell BA, Head of Economics and Business Studies
R Hodges BA, Physical Education
S Hughes BEd, Physical Education
D Jewison MPhil, English
P J Kelly BSc, Mathematics, More Housemaster
D Littler BSc, Computing
Miss A Loudon BSc, Head of Learning Support
Miss E Lucas BSc, Chemistry
D Lynch MA, Religious Education
Mrs F M MacKay BA, Housemaster Junior House
Miss T Madigan BA, Art and Design
J G Mantio BSc, Biology, Howard Housemaster
Miss E Marsden MSc, Physics
Mrs M McCondach BMus, Music
S Mildinhall BA, History
Miss M Mitchell Cert Ed, Mathematics
G K Moran BEd, Director of Sport
D Moyes BA, Classics, Campion Housemaster
Miss K M Mullooly BA, English
O M Newton BA, Religious Education, Owen Housemaster
P H N O'Dwyer BA, English, Activities Coordinator
Miss H Olizar MA, Junior House
Miss E O'Neill BSc, Biology
Miss S J Owen BA, English
R Pointon BSc, Mathematics
M Porter PhD, Head of Chemistry
W Poza MSc, Chemistry
P Read BA, Physical Education
Miss F Reichmann BA, German
P D Richardson BSc, Physics
A Rigano BA, Art and Design
J Rodmell MA, German
A Rubio BSc, Mathematics
Mrs V Sanchez BA, Spanish
M P Sharman MA, Head of Mathematics, Director of Staff Administration
M Smith MA, Religious Education
J H S Stobbs MA, Head of Languages
Miss C M Stoner BSc, Design and Technology
D B Sullivan MA, Head of Classics
G T Taylor BA, Classics
D M Terry MA, ARCO, ARCM, Director of Music
R Tilbury MA, Head of English
P Virgili PhD, Chemistry
M Ward BMus, Head of Academic Music
H Warner BA, History
Miss S Watson BEd, Art and Design
B Williams BSc, Science
Mrs S Wilson BA, English
D Yeates MA, Religious Education

NON TEACHING STAFF

Chaplains
The Revd George Bowen, Senior School
The Revd Edward van den Bergh, Junior House
Headmaster's Office
Miss K Haddy BA, Headmaster's Secretary
Procurator's Office
A Jones MA, Procurator
Mrs M Loudon, Finance Officer
Registry
Miss J Darling, Registrar
Miss M Lago, Receptionist
Miss K Helevuo, Registry Secretary
Mrs B Wlodek, Sixth Form Registrar
Development Office
Miss J McRoberts, Development Officer, Director of the Arts Centre
Miss H Cocks BMus, Music Administrator and Development Secretary
Mrs H Kennedy, Shop Manager
Education Support Services
S Wills BSc, IT Network and e-Learning Manager
Miss A Kujawa MA, Administration Support Officer
Miss C Coles-Lockwood MA, Examinations Officer
D Lasso MCSE, IT and Media Technician
A Cheal BSc, Librarian
Mrs S Bhargava MA, Librarian
B Maguire, Learning Mentor, Physical Education
Teaching Assistants
Miss B Casino
Mrs M Elkington
Mrs M Green
M Hickey BA
Miss R Jarrett
B Paull BA
L Poza
S Wickramaratne BA
Sports Staff
S Lawrence, Rugby Coach
R Lewis, Rugby Coach
K Wood, Rowing Coach
Technician Services
J Haugh BSc, Biology, Senior Technician
Miss A Perez-Gomez BSc, Chemistry Technician
Miss M C Perez-Gomez, Lower School Science Technician
Mr Ekanayake BSc, Physics Technician
Major WAG Coombes MBE, Workshop Technician
J McGrane, Arts Centre Technician
Estate Management
Mrs P Chandler BSc, Estate Manager
E Brown, Schoolkeeper
J Josephs, Schoolkeeper
P Lada, Schoolkeeper
R Rocha, Swimming Pool Manager

Governors, Staff and Pupils

PUPILS

Junior House

George Abbott
Jack Abbott
Mathieu Arnaud
David Barry
Constant Baudin
Lukas Bengtsson
Jude Bertwistle
Linus Blaney
Luke Borrel
Redmond Bowcott
Zane Burton
Oisín Byrne
Frederic Campione
Yxzyl-Kameron Carandang
Jacob Carey
Massimo Chiocca
Jack Clements
Maurice Cole
Dylan Connolly
Vittorio Cuneo-Flood
Thomas Curtis
Juan Cuzme Rigo
León Cuzme Rigo
Luca D'Amico
Leo De Flammineis
Charles Dean
William Delargy
Jules Deruelle
William Diffey
Gabriel Doherty
Lorenzo Dufour
Oisín Duggan-Dennehy
Hugo Farmer
Martin Fedenczak Garcia
James Gardner
Felix Harvey
Luca Hayes Lorente
Harry Holmes-Milner
James Ho-Terry
David Howells
Daniel Hutton
Nicholas Janicki
William Jeffs
Nicholas Kiely
Michael King
Charles Kingsmill
Maximilian Kinsky
Russell Lobo
Sebastian Massey
Charles Mawson-Smith
Seán McHugh
Eoin McKenna
Mark Miskelly
Thomas More
Shay O'Connor
James O'Keeffe
Harry O'Sullivan
Ejike Okpara

Sebastian Ostoja-Petkowski
Elia Paolucci
James Perillo
Maximilian Pintaritsch
Alfred Quantrill
Dominic Quinn
Patrick Read
Thomas Richardson
Luca Slade
Benjamin Smith
Oliver Smith
Tobias Stewart
Timothy Taylor
Jonathan Teixeira
Benedict Verdin
Antony Waldron
Oliver Waldron
Seán Walker
Oliver Ward
Zacharias West
Tycho Williams
Elliot Wolfe
Xavier Wood

First Form

Steven Albuquerque
Felipe Alves
Matthew Asante
Ronan Atterbury
Anthony Awoyomi
Connor Baird
Maximiliano Barria Rodriguez
Marco Belsito
Hunde Berri
Barnaby Blackwood
Benedict Blaney
James Boohan-Makhlouf
Kamil Boulia
Ciaran Bradbury-Hickey
Evan Brennan
Julen Brennan-Garmendia
Aidan Brickley
Samuel Bricout
Colm Brito
Oliver Brydges
Christopher Byrne
Kyle Cajigas
Pádraig Callcut
Alfredo Cassidy
Matthew Cassidy
Declan Casswell
Enrico Cauilan
Garjon Chan
Orin Chapman
Emmanuel Chateauneu
Adrian Cheung
Joseph Choueifati
Calder Christopher
Julian Chrobak

Robert Chudzik
Miles Clarke
Antonio Clegg Gonzalez
Rory Conmee
Davide Correia
Lenny Cossey
Giovanni Crocioni
Finlay Curran
Nathan Daniel
Alexander Davis
Luca De Flammineis
Julian De Zoysa
Jacob Devitt
Aaron Dias
Aidan Dike-Lawlor
Finn Doherty
Thomas Doyle
Oliver Dunning
Joseph Eckert
Benjamin Edeh
Charbel Eid
Adam Feeley
Michael Fennell
James Foley
Jack Foley Rusbridge
Marco Foster
Billy Gallagher
Charlie Gallant
Nicholas Gardner
Anton Garrido Ybanez
Andrea Garzolini
Ronan Gillibert
Malachy Green
Ciáran Hallbery
Conor Hanley
Joshua Hemingway
Stuart Hewins
Carlo Hulme
Felipe Hurtado Taborda
Hector Husselby
D'Carlos Ikuomola-André
Joseph Jarman
John Jerere
Brian Jimenez
Edward Joannides
Fergus Jones
Miguel Joubrael
Stanislaw Kaleta
Zuhair Kazanji
Jack Keating
Finn Kernan
Francis Keryakoz
Robert King
William King
Wenzel Kinsky
Shaun Kolade
Rikardo Kolaj
Terence Lanzalaco
Jason Lightbody

Patrick Lloyd
Edward Lofts
James Lorimer
Lawrence Lowe
Fintan Lyons
Joseph MacGloin
Kristopher Magee-Foster
Simonpietro Magrelli
Alexander Maljkovic
Pietro Manca
Benedict Manfield
Finlay Martin
Samir Mateo Araujo
Adam Mather
Charlie Mathews
Nicholas Mbugua
Matthew McCaffrey
Sean McCarthy
Connor McDyre
Ethan Mebrahtu
Louis Milne
Christian Moloney
Michael Momodu
Christopher Morris
Thomas Mulcahey
Michael Murphy
Cormack Mylchreest
Jules Nimmo
Olumese Nyamali
Alex O'Carroll
Joseph O'Dwyer
Nicholas O'Keeffe
Joseph O'Sullivan
Sean O'Sullivan
Jerzy Oborski
Robert Ojeda-Sierra
John Olid Aguiling
Maurice Oliveira Fitzpatrick
Bradley Paul Ibanez
Kevin Perera
James Phillips
Alexander Pienkowski
Theodore Pinnock
Francesco Polverino
Aidan Preston
Donnell Quarshie
Dominic Raccani
Michael Raleigh
Seamus Ridewood-Byrne
Luke Rolt-Bardot
Hayden Rose
Nicolás Rossi-Rolando
Thomas Russell
Julian Saade
Joshua Santos
Cameron Smith
Marcus Smith
Ryan Smith
Jack Springate

167

The London Oratory School – *Appendices*

Jack Stevens
Nicky Stevenson
Noel Sugunaraj
Thomas Sylvester
Carlos Symes
Alexander Taylor
Daniel Teklemariam
John Thai
Grzegorz Todryk
Thomas Trustram Eve
Antonio Vazquez de Parga
Joseph Verdin
Bertie Viegas
Daniel Wakefield
Toby Ward
Samuel Wareing
Edward Warren
Tobiasz Watrobski
Samuel Wedgwood
Barnaby White
Lucas Wieringa-Diaz
Dylan Williams
Theo Wilson
Henry Winter
Francis Wood
Henry Wood
Daniel Yañez-Cunningham
Peter Zaki

Second Form
Joseph Alakija
Billy Allday
Danil Almeida
Riccardo Alò
Liam Aslin
Callum Ayres
Vito Balboa
Matthew Barrett
Iudaeus Beleno
Finn Bengtsson
Luca Bentivoglio
Patrick Bessa-O'Sullivan
Finn Bowcott
Samuel Brading
Adam Brown-Sadowski
Joshua Burnand Witter
Joseph Bushell
Edward Campbell
Thomas Candia
Euan Carr
Thomas Carter
Sebastian Clifton
James Coltman
Umarr Conteh
Joseph Conway
Rory Conway
Milo Cooper
Oliver Cox
Aidan Crotty-Joyce
Dylan Cuizon
Carl Curtin-Giddings

Zané-Tiago Da Silva
Samuel Dalton
Benjamin Davidson
Cyprian Davies
Daniel Dias Sayali
Luca Digrandi
Marques Doherty
Jai Douglas
Oliver Douglas-Jacobs
Jacob D'Souza
Alexander Eaglestone
Daniel Eisho
Dominic Enright
Peter Fadian
Alessandro Feret-Fillon
Elwyn Fernandes
Inigo Fernandez-Cuervo
Hugo Ferreira
Lorcan Flahive
Jared Forrest
Savio Fung
Donovan Gabriel
Daniel Gallant
Marius Gardner
Matteo Garitta
Luca Garzolini
Matteo Gibbs
Shane Gill
Niall Gillen
Benjamin Gompertz
Dylan Grant
Alexander Guest
Fintan Hall
Joseph Hargreaves
Rory Harrington
Joseph Harrison
Rory Hart
Benedict Harvey
Thomas Hawkey
Benjamin Haynes
Ellis Hennessy
Oliver Higgins
Harvey Hill
Alexander Hogan
Edgardo Honrada Junior
Anthony Ho-Terry
Benjamin Hovey
Jack Hughes
John James
Bartosz Jarosz
Edmund Jenkins
Huw Jenkins
Francis Jinks
Anthony John-Cyrus
Ethan Jones
Oisín Kearney
William Kearney
Max Keenleyside
Niall Kelly
Dejen Kidane
James King

Felix Kirby
Samir Knights
Jakub Kowalski
Robert Kummelstedt
Brian Kwizera
Oliver Lally
Ezekiel Largie-Poleon
Isaac Lautier-Byrne
Tobiloba Lawson
Thibaud Le Calvez
Blaize Lee-Blackwood
Christian Leonard
Edmond Lewin
Alexander Lewis
Dillon Love
Noah Macleod
Roland Maryniak
Giuseppe Maurino
Marcus Mazuri
Kai McCarthy
Joseph McCormick
Ruairi McDonald
Matthew McDowell
Elliot McHugh
Ciarán McKenna
Evan Mebrahtu
Ryan Milne
Oliver Modi-Celda
Joel Moffett
Eduardo Molin-Cobos
Euan Moore
William More
David Morgan
Daniel Moriarty
Joseph Moriarty
Liam Mugwanya
Jack Murphy
Samuel Nabli Lopez
Michael N'Jai
Oliver Nolan-Davies
Euan Norris
Cassius O'Connell-White
Liam O'Dwyer
Louis O'Regan
Alexander O'Sullivan
Cian O'Sullivan
Michael Omisore
Emmanuel Osmond-Igomu
Alessio Paolucci
Marco Papaccio
Louis Penner
Alexander Pereira-Barker
M A Dellon Perera
Theo Pescheux
Wiktor Pienkowski
Joseph Pongràcz
Joseph Poulter
Owen Raccani
Nyan Raess
Nicholas Rayner
Dean Rebello

Daragh Rolls
William Ross
Conor Sheridan
Stefanos Stathis
Caleb Steel
Daniel Sunil
Daniel Sweeney
Joseph Tamborini
Jack Taylor
Luke Taylor
Leo Taylor-Pascal
Kacper Tomon
James Trustram Eve
Viktor Turzynski
Luca Wadham
Oliver Walsh
Henry Ward
Joseph Ward
Abib Wellington
Rory White
Jasiah Williams
Noah Wilson
Ronan Wilson
Theodore Wood
Fabian Worthington
Elroy Xavier
Aleksander Zarebski
Alexander Ziniak

Third Form
Aaron Albuquerque
Riccardo Alexander-Greenaway
Edward Allaker
Michael Alonga
Lucas Alves
Joshua Andrews
James Bailey
Alexander Baldwin
Gianluca Ballarini
Emmanuel Balogun
Edward Bambury
Paolo Barnett
Patrick Barton
Hugo Baugh
Jakub Bednarski
Oliver Blower
Niall Bones
Zachary Buckley
Arthur Burrell
Joseph Callan-Shropshall
Matthew Candia
James Canning
Jonathan Carneiro
Daniel Carr
Michael Choong
Tiernan Clarke
Milton Coutinho
Joseph Cracknell
Aaron Cronin
John Cruz Rodrigues
Michael Cusack

Governors, Staff and Pupils

Cosimo de Barry
Victor De Oliveira Camillo
Frederic de Soissons
Juan Dagorret Martinez
Charles Desa
Benjamin Dickens
Daniel Docherty
Tomás Duarte
Cormac Dullea
Christian Dunne
Saimon Eisho
James Emery
Joseph Evans
Patrick Farrell
Oliver Farrugia
Jeffrey Fernandes
Lee Fernandes
Santiago Fernandez-Cuervo
Beltrán Field
Justin Finn
Aldridge Fisher
Sean Foley
Mark Forss
Leonardo Franchini
Ryan Gallagher
Nicolas Garrido Ybanez
Orlando George-Ibitoye
Tyreece Germain-Andrews
Klodiano Gjergji
Aaron Gnanabalan
Sergio Gonzalez Navarro
Luke Gough
Mathieu Graffin
Vincent Gray
Maximillian Green
Joseph Griso Dryer
Patrick Grzybowski
Gregory Hadeed
Oscar Hale
Peter Hardman
Matthew Hardy
Rory Harper
Alexander Harrington
Thomas Holden
Edward Holmes-Milner
Pedro Humphreys
Solomon Ishaq
Lucas Jones
Timothy Jones
Jesus Jose
Sebastian Joseph
Ciaran Kelly
Simon Kelly
Aedan Kerrigan
Aaron Keshwala
Scott King
Daniel Kitto
Patryk Korczak
Jaroslaw Krzystek
Oscar Lang
Jude Lowe

Ewan Lury
Kieran Lyons
Roderick Macdonald Hill
Brendan Machell
Edward Makin
Milan Maljkovic
Rónán Maloney
Hugo Manfield
Joseph Marshall
Michael Matthews
Conner McCarron
Fraser McKillop
Ciáran McLoughlin
Edward McNestry
Frederick Meinertzhagen
Sebastian Mendez
James-Paul Merlino
Laurence Mohan
Matthew Monk
Archibald Moore
James Mordaunt
Christopher Morris
Reece Moss
Marcelo Moura
Christian Munoz
Gabriel Naginski
Franco Nazareno
Julius Norris Boheimer
Cecil North
Filip Nykiel-Jastrzebski
Piotr Nykiel-Jastrzebski
Jack O'Carroll
Michael O'Connell
Jack O'Donnell
Henry O'Meara
Jonathan Ogodo
Thandy Ogunna-Nwokie
Alejandro Ortiz
Hubert Ostoja-Petkowski
Oliver Oufi
Joseph Oyeyinka
Benjamin Phelan
Stephen Pickett
Conall Preston
James Proudfoot
Peter Puhalla
Anthony Quaradeghini
James Quin
Milo Quirke
Benedict Rangasamy
Odhran Redmond
Danny Reilly
Dominic Riddle
Connell Ridewood-Byrne
Wiktor Rogala
Daniel Rooney
Mateo Rossi Rolando
Joseph Rowe
Dario Ruiz Gonzalez
Jimmy Sarzosa Llerena
Luca Seemungal

Benjamin Shardow
Thomas Simpson
Gilles Sinclair
Charles Smith
Philip Smith Mazacote
Michael Soares
Will Stapleton
Caius Stephenson Py De Mello Silva Camara
Stefan Suchcitz
David Sylvester
Marc Szwagrzak
Richard Szyszko
Alexander Teixeira
Omar Thomas
Calum Thompson
Jacob Tildesley
Eric Tishler
Peter Utley
Kevin Valenzuela
Michael Villar
Séan Von Hagt
Harvey Vowls
Cormac Walsh
Michael Walsh
Joseph Wedgwood
Finlay Wells
Alfred Whillis
Bruno Wieringa-Diaz
Nathan Wilson
Alexander Winter
Jakub Wojcik

Fourth Form
Marcellus Augustine
Simon Adams
Somar Albani
Michael Appiah-Charway
Daniel Ayres
Zygmunt Bannock
Yobel Bariagaber Ermias
Henry Barrington
Maximilian Bengtsson
David Bick
Sean Bird
Zachariah Biriyok
Nathaniel Blake Hugill
David Bloomfield
Conor Bowditch
Daniel Breen
Gonzague Brochard
Aidan Brophy
Evan Bryant
James Butler
Anthony Byrne
Kenneth Cajigas
Arthur Campbell
Ruairi Carey-Furness
Luke Carrigan
Joshua Carson
Stephen Carter

Carlo Caruso
Colm Christian
Tobias Clarke
Conor Connolly
James Connolly
Cormac Conway
Jahmal Coppin
William Corp
Finlay Coward
Liam Cremin
Daniel Cruise
Kieran Cullen
Jack De Guzman
Hugo De Oliveira Camillo
Benjamin Delaney
Callum Dias
Michael Doig
Oskar Domagala
Ciaran Downes
Rory Duncan
Liam Dunsby Sircana
Laurence Dynes
Karim Eid
Marlon Erazo Vasquez
Jack Farmer
Alexander Farrugia
Jason Fernandes
Tomas Fernandez-Cuervo
Joshua Ferreira
Brandon Forrest
Jamie Galal
Tomas Garau
Thomas Gawda
Philippe George
Luca Ghafourpour
William Ghazi
Conor Gillen
Theodore Goodliffe
Harvey Grace
Gianluca Granelli
Michael Griffiths
Donn Guray
William Harris
Oliver Hart
Cameron Haughton
Thomas Hembrey
Shea Holloway
Stefan Holst-Roness
Harold Honrada
Andrew Howell
Ostap Hrynchak
Brandon James
Angus Johnston
Luke Kelly
Luke Kennedy
Naod Kidane
Alexander Kwaskowski
Jonathan Lau
Edward Lawlor
Benito Leus III
Jack Liddy

Robert Lipinski
David Lloyd
Frederick Lloyd
Jose Lopez
Samuel Lowe Bell
Kevin Lozano
Aengus Lynch
Sean Mahendran
Edward Malaluan
Giovanni Manca
Oliver Mattar
Nicholas Maury
Niall McCarthy
Riordan McCready
Ryan McCready
Gabriel McGowan
Fenton McHugh
Harry McHugh
Matthew McInally
Gregory McManus
Francis Mendy
Andrew Mensah
Maximilian Mika
Louis Moffett
Henry Moriarty
Oliver Murphy
Felix Nash
Alexander Niang
Samuel Nicholls
Michael O'Connell
Ronan O'Connell
James O'Connor
Shane O'Leary
Thomas O'Rourke
Kevin O'Shea
Paul Obanya
Oscar Ogrodnicki
Efehi Ohen
Enyinnaya Okpara
Igor Oliiarnik
Dean Omardin Dos
Oluwafemi Omotosho
Daniel Ortiz
Josiah Oyeyinka
Hubert Palczynski
William Pattle
Chrishan Perera
Marc Plantenga
Thomas Pongracz
Robert Postle
Rory Poulter
Luke Pullinger
Daniel Raad
Shaun Rabot
Navin Raess
Jhon Rafferty
Sean Raleigh
Finbar Reid
James Reilly
Jethro Robathan
Joao Rodrigues

Alexander Ross
Harry Rowley
Thomas Russell
Joseph Russell-Bishop
Matthew Saldanha
William Scantlebury
Robert Shanahan
Sergey Sheremet
Stuart Sinclair
Gregory Slevin
Dara Spring
Laurence Stables
Darnell Stanislaus Gilbert
Lawrence Steel
Edward Stein
Luca Stock
Nathaniel Szerezla
Jose Taguba
Gianluca Tartaro
Krystian Tlak
Joseph Tullett
Harry Turzynski
Kai Udondem
Zane Utley
Oliver Van Goethem
Alexander Wakefield
Aodhan Walsh
Matthew Walsh
Dominik Waluszewski
Henry Wareing
Jakub Watrobski
William Watts
Giles Williams
Oliver Wright
Jack Zammit

Fifth Form
Anthony Abbott
Ricardo Abreu
Gonzalo Aguilera Y Rodriguez
Rohan Alexander
Jan Andrzejczyk
Jeremy Ansbro
Cormac Auty
Angus Bamford
Marcus Barratt
Nicholas Barrett
Sam Barton
Jack Beaney
Jake Bedford
Jack Billing
Gerard Black
Harry Blades
Alexander Blaney
Theo Boheimer
William Brassington
David Bull
Declan Burke
Michael Burrows
William Byrne
Gabriel Carberry

Martin Carrere Boronig
Massimo Casali
Zachariah Casswell
Ruari Chambers
Tom Chambers
Luca Charles-Valentine
Joseph Chen
Oliver Clark
Tomas Clarke
Luis Coelho Domingues
Melcom Coutinho
Toby Curran
Joshua Dalton
Noah Daly-Jones
Richard De La Cruz
Dominic de Soissons
Matthew Delargy
Samuel Dickens
Matteo Digrandi
William Doherty
Alexander Dooling
Frederick Dormon
Patrick Dunne
Gaspard Dupuy d'Angeac
Ehizenaga Edevbalo-Ehizode
Thomas Evan-Hughes
Frank Farci
Eamonn Flannery
Joseph Ford
Jon Forss
Emmanuel Galan
Oliver Gatland
Conor Gilmartin
Lewis Grosvenor
James Halsey
Dylan Hanley
Frederick Hardman
Thomas Hargy
Patrick Hayes
Dylan Hazelden-Kingdon
Jonathan Holbrook
Joseph Holden
Patrick Holian
Joseph Holmes-Milner
Dennis Houston
Edward Hughes
James Hussey
James Ireland
Norbert Janicki
Curtis John-Cyrus
Pierre Joiris de Caussin
Connor Jones
Edwin Jones
Iolo Jones
Cian Jordan
George Kearney
Max Kent-Bond
Charbel Khalil
Christopher Khan
David Kiely
Archibald Knox

Thomas Knox
Vladimir Krasnojon
Liam Krawczyk
Daniel Lally
Alastair Lane
Alex Lant
Benjamin Lavin
Fergus Lawlor
Jordan Le Blanc-Burrows
Gautier Le Calvez
Jonathan Lewin
Thomas Liddy
Gregory Loftus
Thomas Longfellow
William Lord
Conor Maloney
Thomas Maton
Calum McDonald
Joseph McDowell
Samuel McHugh
Elliot Mead
Daniel Meinertzhagen
Jakub Mieszkowski
Ethan Moore
Lorcan Moore
Samuel Moriarty
Prince Mwalimu-Sabiti
Samuel Newton
Luca Nicolaou
Richard O'Carroll
John-Joe O'Connor
Felim O'Doherty
Joseph O'Halloran
Adedeji Olaonipekun
Kwaku Osei-Yeboah
Michal Ostrowski
Finn Pace
Luca Papaccio
Mic Pasterny
George Pearce
Bevan Pereira
Louis Pescheux
Matthew Pickett
Jack Pinder
Joseph Pinder
Patrick Pinder
Sebastian Pipins
Conrad Pollock Spadavecchia
Moni Primo
Jack Proudfoot
Thomas Quin
Matteo Quirke
Patrick Raccani
Joseph Ragheb
Darnell Rainford
Paul Rainsford
George Ridewood-Byrne
Patrick Ridewood-Byrne
Joshua Rodriguez-Broadbent
Isaac Roe
Aaron Rose

Governors, Staff and Pupils

Zachary Rose-Witter
Oliver Salmon
Sergio Salveti
Tobias Sanger-Sumner
Zakery Shelley
Callum Shortland
Michael Siravo
Joseph Stapleton
Joshua Steel
Lucas Stephenson Py De Mello e Silva Camara
William Sterlini
Matthew Thoumine
Daniel Titherington
Louis Treneman
Adigwe Uraih
Berkeley Vago-Hughes
Christopher Van Hek
Harry Vigolo Da Silva
William Vigolo Da Silva
Jack Wedgwood
Jack Wells
Jordan Williams
Ethan Wolfe
Elton Xavier
David Young
Edward Young
Alexander Zuntner

Lower Sixth
Jose Afonso
Joanna Alstott
Olivia Anderson-Davies
Joe Antoun
Harry Attard
Maclyn Augustine
Joshua Balacky
Guillermo Banerjee
Roman Bannock
Bartholomew Barrett
Luca Barrie
William Barrington
Christian Beecheno
Erik Benchak
Matthew Blasik
Connor Bourke
Connor Breslin
Elliott Bridges
Conor Bright
Joseph Brophy
Myles Browne
Leo Brydges
Paul Buchinger
Alexander Buckley
Georgia Burnand Witter
Peter Bushell
Ciaran Byrne
Alfred Callan-Shropshall
Daniel Campbell
Andrea Carroll
Daniel Casey

Joshua Casey
Nathan Cefai
Oliver Chesterman
Konrad Chudzik
Ryan Chung
Hugo Clancy
Caspian Clifford
Fergus Coady-Booth
Thomas Collinson
Anna Coughlan
Matthew Coutinho
Harry Cox
Matthew Cracknell
Isabella Crook
MacCartney Cruz
Tara Cummins
Matthew Daly
Benedict Davies
Cillian Davis
Felix de Meeûs d'Argenteuil
Tobias Deckker
Tamara Deidier
Jack Donohue
Isadora Dooley-Hunter
Alfie Douglas-Jacobs
Thomas Edge
Simeon Elderfield
Fryderyk Eldred-Dutton
Thomas Emery
Felix Faillace
Matthew Falcone
Olamide Fayankinnu
Charles Fernandes
Pasquale Ferrara
Lawrence Finn
Declan Flahive
Gianluca Floris
Lauren Flynn
Aidan Foley
Neil Foley
Adrian Francis
Eamonn Gadd
Rosa Gane
Tomas Ghemit
Fintan Gillen
Ali Golchin
Jamie Gosnell
Aodhan Green
Tobias Guppy
Zack Hachem
Thomas Hall
Henry Hanifan
David Hannah
Olivia Hardy
Christian Hayes
Cathal Holloway
Alfred (Simon) Hunt
Samantha Hurley
Dominic Hurst
George Hutchinson
Owen Jenkins

Aphra Joly de Lotbinière
Nathaniel Kabiri
Marie-Isabelle Kaminski
Daniel Kaniowski
Eoghan Keasler
Aran Kelly
Rory Kelly
Ruairi Kerrigan
Felix Lang
Jakub Laska
Jack Lawton
Alexander Layng
Jack Lee
Giles Leigh
Alejandro Lopez-Martinez
Daniel Lord
Eliot Lord
Mallory Lord-Kear
Jonathan Lynch
Oscar Maclagan
Liam Maher
Farrell Mahon
Mario Manca
Marianna Marcelline
Robin Marsh
Antonio Masella
Lewis McCaffrey
Thomas McCormick
James McDonnell
Declan McGarry
Niamh McKenna
Oliver McLaughlin
Caitlin McManus
Daniele Mega
Christian Mendez
Lena Mendy
Lucy Miles
Tom Miranda
Kieran Moggan
Anna Morris
Connor Moylan
Sofia Munoz
James Murphie
Maria Nadarajah
Massimo Newell
Henry Nicholls
Theodore Nimmo
Adam Nowak
Claire O'Donoghue
John O'Reilly
William O'Riordan
Eimear O'Rourke
Connor O'Shea
Oghenesuvwe Obano
Liam Osborne
Christopher Oufi
Evelyn Pall
Ruth Parker
Joseph Peacock
Blaine Pearce
Leandros Philiotis

Arnaud Plantenga
Gregory Potter
Konrad Pukrop
Emily Raad
Jamie Rea
Kelvin Real Polanco
Tehmina Rego
Sean Reilly
Joshua Renshaw
Alexander Riddle
Christopher Roberts
David Rodriguez Campo
Hugo Ruiz Gonzalez
Kiera Ryan
Thomas Ryan
Madeleine Ryan Tucker
Matthew Ryan Tucker
Oliver Ryan Tucker
Tomasz Ryland
Vincent Saade
Carllo Sabapathy
Tania Sarsam
Alexander Sayers
Peter Shaw
Jasmin Smith
Cameron Steel
Sarah Steel
Benjamin Sterlini
Callum Stewart
Nicolas Stock
Marta Stok
Adam Tamimi
Jacob Taylor
Bianca Thompson
Christopher Thompson
Sophia Thompson
Lavinia Treneman
Jessica Tulasiewicz
Timothy Udeh
Lucien Uwayo
Landon Vago-Hughes
Hazlitt Van Goethem
Benedict Wain-Blissett
Maximilian Wallat
Niall Walsh
Felix Wareing
Luke Weaser-Seychell
Lily Weinbrand
Daniel Williams
Edward Yeboah
Matthew Zammit

Upper Sixth
Jason Abi-Saab
Benjamin Abreo
Peter Adams
Rupert Ansbro
William Antepim
Adrian Arulanantham
Stavro Audisho
Brandon Bakowski

171

The London Oratory School – *Appendices*

Luke Barratt	Milo Dickins	Ryan Kitto	Lorenzo Quirke
Edvardas Bazys	Elizabeth Doherty	Isaac Kizza	Ashley Rabot
Rachelle Bernardino	Christopher Doig	Oliver Krahelski	Maximilien Ratti
Remigiusz Biernat	Liam Donnelly	Oliver Kron	Benjamin Reed
Justin Blagrove	Alexander Doyle	Eric Kummelstedt	Louis Regan
Andrew Bradshaw	Joseph Doyle	Timothy Kwaskowski	Armand Rego
James Brassington	Thomas Dunsby Sircana	Fionnuala Lane	Nancy Relf
Matthew Breen	Spencer Duvwiama	Jan Laska	Fenton Robathan
Christopher Brown	Obiora Elliott	Arthur Le Calvez	Henry Rodriguez-Broadbent
Peter Browne	George Ellis	James Lees	Anastasia Roe
George Bryant	Kyle Farren	Guy Leonard	Sean Ryan
Danielle Buckley	Aaron Fernandes	Callum Lewis	James Schiele
Elliott Caffrey	Jacques Ferreira	Meryl Linnard	Alexander Shickell
Michael Canar	Sean Fitzgerald	Florence Litwin-Roberts	Michael Slade
Anthony Carter	Michael Flannery	Grace Lloyd	Thomas Smith
Giorgio Caruso	Ashley Gabriel	Daniel Loftus	Emmanuel Soile
Kirsty Carvalho	Daniel Galan	Ashley Lord	Abraham Somers Cocks
Luke Casey	Oliver George-Ibitoye	Sebastian Lord	Ryan Sooklal-Grizzle
Sarah Casey	George Ghobrial	Theo Lury	Dominic Speight
Minu Choi	Luke Gompertz	Connor Lyons	Barnaby Stevens
Aoife Clark-McGhee	Charles Govan	Joshua Macabulos	James Styman
Maximilian Cogan	Paolo Granelli	Hamish Maclean	Konrad Subieta
Edward Collier	James Green	Matthew Malone	Gyan Swampillai
Jesse Colombage	Orla Green	Finnian Maloney	Daniel Tavana-Delgado
Liam Connery	Julia Hall	Francesco Manzi	Euan Thomas
Isabel Cooper	Christopher Halsey	Richard Mawuli	Frederick Thomas
Ellie Corkerry	Charles Hardman	James McWalter	Eilish Thoumine
Joseph Corp	Senan Hogan Hennessy	James Mead	Oliver Townsend
Luke Coughlan	Robert Holbrook	Luca Miele	John Tuliao
Liam Cox	Kathryn Howell	Peter Morris	Elisa Turner
Adrian Crimmen	Sebastian Hyams	Dermot Neligan	Dominik Turzynski
Patrick Cronin-Coltsmann	Matthieu Isbell	Maurice Nwakor-Nwanaebi	Jesse Upton
Cora Crotty-Joyce	Michal Jarzembowski	Thomas O'Halloran	Simon Uwalaka
Hannah Crowley	Lucien Jasinski	Eseosa Ohen	Julian Vallender
Thomas Cullen	Rianna Julian	Maria Olszta	Sarah Vaz
Anthony Da Silva	Patrick Kearney	Douglas Osmond-Igomu	Stefan Walecki
Marlena Dachnowicz	Patrick Keefe	Nana Yaw Oteng	Finnian Walker
Christopher Dada	James Kelly	Oluwademilade Oyeyinka	Ruairi Walker
Benjamin Daly-Jones	Troy Kelly-Weekes	Christina Paish	Imogen Warren
Santiago Dantas Iglesias	Matthew Kennelly	Andrew Pickett	Charles Whillis
Gareth Davies	Henry Kirby	Miles Pissarro	Philip Wittich
Jude De Buitlear	William Kirkland-Gallagher	Fraser Price	Phoebe Worthington
Alexander Deamer	Fiona Kitchen	Hubert Puzio	David Zimmerer

Index

Page numbers in **bold** indicate featured quotations
Those in *italics* denote illustrations

Across Trust, the 74
Acton Central School 123
Adams, Alistair 125
Aidan, Sister Mary 48
Airfix and Model Making Club 145
Allan, Kathleen 138
Allen, Ernest (*see* Mowbray, Alan)
Allen Hall (Chelsea) 76
Allington Castle 72
Ancre British Military Cemetery 22
Andrews, Wayne 116
Angel, Mr 151
Angling Club, the 147
Annual Art Exhibition, the 92, 93
Annual Awards Evening, the 62
Annual Camp, the 149–50
Annual Choral Service, the 68, 69
Annual Swimming Gala, the *127*
Antrobus, The Reverend Father 15
Aquinas College, Perth 60, 122
Archer, Tony 85
Artesi, Fabio 130
Artesi, Gianfranco 130
Arthur, Abraham 137
Arts Society, the 112, 113
Ashenden, Simon 77, 93, 103, 111
Assinor, Adrian 129
Artro-Morris, Evan 109, 110
Athena (sculpture) *88*, *89*, *90*, 90, 91
Atkinson O'Sullivan, Fergus 152
Atwell, Hayley *109*, 109
Aust, Derek 35–6, 37

Badminton Club, the 129
Bailey, David 44
Balkin, F 21, 22–3
Ballard, Dr 26, 82
Balliol College, Oxford 18
Bamford, Brian 58, 121, 124, 136
Bannister, Roger 128
Banwell, Mr 144
Barberi, Blessed Dominic 16
Barman, Charles 29, 30
Barn Elms *118*, *124*, 127, 128, *130*
Barrett-Lennard, Father Hugh Dacre 72, 77, 78
Barry, Michael 76, 143
Barton, Glenys 92
Battlefields Tour, the 21, 137

Bazaar, the 27, 28
Beer, Simon 71
Belcourt, Paul *151*, 152
Bell, Mr 83
Belloc, Hillaire 27
Benedict XVI, Pope 72, *72*
Bevan, David 98
Bishop Douglas School 120
Bishop Marshall School (Manchester) 116
Blackley, Thomas 36
Blair, Cherie 57
Blair, Euan 56
Blair, Kathryn 56
Blair, Nicky 56
Blair, Tony 56–7, *57*
Blake, Vera 96
Blandford, Lionel 131
Blight, Mr 33, 133
Blunt, Emily 111
Boileau, Ali 124
Bond, Richard *150*, 150
Bousfield School 41
Bowden, Henry 18
Bowden, John 18
Bowden, The Reverend Father Charles 13–14, 18
Bowden, The Reverend Father Sebastian 13–14, 18–19, *19*
Bowen, Father George 9, 72, 74, *79*, 79, 147
Bowes, Jonathan 120, *121*
Bowles, James 124
Boys Central School, the 12
Bradford Textile Company, the 32
Bradshaw, Laurence 49
Brandt, Mr 144
Braun, Mr 133, 134
Breen, Kevin 98, 98, 99, 100, 101, 102, 110
Brentwood Diocese, the 77
Broderson, Knut Jorgen 41
Brompton and Chelsea Catholic Middle School (*see* Oratory Middle School, the)
Brompton Oratory School Internment Centre (001) 40–1
Brothers of Christian Instruction, the 12

Brothers of the Communauté de St Jean, the 73
Brothers of the Little Oratory 77
Brown, F 116
Brown, Mr 23
Brunel University 130
Brunwin, Mr 72, 108, 137, 139
Bull, David 131
Bull, Mr 124
Burns, James Charles 33, *115*, 115, 116, 118, 125, *126*, 151
Burran, Colin 36, 126
Bushell, J 135
Byrne, Chris 85, 129
Byrne, Michael 123
Byrne, Sean 123

Cadet Band, the 150
Callow, Simon 55, 75, 83, *108*, 108
Cambridge, the Duchess of 155
Cambridge University 41, 77, 86, 104, 124
Camera Club 145
Campbell, Martin 47–8
Campbell, Mr 96
Campion, St Edmund 64
Campion House 58, 74
Campos, Grace 109
Cane, Terence 126
Cann, Bernard 39
Canterbury Cathedral 134
Canty, George 53, **54**, 55, 83
Cardinal Vaughan Memorial School 76
Cariaga, Eugene 123
Carmelite Friars, the 72
Carr, James 37
Carr, Michael 120
Carr, Paul 137
Carr, S A 97, 107, 151
Carragher, Susan 138
Carreras, José 100
Carty, Mairead 112
Caserta Military Cemetery 39
Catholic Blind Asylum (Liverpool), the 74
Catholic Children's Society 74, 76
Catholic Community Service 63
CCF, the 79, *150*, 150–2
Chamber Choir, the 99, 99, 102

Chandler, Paula *152*, 152
Cheeseman, Rene 92
Cheesman, Brian 41, **44**, 67, 82, 83, 85, 97–8, *128*, 128
Chelsea Town Hall 29
Chess Club *143*, 143–4
Central St Martin's College of Art 44
Championship Cup, the 127
Cheal, Andrew 144
Chiesa Nuova (Rome) 11, 99
Children of Mary, the 27
Chingford Aerodrome 22
Christie, Linford 128
Choir of the Chapel Royal 104
Choral Society, the 104
Christian Brothers College, Freemantle 60
Church, J 107
Churchill, Winston 39, 40
Clancy, Liam 128
Clancy, Scott 109
Cleese, John 94
Coburn, Aidan 103
Cole, Charles 101
Cole, Maurice 111
Collins, Patrick 40
Collins, Steve *129*
Compton, Denis 123
Compton, J 30
Computer Club *144*, 144
Concert Band, the 98
Condon, J 97
Condon, Patrick Ronald 39
Confraternity of St Joseph and St Philip, the 149
Congregation of the Oratory (Birmingham), the 18
Congregation of the Oratory (Rome), the 11
Conmael 154
Convent Chapel, the 70
Coro 100
Cottrell, P 97
Cooke, Peter 73
Coombes MBE, Bill *152*, 152
Cooney, Joseph 153
Cosgrave, Mr 31
Coward, Noel 113
Cowdry, George 152, 154

173

The London Oratory School – *Appendices*

Cowdry, Tom 152
Craven, Father 74
Crawley, Mr 133
Crewse, Father Edward *18*, 18
Crompton, Mary 92, 93
Crosby, Bing *106*
Crosby, Mr 83
Crossley, Patrick *119*, 119
Crowley, Mr 151
Crusade of Rescue, the 74, 76
Cubitt, Sir William 154
Cullinan, Johnny 125
Curley, Carlo 100
Curtis, Harry 115
Daily Mail Cup, the *120*
Dale-Roberts, Father 35
Dale-Taggart, Mrs 27
Darling, Jackie 124
Dasent, Mrs 27
DaSilva, Michael 84
Daughters of the Cross, the 15, 48
Davidson, Ian *136*
Davies, Robert (Oli) 85, 86
Dawson, Clare 101, 103
Day of Recollection 73
de Barry, Santiago 137
DeBurgh, Tom 152
Deegan, Dan 93, 94, 95
Delap, Isobel 63, 73
Dent, Mr 108, 124, 146
Denton, John 85
Devaney, Ellis 103
Devereux, Pauline 7, **9**, 59
Dining Room, the 31
Dolan, Michael 124
Dom Bosco Institute (Rwanda), the 74, 75, 79
Donovan, Terence 44
Douai Abbey 73
Dow, Lorcan 119
Downer, Desmond 37, 108
Downing, David 116
Drago, Richard 38
Drama Club 110, 111
du Parc Locmaria, Alain 23
du Parc Locmaria, Gatien *23*, 23
du Parc Locmaria, Yves 23
Duckham, Mr 52
Dudley, Ronald 38
Duffy, Brian 44, *45*
Duffy, John Menzies 13, *13*, *15*, 15, 23, 31, 44
Duffy, Michael 23, 45, 67–8
Duke of Edinburgh's Award, The *133*, 139–40, *140*
Dunne, Harry 127
Durrans, Dr Brian 91
Dyson, Paul 144, 153

Edward House 64, 128, 133
Edwards, Mrs 136

Elizabeth II, HM Queen *94*, 94
Elizabeth Fitzroy Houses, the 74
Elkington, Mr 37
Elliot, Mr 45
Elphicke, Gerald 125
Eltham College, Melbourne 124
English College (Rome), the 77
Eton College 18, 48
Euclidean Society, the 145
Ewing, Maria 100
Exhibition Day 82

Faber, Father Frederick William 11, 12, 14, *18*, 18
Falero, Stephen 99
Farm Lane Care Home 75
Farr, Robert 22
Fathers of the London Oratory, the 7, 11, 12, *16*, 26, 28, 31, 43, 65, 67, 68, 70, 71, 78, 81, 96, 127, 133
Fennell, George 38
Fennessy, Richard 21, *22*, 22
Ferguson, Malcolm 98
Ferris, Pierce 153
Festing, Sir Francis 155
Film Club 145
First Form Choir, the 100
First Form Pilgrimage, the 73
Fisher, St John 35, 64
Fisher House 58, 74, 110
Fitness Centre, the 60, 85
Fitzgerald, Barry *106*
Fitzgibbon, D 107
Fitzpatrick, Mr 144
Flahive, James 125
Flanagan, Paul 93, 100, 103, 110, 145
Fleury, P 135
Flint, Tom 94
Flory, D 28
Flynn, Frank 127
Forbes-Jones, Edward 45, 72, 83
Fox, Matthew 127
Francis House 64, 127
Franks, Penny 146
Fraser, J 107
Fraser, Lady Antonia 146
Freely, Daniel 113
Freely, Martin 113
French, Lord 154
French Society, the 145
Fricourt Military Cemetery 23
Friedrich of Prussia, Prince *40*, 40
Frizelle, Nic 53, 55, 83
Fuge, Anthony 38, 117
Fulham Primary School 75
Fulham Secondary School 93

Gaffney, Ian 48, 48–9, 54–5, *55*, 65, 77, 83, 98, 117, 118, *121*, 130
Gaffney Cup, the 62
George, Father (*see* Bowen, Father George)
George V, King 33
Gesdurian, H 135
Gestra, Ben 58, 64
Gibson, Guy 37
Gifford, David *92*, 92, 93, 99, 101, 109
Gilbey, Monsignor Alfred 78
Girls Choir, the 103
Gasser, Edward 135
Glouchkow, Henri 77, 85, 86
Goldsmith, Henry 40
Gora, Albert 125
Gordievsky, Oleg 69
Gore, Al 102
Grahl, Steven 101
Grand Draw, the 28
Gray, David 72
Greenwood, Mr 45
Gribble, Herbert 68–9
Griffin, John 48, 53–4, **55**, 64, 83
Griffiths, Roy 59, 146
Gudgeon, Humphrey 141
Guildhall School of Music and Drama, the 104, 109
Guinness, Paul 121, 122, 139

Hamilton, Rod 128
Hammond, G 123
Handyside, Mr 97, 98, 158
Hanvey, P 21
Harrington, Paul 58
Harrington, James 76
Harrow School 18
Harte, David 99, 124
Hartigan, Tom 52, 58, 83, 118, 121
Harvey, Peter 151
Harvey, Bishop Philip 76
Harvington Hall 73
Haughton, Catherine 112
Haughton, Kevin **45**, 83, 86
Hawley, Alan *116*, 116
Hayes, Mr 23
Hayes, Nick 154
Hazebrouck Military Cemetery 22
Hazell, Richard 71
Heald, Emma 146
Heenan, Archbishop John Cardinal *53*, 53
Hegarty, B 23
Hendrick, T W 23
Henry, Frank 40
Hickey, Daniel 152
Hickey, Matthew 154
Hill, W 149
Hinsley, Cardinal 72
History Club, the 146
History Society, the 146
HMS *Aboukir* *22*, 22
HMS *Springbank* 40
HMT *Dilwara* 135
Hobbs, Jack 123

Holland, Father 40
Holy Cross Cemetery (Culver City) 106
Hogan, John Dennis Patrick *4*, *32*
Hooper, Mr 82, 124, 158
Hopkins, Anthony 112
Houlihan, Matthew **110**, *110*
House Collections, the 74
House Cup, the *64*, *128*
House Drama Festival, the 92
House Music Festival, the 98, 108
House Rugby Competition, the *115*
Howard, Alan 112
Howard, R 97
Howard, St Philip 64
Howard House 58, *64*, 64, 115
Howell, David **77**, *77*, 77
Howells, Dr 146–7
Hume, Archbishop Cardinal Basil 57, *58*, *71*, 76, 101, 120, *121*
Hurlingham Park 129
Hutchinson, Father *11*, 11, 12

Imperial College, London 45, 86
Isaaks, Mr 54, 86, 144

J M Duffy Testimonial Fund, the 31
Jack, Stuart 154
Jarrett, The Reverend Father 14
Jenkinson, J 44
Jenkinson, John 118, *119*
Jennings, Miss 107
Jeronimos Monastery 135
Jerry, Billy 125
John McIntosh Arts Centre, the 41, 56, 89, *89*, 89–90, *90*, 93, 95, 100, 101, 104, 110, 111, 145
Johnston, Paul 101, 123, 138, 146
Jones, Robert 86, **100**, 100
Josefowski, Paul 92
Junior Drama Club, the *106*, 107
Junior House 57, *58*, *59*, *63*, 74, 93, 101, 105, 111, 139
Junior Strings 98, 103

Kacary, Pierre 77
Kaminski, Stefan 77
Kapica, Nicholas 124
Keane, Father Paul *77*, 77, 109
Kearney, George 131
Keble, John 16
Keele University 86
Kelly, Mr 33, 45, 97, 151
Kelly, Pat 62, 145
Kemp, H 23
Keri Nagy, Chris 152
Kerr, Father Ralph *18*, 96
Kerr, Siddie 33
Kerr, Philip 19
Khan, Peter 144
Kijowski, Jan 128
Kindersley, David 71

174

Index

King's College London 47
Kingsley, Charles 17
Kirby, Terence 39
Knight, Roger 53, 83, 118, 126, 136
Kowalski, Peter 127
Krakow Rakowicki Military Cemetery 39
Kuczynski, Mr 121

Langsford, Rod 92
Lavis, John 39
Leavers' Retreat 73
Leicester, Father 151
Leo XII, Pope 17
Leslaeghe, Mr 23
Lett, Miss 96
Library of the London Oratory, the 9
Liengme, Bernard 45–6, *46*, 62, 77, *82*, 82, 85, 91, 128, 129, 136
Linares, Jessica 94
Literary and Debating Society, the 108, 146, 147
Little, Ray 93–4
Lloyd, Peter 72
Lockhart, Gene *106*, 106
Lockhart, June 106
Lockhart, Kathleen 106
Locock, Mr 143
Lombaertes, Mademoiselle 23
London Academy of Music, the 107
London Oratory Punishment Book, the *84*, 84
London Oratory School Chapel, The 11, 21, 25, 35, 39, 57, *70*, 70–1, *71*, 79, 101, 102, 103, 110
London School of Economics 86
Louca (née Epiphaniou), Lola 68
Loughborough College 85
Lovstrom, Peter 112, 137
Lower School Drama Club, the 111
Lynch, Peter 36, 37

MacDonald, Anthony 92
Mack, James 111
Mackle, Shaun 72
Madigan, John 40
Maguire, Brian 122
Major, John *56*, 56, 89, 100
Major, Norma *56*, 56, 89, *92*, 100
Malaney, Tom *119*, 119
Malone, Eamonn 54, 117, 126
Malone, Simon 135
Manchester Grammar School 48
Manresa College 72
Mantio, Joe *64*
Manzi, A P 149
Marc, Kervin 123, *124*
Marchant's Hill *140*
Marshall, Albert 76
Mary, Queen 33
Marty, Mr 86

Marty, Stef 120
Marx Brothers, the 111
Maryvale 16
Masek, Stanley (Stanislav) 39
Matthews, Mike 58, 64, 74, 84, 121, 123, 136
Matsumota, Mr 41
Matt (cartoonist) *101*
Matusomoto, Mr 41
May, James 104
Mayo, Aubrey Leslie 38
McCall, The Reverend Father 14, 149
McCarthy, Michael 101
McCarthy, Jim 58, 64, 74, 83, *137*
McCowatt, Mr 82
McEllin, John 121
McElroy, J 135
McElroy, Mr 74
McFadden, David 7, 9, 60, 62, 86, 122, 123, **159**, *159*
McGee Renedo, Paul 72
McGinty, Peter 127
McGreal, M 76
McHardy, Father Rupert 9
McIntosh, John 55, 55–6, *57*, 57, 59, 60, 65, 70–1, 84, 89–90, 101, 102, *121*, 131, 136, 151
McKenna, Mr 83
McKrill, Moira 75
McLaughlin, Kevin John 116
McRoberts, Jackie 93
Meighan, Jamie 152
Melvin, Joseph 104
Melvin, Leo 104
Melvin, William 104
Mercieca, Nathan 104
Mezzofanti, Massimo 99
Michael of Kent, HRH Princess 102
Middlesex Cup, the 120
Millais, Sir John Everett 71
Model United Nations, the 79
Mole, Edward 120
Mollard, Christopher 130, *131*
Molly, Miss 55
Monaghan, Mr 45, 47, 83, 151
McMonagle, Rory 127
Model United Nations, the *146*, 147
Montgomery, Mr *83*, 83
Moran, Kevin *117*, *121*, 118, 121
Moran, Kevin 'Junior' 120
Moran, Mike 129
Moran, Patrick 73
More, St Thomas 35, 64
More House 58, *63*, 74, 108
Morgan, Paul 145
Morris, Christian 128
Mortlake Central School 123
Mostyn Williams, Feargal 125
Mottershead, Thomas 22
Mowbray, Alan 23, *106*, 106
Mozoro, Sofia 109

Mullov-Abbado, Misha 104
Mullova, Viktoria 102
Munster, Father 44, 151
Murphy, Bridget 146
Murphy, Gilbert 37
Murphy, Jack (Sean) 111
Murphy, Patrick (P J A) 126
Murphy, R 108
Murray, H 21
Murray, Kevin 128
Murray, Mr 33
Mussolini, Benito 39, 58
Myerscough, Mr 97, 158

Napier, Charles 78
Napier, Father 48, 69, 70, 75, *78*, 78–9
Napier Room, the 78
National Schools Regatta, the *125*
Neville, Lady William 27
Newman, Cardinal John Henry 11, 13, *16*, 16–17, 18, 71, 72
Newman Society, the 146
Newman Wing, the 60
Newton, Isaac 145
Niblett, Richard 101
Nisbet, Barney 119
Nolan, Stephen 117
Novello, Ivor 22

O'Brien, Vincent 53, 55, 83, 86
O'Connor, Rory 89, 99, 100
O'Donnell, Mr 92
O'Dwyer, Paul 130
O'Friel, J P 47
O'Higgins, Sheila 108
O'Keefe, Daniel Patrick 37
O'Malley, W 21
O'Neill, Jack 'Jacko' 33, 53, 64, 82
O'Shea, Maciek 104
O'Shea, Michael 46, 82
O'Sullivan, Edmund 'Ted' 32, 33, *40*, 40, 115–16
O'Sullivan, F 128
O'Sullivan, Father 77
O'Toole, Peter 112
Odiwe, Ian 128
Old Boys' Dinner 33
Old Oratorian Association, the 63
Orat. (*see* Oratorian, The)
Oratorian, The 9, *31*, 32, 48, *53*, 53, 75, 83, 91, 97, 98, 99, 100, *101*, 108, 109, 118, 122, 124, 135, 136, 146, 157
Oratory Central Magazine, The (*see* Oratorian, The)
Oratory Boys and Girls Central Schools 35
Oratory Boys Brigade, the 149
Oratory Boys Central School, the 12, 19, 26, 35, 43, 44, 61, 64, 151
Oratory Boys Free School, the 15
Oratory Boys Middle School, the 15,

18, *81*, 81
Oratory Boys' School, the 13
Oratory Cadet Corps (OCC), the 21, 78, 107, 149–55
Oratory Central School, the 115
Oratory Church, the 19, 58, 62, 67, *68*, 68, 69, 70, 71, *76*, 79, 96, 98, 101, 105, 149, 158, *158*
Oratory Cup, the 127
Oratory Fathers, the (*see* Fathers of the London Oratory, the)
Oratory Fete, the 27
Oratory Girls and Infants Middle School, the 15, 26
Oratory Girls and Infants School, the 15
Oratory Girls Central School, the 143
Oratory House, the *16*, 17
Oratory Middle School, the 13–15, 18, 25, 27, 58, 91, 115
Oratory Parish Magazine, The 9, *25*, 25, 36, 82, 96, 108, 133
Oratory Parish Secondary Free School, the 43
Oratory Primary School, the *14*, 150
Oratory Secondary Modern, the 43
Oratory School, Reading, the 17
Oriel College, Oxford 16
Orsini, Agostino 109
Oscott Seminary 16
Owen, St Nicholas 64, 73
Owen House 58, 62, 64, 115
Oxford University 83, 86, 104, 105, 124

Paolozzi, Eduardo 41, 90, *91*
Paolozzi Gallery, the 93
Parish, Daniel 154
Parsons, Dolores 98
Passage Centre for the Homeless, the 75
Patronal Festival, the 57, 62, 67, 69, 70, 77, 84
Pawley, Edward 39
Peachey, Isobel *94*, 94
Peachey, Roy 109
Pearce, Mr 117
Peri, Lori 127
Perks, Miss 27
Philiotis, Alex 119
Philip House 64, 134
Philip Neri, Saint 7, *11*, *25*, 28, 62, 69, 77, 78, 133
Phillips, Melanie 146
Photography Club 145
Pink, Mrs 96
Pius XII, Pope 154, 155
Plessard (Tomkinson), Zara **109**, *109*, 110
Poliakoff, Stephen 113
Post Tour Concert, the 99
Power, Revd Dr Dermot 76
Power, Gerry 54, 115

175

Pragnell, Harry 21, 23
Prize Day 97
Pugin, Augustus 69
Puppet Club 144
Purcell, Henry 101

Quigley, John 116, *117*
Quinlan, Mr 72, 83
Quinn, Paul 129

Radio Club 145
Radley College 78
RAF Memorial, Runnymede 37, *38*
Ragged School Movement, the 12
Ragged School Museum, the *12*
Ragged Schools 11, 12
Railing, Max 152, 154
Randall, Robert 110
Raw, Brian 147
Red Baron, the (*see* Von Richthofen, Baron)
Renfrew, Lord 90
Ressort, Alex 138
Reyntiens, Patrick 57
Richmond Central School 123
Rigano, Alessandro 93
Roche, Rodney 40
Roche, V 129
Robertson, Mr 13
Rocks, J 97
Rocks, John 37
Rooney, Danny 59, 86, 128, 136, 147
Rooney, Natasha 128
Roots, Peter 39
Rorke, Alfred 21, 22
Rose, Paul 122
Royal Academy of Music, the 104
Royal Marsden Hospital, the 29, *49*, 49
Rugby Tour USA 121–2

Sachsel, Hubert Kurt 41
Sanandres, Ollie 152
Santi, Antonino 54
Saunders, Martin 120
Schola, the 72, 99, 99, 101, *102*, 102, 108
Scholes, J J 69
School Art Room, the 28
School Choir, the 100, 101, 102
School Fund, the 28, 29
School Orchestra, the 99, 103
Science Club, the *145*
Science Society, the 145
Scott, Arthur James 39
Scott, C M A 32, *33*

Scott-Ford, Duncan 41
Seagrave Road 49, *51*
Seagrave Stompers, the *103*, 103
Sebastian House 64
Seijido, Jose 119, 120
Servite Fathers, the 43
Sheehan, Michael 61, 118, 136
Sherrin, George 69
Shirley, Wilfred 38, 108
Shrewsbury School 18
Sisters of Compassion, the 26
Sisters of the Little Way, the 74
Skinner's School 119
Slade School of Fine Art, the 94
Slim, Kim **158**, *158*
Smallbone, Thomas 119
Smyth, Thomas 108
Snowflake School 75
Southwell, St Robert 64
Southwell House 58, 64
Speech Day 47–8, 84, 98
Spencer, Mr 144
Sports Day 119, 127–8, *129*
Spring, Dara 131
SS *Neuralia* 134–5, *135*
Stableford, Will 144
Stapleton, Joe 131
Stapleton, Paul *118*, 118, 120, 128
St Aloysius' School (Highgate) 47
St Andrew's School (Singapore) 122
St Bernard's School 44
St Francis School (New York) 121
St Francis Xavier University (Canada) 46
St Ignatius College 120
St Joseph's College, Galway 121
St Mary the Virgin (Oxford) 16
St Mary's Cadogan Street 43
St Mary's College (Twickenham) 72, 115, 116, 129
St Mary's Sydenham *133*
St Patrick's School 48
St Peter's Basilica (Rome) 73, 99
St Philip's Choir, the 98, 100
St Philip's Hall 31, 33, 44, 70, 92, 96, 99, 145
St Thomas of Canterbury Church (Fulham) 22, 65, 69
St Thomas More School 43
St Wilfrid's Convent 15
Steptoe, George 103
Stewart's Grove 25, 26–33, 40–1, 44, 45, 48–9, 53, 60, 68, 70, 84–5, 91, 102, 107, 108, 144, 145, 151

Stobbs, Mr 93, 103
Streatham Cemetery 36
String Orchestra, the 98
Sullivan, Dominic 82, 151, 152, 153
Sullivan, J 'Snowy' 53, 64
Sullivan, Matthew 129
Summerbell, Dr Laurence 30, 32, 33, 43, 44, 45, 46–7, 61, 62, 85, 97, 116, 117, 143
Sumner, Steven 111
Swift, Michael 119
Sykes, Perry 72
Szydlo, Dr Andrew *145*, 145

Tatton Bower, the Hon. Mrs 27
Taylor, Mr 48
Technology Club 145
Terry, David 101, 102, *105*, 105
Theatre Society, the 112
Thiepval Memorial, the *21*
Thomas, Mark **56**, 56
Thomas, Robert 13
Thorn, Roy *151*, 151, 152, 153
Thoumine, Matthew 131
Tierney, Rory 65, 121, 136
Tighe, Father *127*
Tilbury, Robert 110
Time Capsule, the 91
Tompolski, Ewa 91
Toms, Francis Hamilton 22
Toms, J Wybert 107
Tonypandy *35*, 116
Toomey, Mr 96, 97
Trafford, Jeremy 108, 109
Trafford (Johnstone), Scarlett 47
Trapmore, James 111
Trinity College, Oxford 16
Trinity Hall, Cambridge 78
Trondheim Military Cemetery 36
Tuite, John 141
Turner, Norman 126
Tyldesley, John-Joseph 72
Tynan, Stephen 137
Tynecot Cemetery *137*, 137

Ugoala, Chi 110
Ugoala, Obioma 110, **111**, *111*
University College London 104
University College, Oxford 18
University of Essex, the 77
University of the Arts, the 94

Varennes Military Cemetery 22
Vaughan, Cardinal 67

Veacock, Stanley 21, 22
Vestibule, the *25*
Vilona, Lorenzo 131
Vince, S 97
Virgili, Dr 130
Von Richthofen, Baron 22

Wahnon, Alex 127
Wailen, David 45, 55, 82, 85, 86, 136
Wallington, Leslie 36
Walman, 'Georgie' 82
Walshe McBride, Patrick 111
Walton, Maureen 109, 112
Ward, Thomas 154
War Hammer Club 144
War Memorial, the school *21*, 35, *39*
Ward, Lee 72, 101, *102*, 102, **105**, 111
Ward, Mark 103
Watson, Sonia 93
Wellington College 78, 119
Wells, Jack 154
Wells, L 40
Wembley Central School 123
West Kensington Central School 143
Westerman, Mr 13
Western, Chris 152
Western Fever Hospital *51*, 51
Whiffen, Ronald Charles 39, 117
White, Sam 59
Whitgift School 119
Whitwell, Alan 124
Wilfrid House 64, 128, 133
Wilkes, James 40
Williams, Brian 122
Williams, Dean 153
Williams, Graham 85
Wind Band, the 98
Wilson, David 83, 98, 108, 136
Wiseman, Archbishop Nicholas 12, 16
Witty, Wilfrid 37
Wolfe Ritchie, Mrs 27
Woytyna, Martin 152
Wood, Tom 152
Wootton, James Edward 37
Wright, John 36, 126
Wurstle, Georg 41

Xaverian Brothers, the 12

Young, J B 23
Young Christian Students (YCS) 75, 76
Youth Centre, the 65, 151

Zibelman, Charles 135

RESPICE FINEM

Charity Trust Deed (Modification) Order 1992 made by the Secretary of State for Education on the Twent
Armorial Bearings granted and assigned to the said school and duly recorded in Her Majesty's College of Ar
tory School hath requested the favour of His Grace's Warrant for the granting and assigning of such Arm
according to the Laws of Arms And forasmuch as the said Earl Marshal did by Warrant under his hand an
Crest accordingly Know Ye therefore that I the said Garter in pursuance of His Grace's Warrant and by v
grant and assign unto THE LONDON ORATORY SCHOOL aforesaid the Arms following that is t
Wreath Argent and Gules Issuant from a Celestial Crown Or a demi-Lion Bleu Céleste grasping a Staff Or